TOJO: THE LAST BANZAI

TOJO: THE LAST BANZAI

Courtney Browne

DA CAPO PRESS • NEW YORK

Library of Congress Cataloging-in-Publication Data

Browne, Courtney, 1915—
    TOJO: the last banzai / Courtney Browne.
        p.   cm.
    Originally published: New York: Holt, Rinehart and Winston,
1967.
    Includes index.
    ISBN 0-306-80844-7 (alk. paper)
    1. Tojo, Hideki 1884–1948. 2. Prime ministers—Japan—Biography.
3. Generals—Japan—Biography. 4. Japan. Rikugun—Biography. 5.
World War, 1939–1945—Japan. 6. Japan—History—1926–1945. I. Title.
DS890.T57.B7   1998
952.03′3′092—dc21
[B]   97-29822
                                                                 CIP

Penguin Books Limited, for permission to use selections from
three poems by the Emperor Yuryaku, Emperor Meiji, and
Kaneko Mitsuharu, as they appeared in *The Penguin Book of
Japanese Verse*, translated by Geoffrey Bownas and Anthony
Thwaite, copyright © 1964 by Geoffrey Bownas and Anthony
Thwaite.

Tourist Industry Bureau, Ministry of Transportation, Tokyo, for
permission to use an extract from a poem by Basho, as it appeared in their *Japan: The Official Guide.*

Simon and Schuster, Inc., New York, for permission to quote
from *The Cause of Japan* by Shigenori Togo, copyright © 1956 by
Simon and Schuster, Inc.

First Da Capo Press edition 1998

This Da Capo Press paperback edition of *Tojo* is an unabridged
republication of the edition first published in New York in 1967.
It is reprinted by arrangement with Henry Holt and Company,
Inc. and the Estate of Courtney Browne.

Published by Da Capo Press, Inc.
A Subsidiary of Plenum Publishing Corporation
233 Spring Street, New York, N.Y. 10013

To my wife, Sakaye

Foreword

My interest in General Hideki Tojo as a person, as distinct from the latter-day Ghengis Khan figure of western war-time report and caricature, was first aroused when I saw him seated impassively on trial for his life in the court room of the War Crimes Tribunal in Tokyo in 1947. I began collecting cuttings and material with the object eventually of writing a feature article on the man who in the tense months before Pearl Harbor—virtually a minority of one among doubting cabinet colleagues and senior statesmen—forced through the decision which embarked Japan on the ruinous Pacific war.

The article was never written. There seemed always to be something else to find out about Tojo who, until 1938, was practically unknown, even in Japan. This biography, while not claiming to be definitive, does reveal hitherto little known aspects of his personality. It dispels something of the obscurity of his early life and background. And—within the context of the progress of Japan since Perry—it unravels Hideki Tojo's role in the second great usurpation of power by a military shogunate in Japan.

Many books written about the period and persons involved in Japanese events from 1931 to the surrender in 1945 rely heavily on the Proceedings of the International Tribunal, Far East; the Kido Diaries; and the Konoye Memoirs. This is no exception. Also, particularly valuable as sources of information were *The*

Cause of Japan by Shigenori Togo (Simon & Schuster); *Japan and Her Destiny* by Mamoru Shigemitsu (Hutchinson, London; E. P. Dutton, New York); *Journey to the Missouri* by Toshikazu Kase (Yale University Press; published in England by Jonathan Cape under the title *Eclipse of the Rising Sun*); *Land of the Dragonfly* by Lewis Bush (Robert Hale, London) and *Tojo and the Coming of the War* by Robert J. C. Butow (Princeton University Press).

Other sources have been many and are listed separately, but grateful personal acknowledgment is made to:

Mrs. Katsuko Tojo for her kind permission to use family photographs, to use excerpts from her memoirs and the Prison Diary of Hideki Tojo as published in *Bungei Shunju* magazine, and for much new information given about General Tojo.

Ian Mutsu and Dai Inoshita for valuable assistance in interviewing Mrs. Tojo and other much appreciated help and advice.

The late Gunther Stein, veteran Far Eastern journalist, for the loans of books and for generous help in drawing on his wide knowledge of pre-war Japan and the Japanese military.

My wife, Sakaye, for patient and indispensable assistance in gathering material and in preparing the manuscript.

Contents.

TOJO:
THE LAST BANZAI

Part One

EQUAL WITH THE HEAVENS

*"The Land of Yamato
Is equal with the heavens
It is I that rule it all"*

From a poem
by the
EMPEROR YURYAKU
(418-479)

One

On the afternoon of Tuesday, the 11th of September, 1945, Japanese on the streets leading to the outskirts of bomb-gutted Tokyo watched apathetically as a convoy of U.S. Occupation Force jeeps sped past them. The vehicles bumped over ground pocked and pot-holed, shaking their passengers like dice in a box, and passed through fire-razed wastes which had once been close-packed streets until they came to a house in the Setagaya suburb. It was smaller and more modest than others in the area around it, but more fortunate than many in that it still stood undamaged.

As the jeeps pulled up in front of the house, soldiers jumped out while Major Paul Kraus strode swiftly with his detachment of U.S. counterintelligence men to the door. They were not the first to arrive there. A clamorous and impatient gaggle of newsmen and photographers—preponderantly American—were already crowded in the front garden. Their excitement ascended to a higher key as the Major hammered on the door. The noise of the pressmen subsided briefly while they waited and then broke out with greater intensity as a face appeared at an open side window. It was one well familiar to most of those present, almost the personification of the wartime caricature of the Japanese army officer; shaven head, hooded eyes glittering behind thick horn-rimmed glasses, sparse clipped moustache and parchment features.

The man at the window exchanged a few words with the Major's interpreter, who told him that he was to be taken to Occupation Headquarters. He nodded and indicated that they should go to the front door. Once again the CIC men went to the entrance with the newsmen pressing after them. Then the sound of a shot cracked out from within the house. The momentary shocked silence that followed was shattered almost immediately as the two leading CIC men, pistols drawn, smashed the lock on the door, burst through into the hallway of the house, and kicked open the door of the small side room.

The man who lay back in an armchair, grimacing with pain, his forehead shining with sweat, appeared shrunken and insignificant beneath the large painting of him, bemedaled and arrogant, which dominated the room. He was wearing military breeches and riding boots, and his white shirt, pulled open at the front, was already soaked in the blood from a wound above his heart.

In the room, pandemonium reigned as the newsmen pushed in, shoving and gesticulating. In the confusion of sound the words "yellow bastard" and "son of a bitch" rose above all others. More people, officers and GIs, newsmen and photographers swarmed into the room where the air now hung heavy with tobacco smoke. One of the newcomers, a GI with a cigar in his mouth, looked down at the man in the chair, the life ebbing away from him but still conscious and blinking at the rapid succession of exploding flashbulbs.

Raising his camera he took a photograph.

"Say, bud," he asked, "Who is the character?"

A correspondent, busily making notes, answered offhandedly, "Tojo." . . . The photographer turned to another correspondent. "Say, who is this guy Tojo?"

"Tojo. General Tojo, the Japanese dictator, prime minister at the time of Pearl Harbor," he was told.[1]

Two

The case against Hideki Tojo, as amplified and presented by the lawyers of the victorious Allied powers in 1946, was that he had committed crimes against peace, crimes against humanity, and certain specified war crimes. But behind the formal charges, which ran to many pages and thousands of words, was a basic accusation not spelled out in the legal terminology. Tojo was the archetype of the militarists who had made themselves masters of government in Japan and led the Japanese into a war initiated with treachery and fought with savagery. He was, to mix a few of the epithets applied to him, the "bullet-headed Tojo," the "typical officer of the Kwangtung Army clique," "smart and hardboiled" with an insensate hatred for foreigners, the "bloodthirsty *samurai*" who embodied the "fanaticisms and ferocities of his race." For many, the essential crime of General Tojo was that he was a soldier—not in the tradition recognized as honorable in the Western democracies, but a Japanese soldier. And implicit in this were all the connotations of the more lurid denunciations heaped on Japan by that nation's enemies.

    If there had ever been any possibility that Hideki Tojo would have been anything other than a soldier of Japan, it was eliminated very early in his life. He was born on the 30th of December, 1884, into the family of Hidenori Tojo, a dedicated career soldier who had joined the Japanese Imperial Army at the age of sixteen. By the childhood deaths of two elder brothers, Hideki became the eldest surviving son. Thereafter, tradition and all the disciplines of Japanese family structure required him to be a soldier as his father was, carrying on a profession which, in Japan, had long enjoyed a unique and privileged status.

The *haniwa* burial figurines of baked clay which constitute the first records of the Japanese people abound with representations of mounted warriors on horseback. Their trappings and weapons reveal that the early Japanese clans who settled in the Yamato plain of the main Japanese island, Honshu, came originally from northern Asia across the convenient land bridge of the Korean peninsula. Once there they were impelled by the necessity of battling with the aboriginal Caucasoid inhabitants, the Ainu, to unify under one ruler. In his choice the shamans or holy men of the clans took an important part and invested him with the myth of supernatural descent.

Driven back over decades of struggle, the Ainu fiercely resisted each new advance by the invaders to such effect that in the eighth century the latter suffered severe setbacks. The position was restored only after the fight against the Ainu was put into the hands of a succession of specially appointed "barbarian-subjugating" *shoguns* or commanders in chief who, instead of relying on the large Imperial army of conscripts, formed their own smaller but better armed and disciplined units. These they officered with the scions of the local clan chiefs. Thus was formed what developed into a hereditary class of professional warriors known as *samurai,* who served as retainers of the various lords of Japan.

The *samurai,* in appearance distinguished by his hair, top-knotted and shaven in front, and by his kimono marked with the clan badge, devoted his entire life to spartan living and perfecting himself as a fighting man. He was schooled to extremes of self-control, allowing himself to show "no sign of joy or anger."[1] Socially he kept himself apart from the commoners. It was unfitting for him to engage in any form of trade or even to handle money. Chief of the martial skills in which he was expected to excel was swordsmanship, and the two swords he carried at all times, one long and one short, were as much a badge of rank as weapons.

The *samurai* swords had their special mystique, the large two-handed one from the almost incredible dexterity achieved with it and the legendary exploits which grew around the sword and its exponents. The short one was for decapitating the fallen enemy. In the last resort, it was also the instrument of self-destruction by *seppuku,* more commonly known as *hara-kiri,* literally "stomach-cutting." Instruction in this was a serious part of the training of every novice *samurai* for, by the code, he was given the privilege of self-execution to avoid dishonor and was required to exercise this either to avoid capture or as a penalty for displeasing his *daimyo.* In the grisly ritual of ceremonial disembowelment, a comrade-in-arms would stand by with the long sword to give, if signaled to do so by the victim, the coup de grâce.

If the sword was the most lethal of his visible armory, the code of *bushido* (the way of the warrior) was the *samurai's* most potent unseen weapon. The mixture of religion and militarism was nothing new in Japan. In the eleventh century, sects of soldier priests had established themselves in temples around Kyoto. And it was from the disciplines of Zen Buddhism and its doctrines of indifference to physical pain, evolved in the thirteenth century, that the cult of *bushido* was derived.

Under the first Tokugawa shogun, Ieyasu, it was combined with Confucian precepts and codified, and the *samurai* was incorporated into the political order. In the tightly organized society established by the Tokugawa regime, which usurped power from the Emperor in the sixteenth century, the Confucian observance of filial piety was made law, laying down the pattern of behavior between superior and inferior, the former being required to be benevolent and the latter to be obedient.

That there were lapses from the prescribed benevolence was evident in the bitter phrase *kanson mimpi* ("official honoured; people despised") current in the times. Nor were the *samurai* (who, needless to say, were members of the superior classes) altogether immune from the corruption of power. Some, indeed, gained notoriety as ruffians and some for addiction to earthly pleasures. That they should have become arrogant was perhaps inevitable in a class which numbered among the privileges granted it by Ieyasu Tokugawa that of being permitted to cut down on the spot a commoner "who has behaved to him in a manner other than is expected."[2]

The Tokugawa shogunate, having successfully unified

the country, became aware of a threat from outside. The advent in 1543 of a China-bound Portuguese ship driven ashore by a storm had started off the first intercourse with the West. Later ships bearing missionaries brought a large area of the southern island of Kyushu under the alien Roman Catholic faith. It was a development which the authoritarian Tokugawa rulers, whose Buddhist priests were virtually officials of the state, could hardly have regarded with favor. The subsequent arrival of galleons from the Philippines, where Spanish soldiery had followed Catholic priests and made the islands into a colonial possession, and, shortly afterward, an uprising by the Christians of Kyushu, decided the shogunate on drastic measures. The rebellion was put down with ghastly carnage and the surviving Christians, Japanese and foreign alike, were hunted down ruthlessly. Those who did not recant under torture were executed.

Thereafter, every Japanese family was required to register at a Buddhist temple; the building of ocean-going ships was forbidden; and Japanese were not permitted to leave the country on pain of death. The same penalty was prescribed for and, in a few cases, exacted from foreigners who tried to enter the country. Only a few members of a Dutch trading post in Nagasaki were permitted to remain, subject to severe restrictions on their movements, and until the Tokugawa regime collapsed in 1876, this was almost the sole link between Japan and any other country.

As the Swedish scholar and traveler Dr. Thurnberg, one of the few foreign travelers permitted to visit the country, wrote in the eighteenth century, the Japanese had not been "corrupted by the Europeans that have visited them . . . they have chosen to retain their ancient and primitive mode of life."[3] But if the Tokugawa rulers had placed Japan out of the main stream of world affairs, their land did not share the colonial fate of other nations in Asia. Nor was Japan to suffer the humiliation and dismemberment of her neighbor and early mentor as, through the nineteenth century, a half-dozen countries fastened on and tore at the great feeble carcass which had once been the illustrious kingdom of Cathay. In Japan the emperors continued to hold their court in Kyoto, but for the next hundred years, from their own capital of Edo (now Tokyo), the Tokugawa family wielded the real power, which rested on the existence, privileged and increasingly parasitical, of the *samurai*.

Three

The Tojo family, although not of the higher caste of *samurai*—for there were degrees of class even among them—lived as retainers within the feudal structure and had served a lord of one of the northern provinces for several generations. Hidenori, the father of Hideki Tojo, was born in 1855, just two years after a summer day which was to be recorded in Japanese annals as the Day of the Black Ships.

In July, 1853, a small squadron of American warships under the command of Commodore Matthew Perry sailed into Tokyo Bay. They had come uninvited and bore a note from the President of the United States requesting trading and consular facilities. The note and its bearer did not neglect to stress the mutual benefits which these would bring; but more convincing to those ashore than any diplomatic persuasion was the modern armament bristling from the sides of the battleships and the black smoke belching from the stacks of two of them, which moved independent of sail or wind. Strange and foreboding, their coming marked the end of over two centuries of feudal hermitage for Japan.

For the Americans and the other western nations who followed this exercise in nineteenth-century gunboat diplomacy, the intention was no more than to open up another area in Asia for commercial exploitation. It could scarcely have been anticipated that this backward oriental kingdom which had asked only to be left alone would, a few decades after its rude awakening, become a serious new contender for power in the Far Eastern arena. Yet, there was ample warning for those who could have read the signs.

Before leaving, saying that he would be returning for a reply the following spring, Perry presented his unwilling hosts with a brass cannon of the latest design, possibly to impress upon them the daunting firepower that lay behind his country's request. When Townsend Harris, the first U.S. Consul, was installed ashore the following year, he noted that the Japanese authorities had sent "two handsome brass howitzers, copied in every respect from one Commodore Perry gave them."[1] A few years later, a British official was presented with an excellent copy of a breech-loading rifle, one of many made from a gift recently made by a visiting British naval officer.

The western cannon that had boomed out in salute across the shimmering waters of Tokyo Bay had done more than force the door of medieval Japan. For the Tokugawa family the guns sounded the end of their long years of rule. And their downfall came, ironically, because they were no longer capable of enforcing their policy of exclusion in the face of this technological challenge from the west. Enraged and alarmed by the alien intrusion, the lords of the powerful Satsuma, Choshu, and Tosa clans united and, raising the cry "Revere the Emperor; expel the barbarian!" overthrew the shogunate. In so doing they could scarcely have expected that this would accelerate the very processes they had aimed to halt.

Now installed in the northern capital of Edo, later to be renamed Tokyo, the younger Emperor Meiji, advised by a cabinet of enlightened and aristocratic advisers, was heading what the historian Basil Hall Chamberlain described as the most sudden and the wisest *volte face* in history. Far from expelling the foreign barbarians, he was, with his government, pressing on with modernization and westernization. In the land there had been unleashed a veritable frenzy of activity. "Schools were opened for the study of foreign languages, academies shot up where youths could receive instruction in military and naval tactics; raw recruits were drilled; foundries and smithies sprang into existence, and belfries were molested to furnish metals for arsenals."[2]

Missions were sent abroad to study, and so ardent was the desire to learn from the occidentals that even the wearing of western dress was made mandatory for government ministers and officials. *Fokoku-kyohei*—"rich country; strong arms"—was the new cry. United again under the illustrious descendant of the Imperial line, the islands of Nippon were not going to submit to being, like China, the unhappy cockpit of contending alien powers. The spirit of the times was expressed by several of the important clan chiefs when they voluntarily gave up their lands to the Emperor. "Thus," they declared, "our country will be able to rank equally with the other nations of the world."[3]

Other lords, less willingly, yielded up their fiefs when "invited" to follow this patriotic example, and under a new prefectural system of government private domains were abolished. But whereas it was possible to give the comparatively small number of *daimyos*—now given titles in the European tradition—a place in the new society, the *samurai* presented a much greater problem. There were estimated to be close to two million hereditary warriors with their families who had been deprived of the lordly patronage on which they had depended. As many as possible were given police posts and other official positions, but unavoidably many were left to their own resources, a sorry prospect for a class who had for centuries been schooled to despise all forms of common work or commerce.

It was open to some to follow their profession of arms in the newly formed Imperial forces, but the opportunities here for the relative few were more than offset by the fact that the remainder, by the creation of a conscript army, had lost their status as an exclusive military caste. New laws were passed to do away with the old *samurai* image; their distinctive hair style was frowned on; clan badges were not allowed to be worn; and the final turn of the screw came when they were forbidden their ancient right to carry in public the swords which marked them from all other men.

Young Hidenori Tojo was among the people affected by these innovations. In 1871, his family impoverished and made masterless by the breaking up of their clan, the sixteen-year-old lad made his way to Tokyo and joined the Imperial army. He was more fortunate than many not only in finding a place in the new order but in his modest birth. This enabled him to enlist as a common soldier, a rank which higher-caste *samurai,* oppressed as much by pride as by poverty, would have disdained to accept.

While it was comparatively painless for Hidenori Tojo to change in a society where, in any case, his place would have been limited and relatively inferior, the sudden stripping away of generations-old power and wealth from the lords and *samurai* who had so much more to lose provoked the most bitter reaction. Moreover, there was considerable dissatisfaction among certain of the leaders who had supported the Emperor against the Tokugawa usurpers and who now felt themselves betrayed. Under the restoration they had expected rewards rather than deprivation. And now the Meiji government declined to engage in an expedition against Korea and China which, it was argued, would give appropriate employment to large numbers of masterless *samurai.* The discontent finally erupted violently in a bloody uprising of certain of the clans against the Emperor and those who supported him.

The civil war of 1877 was, in military terms, essentially one of a rebel *samurai* army pitted against the new national one, mainly conscript, but armed with modern weapons and disciplined in western tactics. In this struggle Hidenori Tojo, as a regular army sergeant, fought against the class into whose service he had been born, and so distinguished himself that he was raised to the rank of lieutenant.

The months of battle which followed were marked by all the ferocity of civil war and casualties were heavy on both sides. It ended when, with his armies decisively defeated, the rebel leader, the lord Saigo, took his life in the traditional *samurai* manner by *hara-kiri.*

The crushing of the rebellion signified much more than the collapse of feudal opposition to the government and the new order. In the conflict the regular soldiers like Hidenori Tojo and the conscripts who had fought along with them had shown that the valor and martial skill which had made the *samurai* elite such formidable fighters could be found in all the levels of the nation.

To the Japanese, with their abiding veneration for the past which no amount of modernization was ever entirely to eradicate, the warrior spirit of ancient Yamato was seen not to have ended with the defeat of the *samurai* but to have passed on to those who had prevailed over them. The officers of the new Imperial army were the heirs of the *samurai* and the inheritors of their code of *bushido,* a belief that was fostered by members of the knightly caste from clans loyal to the Emperor and already in the army. It came with the force of an almost divine revelation that out of the fire and blood of civil war such men, armed with the weapons of the new age, had been forged into a mighty instrument of national power.

Seventeen years later—a little over thirty years since Commodore Perry's first peremptory knock on their doors—the Japanese, now with black ships of their own, were ready to use this instrument to stake their claim to Korea, then a part of the disintegrating empire of the Manchu rulers of China.

Four

Broken only by the narrow Shimonoseki straits at its southeastern extremity, the Korean peninsula constitutes a natural land bridge from the mainland of Asia to the islands of Japan. It was through the "land of the morning calm" that much of the culture of Cathay had flowed to Japan. It was from Korea, too, that the Mongol emperor, Kublai Khan, mounted his great armada for the conquest of Japan in 1281. Only the timely intervention of a typhoon, thereafter venerated by the Japanese as the *kamikaze*—the "divine wind"—saved Japan from becoming, like the ancient kingdom of Korea itself, a province in the great Khan's realm. The Japanese never forgot that Korea was "a dagger pointing at our heart."

The Japanese victory in the brief war which they picked with the Chinese in 1894 was not a glorious one. The government of the Manchu empress in Peking was weak and corrupt, the fossilized shell of what had been the center of a great empire and civilization. The Chinese troops opposing the Japanese were miserably led and worse equipped. Nevertheless, the Japanese, flexing their muscles for the first time, were astonished and almost hysterically jubilant at the success of this, their first international adventure, the extent and direction of which boded so much for the future.

In the process of chasing the Chinese out of Korea, Japanese troops had crossed the Yalu river, occupying the

Liaotung peninsula and Port Arthur in Southern Manchuria. There, Hidenori Tojo and other young officers in the Japanese expeditionary force were getting their first conqueror's glimpse of the land which was to become the Mecca of the Imperial Army's career officers, the place where they had to serve to gain not only merit but advancement. Exhilarated by their easy victory, they were savoring the taste of power and prestige as members of an army of occupation, uninhibited by the restrictions of service in their homeland. Their stay on this occasion, however, was to be a brief one.

The Chinese, in no position to resist Japanese demands, ceded Japanese-occupied southern Manchuria and the island of Formosa and gave up their dominion over Korea. But the Chinese peace mission had barely time to return to Peking before the ambassadors of Germany, France, and Russia made it known to the government in Tokyo that their governments were not prepared to accept the Japanese presence in Manchuria.

In the hardly concealed threat behind the diplomatic wording, the menace of Tsarist Russia with its military bases in northern Manchuria loomed largest. The ministers of the Meiji government had little choice. Mortified though they might be, they knew that Japan on its own was not strong enough to challenge a combination of three great powers. The howl of rage which went up in Japan at what was to become known and execrated as the "Triple Intervention" was calmed only when the Emperor, addressing the people through an Imperial rescript, told them that they must "bear the unbearable."

Over in Manchuria the soldiers of the Imperial Army heard with anger and incomprehension the order to yield up the ground they had fought for. They marched out, but unwillingly and resentfully, only too ready to listen to the superpatriots at home who accused the politicians of surrender to foreign pressure, craven betrayal of the soldiers' sacrifice and valor, and above all, misleading the Emperor with "insincere advice."

Despite this setback, Japan had held on to Formosa and expelled the Chinese from Korea, but the intervention had a profound effect on a country single-mindedly set on being no less than equal among modern powers and sensitive in the oriental way to loss of face. More soberly than the extremists, the Meiji government was drawing its own lesson from this confrontation with the realities of international life. Count Hayashi, a leading member of the government, noted that Japan had to "continue to study according to western methods, for the application of science is the most important item of warlike preparations that civilized nations regard."[1]

It was with a nation in this mood that direct political power was given to the armed services by allocating the posts of navy and war ministers to senior officers on the active list. The intention was simply that the armed forces should have a say in the allocation of budget funds at a time when their expansion was of vital national importance. The long-term result was to be the erosion of civilian control of the generals and admirals, which is essential in a democratic state.

So it was that when Lieutenant Colonel Hidenori Tojo returned from Manchuria, the aim of mere equality with other nations was already being discarded as overmodest. In the modern game of international power it was plain that those with strength and the will to use it were more equal than others. Almost half a century later it was to be the destiny of his son, Hideki (then eleven years old) to lead his countrymen into a total war that was Japan's ultimate expression of this belief. But the first step had been taken. Japan had turned the Korean dagger in the reverse direction—pointing at China.

Five

The family home to which Hidenori Tojo returned in 1895 was simple, almost severe. Japanese officers were expected to be austere in the image of the *samurai*. Economics, in any case, made ostentation or gracious living out of the question for the majority of Japanese officers who did not enjoy private means. Although as a class they might have the respect of their nation and as individuals the deference of their neighbors, they were not highly paid.

For the young Hideki the extremes of indulgence at home and strict discipline at school—traditionally the lot of the young Japanese male and blamed by psychologists in later days for many of the less attractive aspects of his behavior—were present in marked degree. His mother, the daughter of a Buddhist priest, has been described as "a very difficult woman," given to outbursts of hysteria. She was, perhaps, no more difficult than might have been expected from a woman who had borne seven children since her marriage at the age of seventeen, who was compelled to take in sewing work to eke out the family income, and who, because of her husband's prolonged absences, had to deal with a large family very much on her own. In this family environment, and in a society where Confucian precepts of obedience and respect for the position of an eldest son were strongly held, it is scarcely surprising that as a schoolboy Hideki Tojo exhibited many of the traits of the spoiled brat.

He was opinionated, obstinate, and quick to pick a fight. On the credit side, having got into one, he showed considerable personal courage and tenacity in seeing it through. At school he was no more than an average student, but comparison with relatively carefree standards in Britain or the United States would be entirely misleading. The Japanese schools of Tojo's youth were relentlessly competitive in character, and there was no nonsense either in studies or sport about it not mattering if you won or lost but how you played the game. Nor was there anything like the western tradition of commiseration with the loser. Losers were weepers and—very often—suicides.

In his youth he suffered more than usually from the bad complexion which is so often the bane of adolescents. He was short-sighted and his physique generally such as to cause wonder, when he entered a military preparatory school at the age of fifteen, at how he could ever have aspired to be a soldier. At the school it quickly became apparent that the injunction of the Tokugawa shogun, Ieyasu, to his subjects: "Avoid things you like; turn your attention to unpleasant duties" had particular meaning for him. With no outstanding ability, plain hard work would be necessary to keep up with or beat the other students. He developed a morbid capacity for it, applying himself to such effect that he excelled colleagues possibly more gifted intellectually but lacking his own driving intensity of purpose. His success left him with a humorless, almost superstitious belief in the dividends of application and the power of will. "I am just an ordinary man possessing no shining talents," he later told a group of students. "Anything I have achieved I owe to my capacity for hard work and never giving up."

In 1902, Cadet Tojo entered military academy, having chosen the infantry as his arm of service. In the ordinary course of events he would have stood with other successful graduates three years later at a commissioning ceremony, probably witnessed by his father with the grave approbation proper to one who was now a full colonel. But events were fast moving to a crisis in Japanese history.

Over on the mainland, the turbulent Koreans, sometimes described as the "Irish of the Far East," had been taking no more kindly to Japanese protection than they had to that of their erstwhile Chinese overlords and were showing signs that they took their newly gained autonomy far more literally than their Japanese "liberators" had ever envisaged. It was a situation that the Tsarist government was quick to exploit. In 1903, Russian troops, despite angry Japanese protest, moved down from their Manchurian bases into north Korea, ostensibly to protect a forestry concession granted them by the Korean government in Seoul.

The Japanese, with the Russians' part in the Triple Intervention of 1895 still rankling, were in no mood to step down again. And this time they were not alone. A five-year treaty with Great Britain had been negotiated when Britain was fighting the South African Boers and wanted Japanese support if any of the European powers attempted to take advantage of the situation in the Far East. This treaty now ensured that no such European combination of nations as had threatened in 1895 would intervene in a Russo-Japanese showdown.

On the evening of the 8th of February 1904, while their diplomats were still negotiating in Moscow, a Japanese battle fleet struck at the Russian Pacific squadron lying at anchor in Port Arthur. Just as in the assault on the Chinese ten years before and as it was to happen at Pearl Harbor thirty-seven years later, the Japanese attacked without formal declaration of war. This was not made until the 10th of February, and by that time, with Japanese troops closing in on the Russian garrison in Port Arthur, the eldest Tojo had once more gone to war.

Six

The war against the Russians was for the Japanese an unbroken series of brilliant victories on land and sea over an enemy established as a world power since the days of Peter the Great and, on paper, disposing of infinitely greater strength. On land the Russian soldiers fought with stubborn courage but still thought and acted in terms of a static Crimea-type war. The Japanese moved rapidly, attacking relentlessly under officers like Hidenori Tojo, trained by Prussian instructors in the tactics that had scythed through the French lines at Sedan. Superbly disciplined, they performed epic deeds of valor without regard to casualties.

Port Arthur finally fell after a long and costly siege on the 31st of December, 1904; Fieid Marshal Oyama took Mukden, the Manchurian capital, on the 16th of March, 1905. When the Russians tried to reinforce their Far Eastern navy by dispatching their Baltic Fleet to the Far East, it was met on the 27th of May, 1905 by the force under Admiral Togo lying in wait for it in the Tsushima straits and was shattered in a two-day battle.

In Japan patriotic enthusiasm was fever high, increasing with every victory. Nowhere was it higher than in the military academy where Hideki Tojo had celebrated his twenty-first birthday on the day before Port Arthur was taken and where he and his fellow cadets impatiently awaited the time when they could join their embattled fathers and elder brothers overseas. For the young

Tojo that day came just after the fall of Mukden, when he was commissioned second lieutenant.

The young officers who strapped on their *samurai*-style swords and sailed for Manchuria in the spring of 1905 set out with high hopes that they would go side by side with their triumphant countrymen on the flood tide of victory. But what Hideki Tojo and most of them were to know of the Russo-Japanese war was to be the boredom of garrison duty and the frustration of seeing their chances of battle taken away in the anti-climax of a negotiated peace.

All the victories on land and sea and patriotic fervor in the homeland could not change the fact that by not taking Port Arthur quickly after their surprise blow, Japan had missed the opportunity of the speedy and decisive victory she needed. The glittering military successes and the heroic sacrifices of her soldiers and sailors, in somber terms of manpower and economics, had mounted to a cost of pyrrhic proportions.

The loss of over two hundred thousand men had bled white Japan's capacity to provide trained replacements. The politicians at home were realizing, too, even if the soldiers and civilians did not, that patriotism was not enough. The national treasury was empty; international credit was exhausted. For the second time the Meiji government was forced to bow to the inevitable. An approach was made to President Theodore Roosevelt of the United States to use his good offices in bringing the war to an end. The fact that this overture was made by their own government was unknown to the broad mass of the Japanese people who knew only of the triumphs and were ecstatically confident that complete victory over the Russians was just within their grasp. When the terms of the Treaty of Portsmouth, signed on the 5th of September, 1905, were made known, the anger in Japan exceeded even that of the time of the Triple Intervention. Japan had got the Russians out of Korea—the issue on which the war had been fought—and regained the treaty rights in Manchuria taken away by the Triple Intervention. Russia had ceded the southern half of Sakhalin island with its valuable fishing grounds. But no war indemnity, as traditionally exacted from vanquished by victor, was to be paid by the Russians.

For the Japanese there was only one explanation, one

which their government to its lasting discredit made no effort to correct. Japan had once again been cheated by western intervention and this time their fury was turned on the Americans. Again the ultranationalists whipped themselves into a frenzy of rage. In Tokyo rioting crowds demonstrated, attacking police boxes and setting fire to streetcars, and the ugly situation was brought under control only by the declaration of martial law.

In Manchuria, where the hardships of fighting in a bleak vastness had inspired a Japanese version of "It's a Long Way to Tipperary" in a dirge-like ballad which told of "a lonely country far from home," most of the conscripts were as glad as any soldier in the world at the thought of getting back to wives and families. This sentiment was not shared by their regular officers. Conscious only of the army's achievements and what these had meant in sacrifice, they knew even less than the people at home of the hard facts which had cut short the war and their chances of military luster. For Hideki Tojo and other newly commissioned regular officers, too, there was more than just the prospect of death or glory snatched from them. The opportunity of quick promotion, probable in war, was now replaced by the certainty of waiting in the slow moving queue for routine peacetime advancement.

The elder Tojo returned, early after the peace, a sick man. Not all of the casualties in the Japanese ranks had been from bayonet or gunfire. No less than twenty-seven thousand had perished from disease and Hidenori Tojo never entirely recovered from the after-effects of beri-beri contracted in the campaign. His son stayed on to complete his tour of garrison duty in Manchuria and returned in 1906. Three years later he married Katsu Ito, a young lady from Kyushu who, at the time of their wedding, was a student at a women's college in Tokyo.

The nineteen-year-old Katsu was a relatively emancipated young lady for a Japanese girl of the period and it was generally agreed by all who knew her that she was not cast to settle down to the self-effacing role of a Japanese wife. Daughter of a small land-owner who was active in local politics in Kyushu, she was one of a minority of women in her day who had aspired to higher education. "You could say that I tend to be headstrong," she admitted, "and I don't take easily to having my mind changed."[1] Also untypical in the match of this girl with a mind of her own and the stiff-necked, uncommunicative young Hideki was the manner of their marrying. Theirs was not the loveless contract of the traditional Japanese arranged marriage of partners picked out by their parents.

Through mutual friends Katsu was being sponsored by the Tojo family while in Tokyo and often visited the household. Hideki Tojo, very soon after their first meeting, had taken the initiative, indicating to his parents that this was the girl he wanted to marry. Tojo's mother, although she had taken a liking to the girl and yielded to her son's wishes, was not prepared entirely to overlook the unconventional nature of the match. For some time the Tojo parents declined to enter Katsu's name in the family register, perhaps thinking that the marriage would not last. The Japanese mother-in-law was, in any case, able by custom to exercise almost tyrannical power over a young bride, and the elder Mrs. Tojo was not an easy person to get on with. For some time Katsu wondered if it would not after all be better for everyone if she left, but her husband's kindness persuaded her to stay.[2] Despite this early opposition, or perhaps because of it, the union was a genuinely happy one. Katsu bore the first of their seven children in the Tojo family house in Tokyo in 1911. Seventeen years after Tojo's death, she recalled her husband with sorrow and affection.

"There is still not one day when I don't think of my husband. Every morning I go to the family altar where his picture is and my tears flow, not because it is painful to recollect memories of him but because he was a warm person. He was a man of few words and he did not fully express himself, so people did not always understand him. When he was alive I always consulted him before I did anything. I wasn't forced to but I knew it would please him and, from the bottom of my heart, this was what I wanted to do. Even now I try to do what he would want. For instance, they are repairing the road in the front of the house now. I give the laborers tea in the morning and at noon and perhaps cook some noodles with eggs later for them. It is almost as if I could hear my husband say 'It is good to be nice to people.' He liked that sort of thing."[3]

With the responsibility of marriage and a family and the example of his father who had risen to the rank of general, the pressure on Hideki Tojo to succeed was greater than ever. Still a second lieutenant, with a medal and not much more to show for his service overseas, he applied himself more grimly than before to his profession, working long hours with obsessional concentration. Routine promotion to full lieutenant came at the age of twenty-three and six more years were to pass before he attained the rank of captain. Nevertheless, proof came—if he needed it—of the rightness of his creed of hard work when he was selected for a vacancy on the coveted staff officers course. He was approaching thirty when he graduated from staff college, but with his staff qualification he was at least assured of not being compulsorily retired at an early age, as was apt to happen to less successful army officers.

In the meantime, for the nation an era had passed. In 1912 the revered Emperor Meiji had died, bringing to an end the eventful period in Japanese history that bore his name. His demise was marked by great public mourning, highlighted by the suicides of General Nogi and his wife by *hara-kiri* as a gesture of grief for the passing of their lord in the tradition of the ancient *samurai* retainers. It was well known that the chivalrous and gallant victor of Port Arthur also intended his death to atone for the terrible loss of life among those, including his two sons, who fought under him.

A few months later the Tojo family went into its own personal mourning for General Hidenori Tojo, who finally succumbed to heart trouble. The general died at the age of fifty-seven, an extraordinary man in his own right whose rise from modest origins to high rank and distinguished service typified the fantastic change and progress of the Meiji era. As with Nogi, there was a certain melancholy appropriateness in his death as the era ended.

Whatever else Japan had achieved in the Russo–Japanese war, it had left no doubt of its claim to acceptance as an international power, which was confirmed at the outbreak of the First World War in Europe by the Japanese entry on the side of Britain and her allies, among whom were included Japan's erstwhile enemy Russia. For Tojo personally the war was much a case of history repeating itself. At the time that war was declared he was still at staff college. By the time he passed out in 1915 it was quite obvious that Japan's participation in the war was going to be almost entirely naval, leaving the army on the sidelines with no role to play.

For Japanese leaders the war convulsing Europe was a distant affair. In the Pacific, Japanese naval forces, quite legitimately within the context of hostilities, occupied German-held islands in the Pelew, Caroline, and Mariana groups—islands like Truk and Saipan. From these, Japanese troops were to be blasted out thirty years later, but at the cost of many thousands of American lives.

More significant was the opportunity the war gave for Japan to consider the possibilities in China. There, at a time when the colonial nations of the west were locked in a life-and-death struggle, the Japanese had a free hand that was too good not to be tried. They took the German-held port of Tsingtao and soon afterwards the Chinese were presented with a series of "requests" which, if granted, would have made China virtually a Japanese protectorate.

Those who led Japan at the time might have seen—and far-sighted Japanese did see—danger signs for the future in the reaction to what became notorious as the Twenty-One Demands. China, now a republic and with nationalist feeling rapidly growing, vehemently opposed further Japanese usurpation of its sovereignty and territory; Britain warned its ally of the consequences of overreaching itself. Japan might have risked disregarding both of these countries, one weak and the other pitting all its available strength against Germany. But from America, strong and not yet at war, came the sternest protest. The most extreme of the demands on China were dropped, though not without virulent criticism by the ultranationalists of the alleged cowardice of the Japanese government and of, to them, this additional proof of America's hostility toward Japan.

All of this Captain Hideki Tojo was aware of as a spectator. Apart from a short spell in Siberia as a member of the Japanese contingent in the short-lived and ill-conceived Allied intervention against the Bolsheviks who had seized power in Russia, he had served out the war in routine staff and regimental posts. But the Captain's dogged and efficient service had not gone unnoticed. In the higher echelons of the War Ministry, where he had briefly occupied a junior staff officer's desk, Tojo had been selected for an assignment that would remove him for a time from the routine of ordinary military life.

Seven

Much was to be made in later years of Hideki Tojo's lack of knowledge of the west, and it was commonly assumed that he had never traveled beyond China. Certainly when he was being interrogated during his trial as a war criminal he revealed, for one who had wielded such power and exercised such a fateful influence in the affairs of mankind, an astonishing ignorance of the world outside of Asia. But three of Tojo's earlier years were spent in Europe and he had even journeyed through the United States.

In 1919 he was posted abroad, serving briefly in Switzerland and then in Germany as military attaché. Japan's officer corps had been modeled on the German pattern and to have studied in Germany was to be a member of an officer elite. For Tojo, whose father had also been sent to Germany, his journey had all the significance of a pilgrimage. The fact that his time in the country was spent in the aftermath of its World War I defeat appeared not to have affected his attitude. Post-war austerity there struck a responsive note in one imbued with the concept of frugality and denial of creature comforts in the *samurai* tradition. He admired the fortitude and toughness of the German people and often commented afterwards on their ability to stand up under hardship and suffering, saying that the Japanese could learn much from the Germans. And, for a military man, study in the vanquished country was not such a futile exercise as might be supposed. The Prussian military caste had emerged almost intact from the war, its members already regrouping and forming into the nucleus of an army that was to serve Hitler so well.

It was the more unfortunate that since his knowledge of Europe was confined to Germany and to the narrow military field, Tojo's years in the west gave him only a short time to gain some firsthand knowledge of the United States. When he returned to Japan in 1922 on completion of his tour of duty, his homeward journey took him across the United States. He observed a country, in contrast with Germany, rich and apparently untouched by war. He saw a people, compared with the formal Teutons and his ultra-formal countrymen, casual to the point of being undignified, thoroughly unmilitary and uninhibitedly dedicated to the pursuit of material prosperity. This brief and superficial encounter left him with convictions that were to prove as fatal for him and his country as his uncritical admiration of Germany. America might be materially strong, he concluded, but she lacked the spiritual strength of the Japanese, a dangerous opinion in itself but the more so in one who held as an article of faith that purpose plus hard work would inevitably prevail over mere material factors.

When Major Tojo returned to Japan in 1922, he was coming up to the age of forty but looked older than his years. He was balding and the close-cropped military style further accentuated the bare expanse of skull. The clipped moustache cultivated from early manhood, sparse and graying, grew over a mouth habitually compressed, and the hard glitter of the eyes behind the horn-rimmed glasses was as much responsible as the cutting edge of his tongue for his nickname *"Kamisori,"* or "Razor" Tojo, by which he was to become widely known. His uniform hung loose and looked ill fitting on a scrawny but wiry five feet four inches. The nervous energy and combativeness of his youth were now contained within a tough shell of severity which habitual self-discipline and the restraints of military life had inculcated. But his rapid, staccato manner of speech and the impatient outbursts that were to become more frequent as he rose higher in rank betrayed that the temperament of the young Hideki was still there.

As a soldier, he often told people, he was on duty twenty-four hours, and long after other officers had gone, the lamp would be burning in Tojo's office. When quartered with his family, he habitually brought home military manuals and papers, working at them with relentless concentration for long periods. What time he spared himself for relaxation he spent with his wife and children. Hobbies or sports he had none and, he always insisted, his hobby was his work. Personal indulgences were few. He had a liking for sweet Japanese rice-cakes, often helping himself to two at a time, but he ate sparingly, saying that too much food made him sleepy. The strongest drink he permitted himself was coffee and Mrs. Tojo would serve him up to six cups when he was working at night. Tobacco was his only uncontrolled weakness. He was a nervous and compulsive smoker, getting through sixty cigarettes a day but often stubbing them out after a few puffs, to the distress of his wife who deplored the waste as well as the effect on his health. He knew that he smoked too much, frequently saying he ought to give it up. Once he did, with his wife's encouragement, for a whole year. Then one day he announced abruptly that he was going to start again. "It's the only pleasure I have," he told her.[1]

Outside of two friends he had made while at military academy, he had few others. Both of these, Tetsuzan Nagata and Hisao Watari, also became generals but were fated for early death —one by an assassin's hand and the other of pneumonia while serving in Manchuria. His relations even with military men were on a colleague rather than a crony level, always inhibited by his brusque manner and unyielding observance of service protocol. He had little time for civilians, although later in life he became acquainted with some who served under him in government and with a newspaper columnist whose devotion penetrated even Tojo's habitual reserve. Much later he got to know Giichi Miura, an exponent of rightist philosophy whom he particularly admired for the clarity with which he expounded the concept of *kokutai,* a mystic and untranslatable term signifying the oneness of the Japanese state and people with their divinely descended Imperial line.

The spectacles that corrected his ocular shortsightedness did nothing, unfortunately, for the mental myopia he was cursed with. He never lost the ideas and prejudices formed in these early years. Constant and basic in his thinking was that the contest with Russia, unfinished in 1905, must ultimately be fought out to achieve Japanese domination, or as he called it in the terminology

30

of his day, Japan's destiny in Asia. Russia was, and remained for him, the first and last enemy.

In his earlier days he had a grudging understanding for the older colonial nations whose military conquests and self-interest he could appreciate; but America was, to him, an unwanted arbitrator and intruder in Asian affairs. He could never accept that a nation with its own recent expansion in Mexico, Cuba, Hawaii, and the Philippines, and on whose possessions Japan had no designs—at least at that time—could have any honest motive for standing in Japan's way. The mixture of a profession of lofty ideals with the eye to commercial advantage that keynoted American policies in the Far East he regarded as hypocritical. To this irascibility and contempt for America was added the consciousness of American discrimination against his race.

Of all the oriental peoples, the Japanese are the most racially conscious. Indeed, the notion of the ethnological superiority of the Japanese as pure in strain and divinely descended was centuries old in Japan long before the first nineteenth century European exponents of the myth of Aryan supremacy were born. Ironically, in the Germany that Tojo knew there was no race problem or, at least, it was not then an open issue. Former corporal Hitler was just one of the faceless multitude of demobilized soldiers, and more than a decade was to pass before he and his Nazi adherents were to implement the principles of the pseudo-science of the master-race in Europe. Between the United States and Japan, on the other hand, race had already become an issue at the time that Tojo passed through.

Soon after Tojo had returned from Manchuria sharing the widely held conviction that American interference had deprived Japan of the fruits of victory over the Russians, he and thousands of his countrymen saw insult added to injury when there were moves in America to include Japanese in anti-immigration laws passed to prevent the further entry of Chinese laborers into the United States. Angry demonstrations were provoked in Japan and bitter protest came from the Japanese government. The proposed legislation was, for the time, dropped, but the damage was done as far as Tojo and many other Japanese were concerned.

The Japan to which he returned had already graduated from the guided democracy imposed at the hands of the Emperor Meiji and his advisers. The health of the Emperor Yoshihito, poor when he inherited the throne, had deteriorated physically and mentally. For the remainder of his reign, the *Genro,* or elder statesmen, who comprised the advisory council to the throne, were preoccupied with grooming for his future role of sovereign the Prince Regent, Hirohito, a young man who dutifully applied himself under their guidance but whose interest in the exercise of power was probably exceeded by that in his hobby of marine biology. Government had settled down to a two-party system of parliamentary rule and now, as a modern industrial state, Japan was enjoying a postwar boom.

For Tojo this combination of civilian, nonaristocratic rule with concentration on material prosperity must have appeared disquietingly similar to the conditions and attitudes he had noted briefly and disapprovingly on his passage through the United States. For the next few years, from his new post as instructor at the Military Staff College in Tokyo, from which he had graduated as an honors student in 1915, he had ample opportunity to observe that the army, far from sharing in the new prosperity, had actually declined in prestige. What was more, it was being openly questioned if the money spent on the army was really justified. It had, after all, taken no part in the major war just concluded and almost two decades had passed since the glorious victories of the Russo–Japanese war.

If the soldiers had taken no part in World War I, the merchants and industrialists of Japan, mainly grouped under four giant and all-embracing *zaibatsu* family organizations, had been extremely active. Much of their profit came from the direct supply of ships, equipment and materials to the embattled nations of Europe, and a lot more through expansion into those nations' traditional markets in Asia. As opportunities in commerce and industry beckoned, bright young men no longer aspired to be officers in the services. The pay of the Japanese officer, never high, now lagged even further behind in relation to that of other professions. For the junior officers in particular, there was the feeling that their profession held little future and a falling status. There was the chagrin, too, of knowing that, in cash, they were worth little more than a despised clerk in a bank or in one of the *zaibatsu* (great company) offices.

The postwar boom was, in fact, actually fading on Tojo's return. With a population more than doubled to fifty-four millions since the beginning of the Meiji era, and with an annual increase of almost one million being crammed into the narrow islands, Japan was no longer self-supporting in food. As the cancellation of war contracts began to be felt by industry and the western nations began to compete again in the Asian markets, Japanese industry faced a severe recession. Then, at midday on the 1st of September, 1923, nature took a hand. Just before noon the first tremors of an earthquake, the greatest natural disaster in Japanese history, shook the country, the prelude to six days and nights of unforgettable terror and appalling destruction in which one hundred thousand Japanese perished and the cities of Tokyo and Yokohama were almost totally destroyed.

The enormity of the calamity and its tragic toll of suffering brought immediate worldwide sympathy and offers of assistance. From no country was the response more compassionate than from the people and government of the United States, and in prompt and generous aid to the stricken nation the Americans outdid all others. During and after the ordeal the Japanese army also played an invaluable part in aiding the civilian population and was given a chance for action more positive than military training and more popular than putting down riots, its only role for many years. But the officers and soldiers who looked back with justifiable pride on this soon found themselves, with the Americans, reflecting on the transient quality of gratitude.

Much, if not all, the goodwill engendered toward the people of the United States for their aid in the earthquake of 1923 was wiped out the following year. In 1924 pressure groups in the United States finally achieved the passing in Congress of the Selective Immigration Act. This discriminatory measure, taken against the advice of many liberal Americans, once more raised the race issue between the United States and Japan, where it was bitterly resented as putting Japanese in the insulting category of "coolies" along with the Chinese. Tojo observed at the time that the real reason for the passing of the law was that Japanese immigrants working on farms in the United States were disliked because they were more industrious than American farmers. "It shows," he said, "how the strong will always put their own interests first. Japan, too, has to be strong to survive in the world."[2]

At the same time, the great expenditure needed for rehabilitation after the earthquake in an economic situation that continued to worsen brought to a head the long-standing demand to cut down the armed forces. Despite frenzied protest by the ultranationalists and the utmost military propagandists could do to keep alive the bogey that Japan was encircled by a hostile world and threatened by the Americans, the army was cut by four divisions.

This alone was a serious enough blow for the military and represented a successful assertion of authority by the civil powers. But worse was in the air. The politicians, emboldened by their success, were taking a new look at the wider issue of Japan's relations with China. Doubt was being openly expressed in government and business circles whether Manchuria was worth keeping, whatever its potential value, if doing so incurred the sustained hostility of the Chinese people. And, more ominous still for the army, an additional benefit was being talked of by those who advocated the new approach to China. Without Manchuria, it was asked, what need would there be to keep up the large and costly Kwangtung Army.

Eight

The feeling that there must be special and close ties between Japan and China is almost atavistic in Japanese political thinking. Even since the unhappy chapter in Sino–Japanese relations begun in 1894, there had been Japanese ready to advocate—without noticeable success—that such ties should be achieved by peaceful means and based on assuring the Chinese that they needed Japan.

Now hard facts were beginning to convince where liberal thought had failed. Already harried by competition and severe tariffs in the international markets, a vigorous anti-Japanese movement and boycott of Japanese goods by the Chinese was hurting Japan still more. The prospect of a rapprochement with China over Manchuria, with the twin benefits of increased trade and a considerable cut in military expenditure, was beginning to look like good sense. In July 1929 Premier Hamaguchi, heading a new cabinet, initated a friendship-with-China policy, and, from Nanking, word came from the Kuomingtang government that it was prepared to enter into discussions.

There was powerful and obstinate opposition to such a policy, and it was not confined to the services. Voices both persuasive and loud were raised against it. Where, some demanded, was the guarantee that China would forgive and forget so readily? And if it did, how was Japan's claim to a special position in China to be assured?

More shrill was the denunciation of the superpatriots and those who spoke for the ultranationalist societies—secret and semisecret—that had proliferated in the land. Representing all degrees of chauvinism, belligerence, and mystic belief in Japan's right and duty to be master in Asia, they held all who were suspected of aiming at anything short of this to be traitors.

There were the "Black Dragons" of the notorious Mitsuru Toyama, the doyen of all the extremists, who had connections in high places and enjoyed throughout his long life and career apparent immunity from any form of civil or criminal action. Toyama's organization, old-established and having its beginnings in the Meiji era, was dedicated to extending Japan's sway as far as the Amur River on the mainland. Though given to theatrical gestures and sinister threats, its members did not go in for overt acts of violence, but assassinations of prominent persons were to become an all-too-frequent reminder that some of the more recently formed "blood brotherhoods," such as the "Native-land Loving Society," did not stop at mere advocacy.

Among the individual extremists was the serio-comic figure of Dr. Shumei Okawa, perpetrator of "The Book of the Tiger," a combination of bible and handbook that set out the principles of a one-party state and restated in terms of political philosophy the myths of Japan's divine origin and destiny. Okawa had just returned from Manchuria where for some time he had headed the "research staff"—a euphemism for propaganda department—of the South Manchurian Railway. Back in Japan, provided with apparently ample funds, he was actively pursuing his propaganda work.

Just returned too, from a tour of duty in Turkey as military attaché, was Major, later Colonel, Kingoro Hashimoto. Inspired by the exploits of the Turkish military dictator and reformer Kemal Ataturk, whose "Young Turks" from the army provided a nickname for all future youthful zealots and activists, Hashimoto envisaged Japan similarly purged of weak-kneed civilian government and achieving glorious and heroic dominance in Asia under soldier-administrators. Even as the debate on the new policy towards China was going on, the Colonel was forming the new "Cherry Society," taking its name from the blossom which, from its fall at the peak of perfection, has poetic links with the traditional dedication in life and nobility in death of the *samurai*. The society was to have many adherents, a few of them civilians like Dr. Okawa with whom Hashimoto kept in close association over many years, but it was primarily an extremist fraternity among the armed services. Among the first members who met with Hashimoto at the inaugural meeting were officers just out of staff college who were later to appear in various key posts in the Kwangtung Army in Manchuria.

It was in Manchuria that the hard core of hostility to any accommodation with China was concentrated. Since the war of 1905, a great deal of money and effort had been invested in the development of the country. Businesses had been established and many thousands had emigrated there. In the public sector large enterprises had been set up, dominated by the South Manchurian Railway Company. The presidency of the latter organization had become an important political appointment, and it operated in Manchuria virtually as a separate government regardless of Tokyo-appointed consular officials. Those Japanese who soldiered, worked, and lived there had a vested interest in the proposition that Manchuria, in terms of potential wealth, living space, and prestige, was indispensable to Japan. Moreover, despite a quarter of a century of occupation and consolidation, the inherent insecurity of their situation had accentuated the colonial outpost mentality among them.

From Russia, ruled by Stalin, a tyrant more ruthless than most of the Tsars, there was a triple threat. To the north was the Far Eastern army of the formidable military forces created by the Soviet regime. More dangerous than Soviet soldiers, agents from Moscow were intriguing with local revolutionaries all over the Far East. And in China, the Japanese were particularly exercised by the presence of Soviet political and military experts attached to the new republican Kuomingtang government of Generalissimo Chiang Kai-shek. Japanese fears that such Soviet assistance would lead to eventual domination of China by Russia doubtless underestimated the deep-rooted xenophobia and historic ingratitude of the Chinese, but were, nevertheless, strongly felt.

The Chinese government, resurgent and nationalist, exerted its own persistent pressure. This was increasing as Chiang Kai-shek broke, one by one, the power of the warlords in China proper and drew nearer to a confrontation with the last of them, the foxy old Chang Tso-lin, who was still nominally the governor of the Chinese province of Manchuria. Large numbers of Chinese troops were stationed there, for they had never relinquished their claim to sovereignty. The government in Nanking used all possible means short of war to loosen the Japanese hold.

Internationally they organized support for the Chinese cause, skillfully playing on the sympathy and self-interest of the western powers and especially the United States. In Manchuria itself they attempted to undermine Japanese control by granting concessions to foreign concerns, all of which the Japanese refused to recognize. One of these, a bid by a large American syndicate with U.S. government backing, had done nothing to dispel the cynical belief of many Japanese that behind high-sounding American condemnation of Japanese occupation of Manchuria, there were motives of a good old-fashioned commercial character.

Civilians back in Japan might talk of reducing military strength, but the attitude of those in Manchuria corresponded in their day much more to that of the French *colons* who, a quarter of a century later, were still stubbornly committed in Algeria. They were acutely conscious of the protecting arm of the strong and semi-autonomous Kwangtung garrison, and as was to happen in Algeria, interest in mutual survival had brought between soldier and civilian in Manchuria an unusual degree of common involvement in political and military affairs.

In Manchuria, in a society that depended on it for existence, the army had status and power, a flattering change from the position in Japan where it was under attack both from the axe of the government economizers and from innuendo by those who sneered at the army that never went to war. Here Japanese army officers from Japan were exposed to the theories of the idealists, romantics, cranks and intriguers who had gravitated there. There was already talk of creating a Manchurian state more Japanese than Japan itself, and free of the corrupting combination of big business and alien political institutions. And particularly susceptible among the officers who came were those—now comprising about a third of their number—who had come into the army from the poverty-ridden rural areas of Japan.

There had always been a human surplus in the countryside of Japan that the land's meager return to those who worked it could not support. It was from the country areas that the well-off got their servants, the factories their female sweated labor, and the houses of pleasure their handmaidens. For the men there was the armed services and it was from the farming districts that the rank and file of the regular soldiers and NCOs were recruited.

Those who joined the armed forces either as officers or in the ranks, even the sons of peasants or fishermen who sought escape from extreme hardship and poverty, were likely to find conditions hard. When, in the Meiji era, Japanese missions had gone abroad to choose the best models on which to pattern their own institutions, great care had been paid to those of the army and navy. For the latter the British navy was chosen as being best suited to the Japanese character and requirements. But to the discipline and traditions of the British senior service—faithfully copied and exigent enough in themselves—there had been added austerities and practices of a strictly Japanese conception, as exemplified by the description of a day in the life of the cadets at the Imperial academy at Etajima.

The cadets get up before the crack of dawn. After saluting the Rising Sun they run up to the peak of the mountain, come back and have their morning meal of rice and salt. After four hours of work they get another bowl of rice and at night, after another four strenuous hours, a last bowl of rice with soya beans. And this goes on for four long years.[1]

In the army which, it was originally planned, should be based on that of the French but was swiftly changed to follow the Prussian army after its shattering defeat of the French in 1870, the regimen was even more severe. Those who entered it were subject to some of the worst aspects of Prussian military tyranny combined with flagellant *samurai*-derived disciplines.

On completing his own cadetship, Tojo had taken part in the customary forced march, designed to try the spirit and physical endurance to the limit and as a final test to separate the men from the boys.[2] Training for the ordinary soldiers, second to no army in the world in toughness and thoroughness, was augmented by such institutions as the "ordeal by slapping" undergone by new recruits and described by Hanama Tasaki in *Long the Imperial Way*.

Five old soldiers went down the line without warning, slapping each soldier soundly on his cheek. Those that could not keep their posture of attention were slapped more than the others. The sergeant then demanded of each recruit why he thought he had been slapped. As each gave what he thought might be the answer, he was soundly slapped again. Finally, one recruit, when his turn came said he didn't know. "That is right!" the squad leader said. "When you are slapped, don't give excuses. As His Majesty has been pleased to admonish in his Imperial Rescript, 'Uninfluenced by worldly thoughts and unhampered by politics, guard well your single destiny of patriotism.' Our sole duty is to be patriotic to the Emperor. You need only obey what you are told."[3]

In the army, for all this, conscientious officers maintained the same kind of paternalism for those who served under them which was one of the best traditions between master and man in Japan. This was especially true where the officers—as was common—were appointed to locally raised units and where they, like the men they commanded, had local affiliations. Tojo, for example, accepted that face-slapping was a "means of training" in Japanese families where educational standards were low and that its practice in the armed forces was, therefore, no more than the continuation of a national custom; but his own conscientiousness as an officer was beyond doubt. When, in 1928, he was given his first regimental command, he went to lengths in the care of his men which, although considerable, were not untypical among regimental officers. "The regimental commander," he told a meeting of his company officers when he took over a battalion of the 1st Infantry Regiment in Tokyo, "is the father of the regiment. You are the mothers." He required them to make personal visits to the homes of soldiers who had domestic troubles and even went to the extent of helping men out of his own slender resources. Mrs. Tojo recalled how on one occasion one of his officers, Lieutenant Sato, came to Tojo's house to ask for a loan. One of Sato's men needed thirty yen, the equivalent of a little over ten dollars in those days, which he could not raise himself. Sato thought the regimental commander rather querulous at the time, making much of the fact that although Sato insisted he would repay the money, he did not know when. Here was a Lieutenant Colonel, as Sato put it, holding "an Imperial Council meeting for a mere thirty yen." Tojo left him in the hallway for a time and eventually returned with the money, saying, "Here it is. Come again if you need some more," and enjoined him to continue caring for his men. "The fact was," Mrs. Tojo said, "an unexpected call for even such a small sum as thirty yen had been very embarrassing for our household. While Sato was kept waiting, I had to slip out by the back way to borrow the money from a neighbor."[4]

As yet Tojo had not become associated with any of the political activity rife in the Kwangtung Army and spreading, often through officers who had served in Manchuria, to the army at home. This was not to say that he was unaware of it or that he had any confidence in the politicians. He was to give only too ample evidence later that he despised and distrusted them. But as a hard-working and not so young officer—he was now turned forty—political or any other activities would have been a distraction from the serious business of advancing his career in the series of administrative posts in which he had been serving until now. He lived and worked, as military men say, by the book. The time was almost upon him, however, when as a regimental officer he was to be directly concerned with the problems of people that were covered by no military manual.

When the shock of the world economic depression hit Japan in 1929, it was for the Japanese nation a disaster in many ways as tragic as the earthquake six years before and with repercussions more far-reaching. Of all the world's industrial nations, the Japanese were the worst affected. There were few among Japan's millions who were not touched by it, and in some sections of the population the suffering was intense. In the agricultural areas alone more than half of the farmers were engaged in silk production. The shutting down of their main overseas market, the United States, brought widespread distress and then, owing to a disastrous crop failure, conditions of famine. The effects were more than social, although the degradation of poverty and the necessity of selling daughters to *geisha* houses or into prostitution for payment of debts or just to get enough to survive was bad enough.

As the consequences of the world depression bit deep into the nation's vitals, officers like Tojo, who up to that time had considered politics and economics a thing apart, now learned about them in human terms from their men, who brought back pitiful tales of hunger, despair, and often suicide. And there was no lack of people in the army and out of it to point out that those responsible were their own corrupt politicians and businessmen and, beyond them, America and other western nations which, to protect their own interests, had brought this tragedy to the Japanese.

Typically, Tojo was as much concerned for the morale of the regiment as for the welfare of his men. Indeed, he believed that the two were linked. "Soldiers can't concentrate on their duty," he frequently said, "if they have personal worries." He held special meetings of his officers at his home discussing the state of the unit and urging them not to let their men get carried away. It was their special responsibility as officers, he told his subordinates, to bear in mind the future of the country and not to be blinded by more immediate and emotional considerations.[5]

The depression had spared almost no one. In the cities there was unemployment on a scale far exceeding the worst in any western country. Banks failed, and the big industrialists and the four giant *zaibatsu* concerns controlling the bulk of the country's commerce were badly hurt. Those among them who, a year earlier, had been disposed to support a liberal approach to China now hardened against it. With discriminatory taxes and embargoes barring Japanese goods not only from the United States and Europe but from the colonial areas they controlled, they saw the raw materials of Manchuria and China proper and the latter's immense potential market as not merely desirable but vital to survival. Only there could the great powers not shut them out as it suited them. The situation had become too serious to be left to protracted negotiations or the whim of the Chinese.

The friendship-to-China policy was already in ruins when its sponsor, Premier Hamaguchi, was struck down and mortally wounded by the bullet of a fanatic member of the Native-land Loving Society in the early morning of the 14th of November, 1930, on the platform of Tokyo Station. By this time there was no talk of economizing on the armed forces. Fed by antigovernment propaganda, people saw this as throwing away the very tool which could assure Japan's future security, the only argument to convince the stubborn Chinese. And in Manchuria the officers of the Kwangtung Army decided that the time had come for positive action to thwart once and for all the machinations of the Chinese and their own politicians.

Already they had accomplished an act indicative of the desperate measures of which they were capable. In 1928, as the armies of the Chinese generalissimo, Chiang Kai-shek, drew near to the borders of Manchuria, the old Manchurian warlord Marshal Chang Tso-lin had begun to show—as far as the Japanese there were concerned—signs of unreliability. He was suspected, quite rightly as it happened, of being in secret negotiation with the Chinese Kuomingtang government. On the 4th of June of that year, as his train passed over a bridge, it was dynamited by, it was learned much later, a Japanese army unit. The murdered marshal was succeeded by his son who, contrary to the hope placed in him, was showing no more willingness to become an outright puppet of the Japanese army than his father had done.

If the Chinese were taken by surprise in this and in later moves against them, the government of Baron Wakatsuki, who had succeeded the murdered Premier Hamaguchi, certainly had warning. Their Consul General in the Manchurian capital had signaled to Tokyo that "a big incident would break out" when Kwangtung Army units carried out maneuvers in the Mukden area on the night of the 18th of September, 1931. His message, which reached members of the government some ten days before the date given, stimulated the cabinet into some activity and the war minister, General Minami, was persuaded to send an emissary to be on hand to prevent any trouble.

At ten o'clock on the night of the 18th a loud explosion on the railway line near the Chinese military barracks brought a Japanese patrol which "happened" to be in the vicinity to the scene to investigate. They reported that a section of the railway track had been dynamited and that they had themselves been fired on. An hour and a half later, Japanese forces in a sudden attack in strength assaulted and overcame the Chinese quartered in the barracks. A simultaneous attack was made on Mukden itself and by the next morning the city and the airfield were in Japanese hands.

There is ample evidence that the incident was planned well in advance with the heavy artillery used in the fighting moved secretly into position some days before. No request for permission to engage in the operation was made to the government in Tokyo, which was soon made aware that it would have as little say in stopping this private war of the Kwangtung Army as it had in starting it.

A civilian consular official summoned to the Mukden army headquarters was met by the senior staff officer there, a Colonel Itagaki, who told him that the army was now taking the necessary action. The official protested that the affair should not be allowed to get out of hand and that negotiations should follow. His advice and protests alike were ignored. The Chinese, Itagaki insisted, had attacked first and would be dealt with. The honor of the Japanese army and the nation depended on it. As the official continued to protest, Itagaki asked him coldly if he was proposing to interfere in what was now a matter for the army, and to ensure that the official grasped the nakedly martial nature of events, another officer present threatened him with a drawn sword.

War Minister Minami's envoy, Major General Tatekawa, arrived belatedly just after midday on the 19th of September. Like the consular official, he was met by the ubiquitous Colonel Itagaki and was persuaded to go first to an inn to eat and rest instead of direct to military headquarters. There, as he told it later, "I was entertained by *geisha* girls while listening to the sound of firing in the distance." Having gone to bed and "slept soundly," he emerged next day and signaled back to Tokyo that in his opinion the Japanese army in Manchuria was doing no more than defending itself.

With Minami blocking for them in Tokyo, the soldiers of the Kwangtung Army had by January, 1932, reached the Great Wall built centuries before to keep the predatory Manchus out of China proper. A few months later, Doihara, another colonel of the Kwangtung Army staff and a crony of Colonel Itagaki, was installed as mayor of Mukden. And Manchuria, now firmly in the hands of the Kwangtung Army, was later renamed Manchukuo, a so-called independent state under Japanese protection.

Nine

At the time the Kwangtung Army brought off its Manchurian coup, Hideki Tojo was back at a desk in Army Staff Headquarters in Tokyo. Whatever his thoughts were on the army's independent action overseas, since his duties did not call for him to align himself on any political aspects of it, he kept them to himself. With Tojo, the job in hand was what mattered. Characteristically, it was not until 1933, when he was appointed to head the General Affairs Bureau of the War Office, that he first spoke out on political and international affairs.

The bureau, which had been set up as part of the military affairs section of the War Office after the cut of four army divisions in the 1920s, was, in effect, the public relations department of the army. From it were given out the army's views on a wide variety of matters, not overlooking that of the army's 'divine mission' as set out in a pamphlet, published in 1934 and widely quoted, which began, "War is the father of creativeness and the mother of culture. . . ."

One of Tojo's tasks as the new chief was to pronounce on any developments in which the army felt it was concerned. When he took over he may have been surprised at the very wide range these covered, but once appointed, he got down to mastering the details with his usual thoroughness.

Certainly the study of wider issues beyond the strictly

military area—albeit confined to those necessary to argue the army's special case—may have helped to crystallize his views and confirm private prejudices, up to now unvoiced. In fact, it made little difference whether what he said represented original thinking or something he learned in the course of his duties. What made it right for Hideki Tojo in his new job was that it was official. It would have been as difficult to separate his public statements from his own thinking as to isolate Tojo the soldier from Tojo the man.

What he had to say over the period he held the post was repetition and variation on the theme that the destiny of the ancient and great Japanese people beyond the confines of their narrow islands was threatened. The jealousy of the United States, the sinister ambitions of Soviet Russia, and the blind intransigence of China meant that Japan had to rely on her own strength and must be constantly on her guard.

In this last, there was from the army's point of view some reason for concern. By the mid-1930s, something akin to complacency had settled over the land. The army's action in Manchuria, now that it had succeeded, had been accepted by both people and government as a fait accompli and there had been great relief that the direst predictions of those who feared the consequences had not been borne out. America and the western nations had protested but done little else. Japan, denounced by the League of Nations, had walked out, but that body had already, by the withdrawal of the United States early in its life, become largely ineffectual. China, with only moral support from the rest of the world, and far from being able to do anything about the Japanese takeover of Manchuria, had since been compelled to withdraw her troops from the border provinces to make way for extensive Japanese military, political, and commercial penetration in a large area stretching out to Peking.

In Japan itself, with conditions relatively good after the near ruin of 1929, it was difficult for the average Japanese to feel that he was threatened. Giant strides had been made along the road indicated by Count Hayashi after the Sino-Japanese war of 1895. For better or worse Japan was established as a modern industrial nation. Except in the most backward and remote country districts—and even these were served with electric light and power—the standards of living of the Japanese were immutably based on those of the nations of the west. True, they still lagged far behind the most advanced, and in the industrially based economy benefits were unevenly spread. The peasants were still miserably poor and ground down by oppressive taxation. But the Japanese could point out with pride that there was no comparison between their lot and the oriental squalor and omnipresent and apparently hopeless impoverishment of millions of fellow Asians under colonial or semicolonial rule.

The satisfaction was not universal. Along with modern technology and western civilization, there had been imported elements which, to many Japanese, were undesirable and even dangerous. These were the kind of things that had caused the late 1920s and early 1930s to be called the age of "eroticism, grotesquerie, and nonsense." Among them were included the "Modern-garu" or modern girl, shortened to *moga,* the equivalent of the western flapper, with heavy makeup, abbreviated skirts, and shingled or Eton-cropped hair. Included, too, were the "modern boya" (*mobo*), who indulged with the *moga* in such alien promiscuities as walking hand-in-hand or even kissing in imitation of the scenes in the new imported talking pictures.

"Eroticism, grotesquerie, and nonsense" also covered such imports and adaptations as jazz; chorus girls; shows like "Mon Paris," staged by the Takarazuka All-Girl troupes; Charlie Chaplin; dance-halls; the foxtrot and Argentine tangos; French chansons; *avant-garde* painting, sculpture, and their admirers and exponents; and, more sinister, the *"Marx-boya"* students with their unkempt hair, unshaven faces, greasy tattered uniform caps, generally unwashed appearance, and radical thought.

These last represented more than just frivolous outlook, outrageous public behavior, and a potential danger to traditional morality. They were indicative of something which was already felt by the more conservative to be a threat to the state itself. With the consolidation of the Soviet regime in Russia, agents of international communism had been intriguing and working to undermine governments all over the world and nowhere were they more active than in the Far East. Radical thought in Japan had even spread to young officers in the army. For most of them this leaning towards socialism was to prove no more than a first step to conversion to the national-socialist philosophy. This evolved increasingly as left-wing thought became more and more identified with support of Soviet Russia and, therefore, traitorous. Moreover, young officers were returning from military study courses in Hitler's Third Reich indoctrinated with national-socialist ideology. Filled with enthusiasm for Nazi Germany's military resurgence in Europe, they came back, as the young Hideki Tojo had once done, convinced that Japan had much to learn from Germany. In Japan they found common cause with fellow officers and civilians, ultranationalists who were dedicated to doing away with the despised parliamentary system. Indeed, in the Japanese army in the thirties, there were few officers who were not. They were divided only on what form of government should replace it.

Generally they adhered to one of two main factions. There was no formal membership to either and both were composed of an amorphous body of all kinds of individuals and organizations. There was the "Control" group (*Tosei-ha*) which believed in the establishment of a one-party state in which the armed services and the people would be merged into a monolithic political structure based on a war economy. Tojo supported this group as did most high-ranking and senior officers. The policy of the second faction, the "Imperial Way" group (*Kodo-ha*), was perhaps defined as succinctly as it could be by Lewis Bush as "placing faith in divine inspiration."[1] Its exponents, headed by the fire-eating and chauvinistic General Araki, a former war minister, put much stress on reversion to ancient virtues and revival of the traditional martial spirit of Yamato, and called for the sweeping away of the evil and corrupting influence of party politics and big business. Both, needless to say, professed the greatest loyalty to the Emperor. It was to the Imperial Way movement that the most extreme of the ultranationalists, the blood brotherhoods and the mystical cranks, gave their support. And it was among young Japanese, often young army officers, that they found their most willing tools.

Plots for taking over government and carrying out political murders had not been unknown before Premier Hamaguchi was shot down by a member of the Native-land Loving Society in November 1930, but the killing of the diminutive premier set off a whole series of assassinations, attempted assassinations, and coups. People like Dr. Okawa, Colonel Hashimoto and other members of the Cherry Society were back in Japan from Manchuria after the army's independent action there, intriguing and agitating. With Colonel Hashimoto, Okawa planned a series of terrorist acts timed for the 20th of March, 1932, and aimed at setting up a military government with the war minister, General Ugaki, at the head. Among senior army officers alleged to have been involved in the "March Incident" were General Sugiyama, the vice-minister of war, and General Koiso, chief of the military affairs bureau of the army. The plot, apparently, envisaged a large scale disturbance by mobs who, excited by a combination of violent oratory and an issue of free *sake*, would converge on the Diet building. The Diet would then, ostensibly to protect it, be surrounded by troops, and either General Koiso or General Tatekawa —whose dilatory tactics on his mission to Manchuria had greatly contributed to the success of the army coup there—would enter the Diet and call for the resignation of the entire cabinet.

The participation of army officers in the earlier stages of the plot took place during a period of months in 1931 when War Minister Ugaki was absent from office through illness. Ugaki, it seems, knew nothing of it or his own proposed role until, at General Koiso's request, he met Okawa and told him that much as he personally deplored the degeneration of party politics, he would not, as a soldier, have any part of the business. Dr. Okawa took this to mean that Koiso was not unsympathetic. The war minister did not, at any rate, formally denounce the plot or its leaders, but when Okawa approached him again early in March 1932, Ugaki got alarmed and ordered his vice-minister, Sugiyama, and General Koiso not to have anything to do with the affair. Both complied, but not before Koiso had heard that his subordinate at the military affairs bureau, Colonel Nagata, had failed to win support from army officers whose co-operation in the coup would have been essential. Notable among these was General Mazaki, commander of the First Division, who threatened to take action against anyone, whatever his rank or office, who tried to use his troops in such a conspiracy.

Nagata was to bear a grudge against Mazaki from then on—with dire consequences to himself. He was politically active, a leading advocate of the *Tosei-ha,* and listed as a member of *Kokuhonsha,* one of the right-wing patriotic societies. What is interesting about his part in the abortive March Incident of 1932 is that in his book, *Conspiracy at Mukden,* Takehiko Yoshihashi names Hideki Tojo as one of two officers who assisted Nagata in one of the earlier plans for the proposed coup.[2] Nagata was certainly Tojo's old friend from their military academy days and Tojo was, at that time, subordinate to Nagata at the military affairs bureau. Whether or not Tojo was involved—and from the confusion of accounts and the secrecy implicit in the affair there must be allowed a strong element of guilt by association—he was never thereafter associated with any intrigue for the violent overthrow of government. What the failure of the March Incident did produce, in fact, was a definite schism between advocates of the Imperial Way and the Control factions, with the latter concentrating on keeping senior officers of the *Kodo-ha* out of important posts, particularly in the Kwangtung Army, and on exercising political power through the army's representative in the cabinet, the war minister.

Undeterred, Colonel Hashimoto and Dr. Okawa plotted anew for a takeover in October of the same year, this time combined with an elaborate plan to wipe out the government's leading ministers and a proposal to put General Araki in charge of a new government. Once again the scheme was foiled, largely because of the eccentric Okawa's bungling and indiscretion. The ringleaders were arrested just before the coup was due to take place, but no charges were made against them and the officers involved were released and posted away from Tokyo.

The Imperial Way extremists, for a time at a disadvantage, had already resorted to isolated action against individuals they held to be inimical to the the interests of the state. A list of prominent businessmen, statesmen and politicians had been drawn up and, at intervals in 1932, Inoue, a former prime minister, and Baron Dan, a director of the Mitsui commercial and banking empire, were murdered. Inukai, the seventy-five-year-old prime minister, was determined to bring an end to the conflict with China and (it came to the knowledge of the extremists) was in secret touch with the Chinese and was proposing to ask the Emperor to issue a rescript ordering the army to desist from taking any further direct action. Inukai's efforts for peace were stopped when he was shot down by young fanatic members of one of the blood brotherhoods. Over the same period, terrorist bomb attacks were made on the headquarters of political parties, government residences, power stations, police stations, and banks. The assassins were arrested and the organizers of the blood brotherhood, including Dr. Okawa, were later rounded up. Although all received long terms of imprisonment, none was sentenced to the statutory penalty of death.

There was more than a suggestion that the tolerant attitude shown by the army command towards army men involved in the March and October incidents had as much to do with politics as compassion and that their crimes were exploited as a threat to advance the army's political ends. Behind the scenes, high-ranking officers took every opportunity to drive home their claim that, though regrettable, the incidents were but a manifestation of the anger and explosive mood of most of their young officers. They would cease, they implied, only when the frustrations and evils of party politics were eradicated under a government that united the army and the nation. The generals of the Control group in fact used the young extremists, if less obviously, just as the wild men of the Imperial Way faction did. It was a cynical and dangerous game and one which recoiled on them in August of 1935.

Hideki Tojo had left the military affairs bureau to command a brigade in southern Japan, and his friend from military academy days, General Tetsuzan Nagata remained there. A few months earlier, in November 1934, military police, in a sudden swoop, had arrested several young army officers who were accused of planning a series of political killings. A court-martial, held behind closed doors, went on until the following May when the trial was mysteriously dropped and the defendants were released. Allegedly influential in getting the trial stopped was General Mazaki, who was now inspector general of military training and an advocate of the Imperial Way movement.

In August Mazaki was compelled to give up his post, probably from a vague uneasiness on the part of the general staff that the complicity of young officers in extremist plots was getting out of hand, and he was replaced by a Control group man. The resignation was demanded in the name of the war minister, General Hayashi, but Mazaki appeared to have believed and to have repeated to subordinates that the action against him had been instigated by General Nagata.

On the 12th of August, a young Imperial Way adherent, Lieutenant Colonel Aizawa, forced his way into Nagata's office. Aizawa was one of a number of officers who, because of his known ultranationalist views and perhaps also for suspected involvement in the recent plot, had been put on orders for overseas. He was wearing a sword, as he was entitled to do—not the dress sword of western armies but a deadly razor-keen *samurai* weapon. Drawing it, he slashed at Nagata and, as the general tried to escape, hacked and stabbed him to death. This done, he calmly returned to his quarters to prepare to leave for his new station. Surprise, apparently, was his dominant emotion when the military police came to seize him.

It was surpassed by the shocked reaction of the senior officers now that the fanatic hand of the Imperial Way faction had been turned not on civilians but on one of their number. Ironically, Nagata had been one of those who, at the time of the October incident in 1931, had argued that the officers implicated in the conspiracy should not be formally punished because patriotism and youth had led them into it. After Nagata's murder there was no question of excusing the assassin on account of youth or idealism. Aizawa was tried and, despite much emotion fanned by sympathizers, he was condemned to death and executed.

With the death of Nagata, Hideki Tojo lost an old and good friend, one who had often asserted that Tojo would rise to high rank in the army. It was his friend's murder which now set in train events that were to put Tojo on the way to office more exalted than Nagata could have envisaged. While the trial of Aizawa was still going on, the war ministry and army general staff rushed measures for the tightening up of discipline. More Imperial Way adherents were removed and posted away from the capital; units known to contain extremist elements were alerted for overseas service. The reliable and efficient Hideki Tojo, promoted to Major General, received his orders to take over one of the most sensitive and potentially one of the most powerful posts in the Japanese army. In October, 1935 he embarked to head the Manchurian army gendarmeries, the Kwangtung detachment of an organization which became better known and infamous later by its Japanese name, the *Kempeitai*.

Ten

In the few years of its existence, the Japanese maintained the fiction that the renamed Manchukuo (the Land of the Manchus) with a Japanese-appointed puppet Emperor of the old Manchu royal house was an independent state. The fact that it fooled no one, not even the fascist powers who recognized it, did not concern them. But the pretext of the independent state of Manchukuo served as much as anything to insure its firm control by the occupying Kwangtung Army, by circumventing direct government from Tokyo. The country was run by a consortium of businessmen, local civilian officials, and army officers, and it was the latter who had the final say, notably Lieutenant General Itagaki, the commander of the Kwangtung Army who had been so deeply involved in the 1931 action.

On his arrival in Manchuria, Tojo showed that he was going to take no part in, nor would he tolerate any unofficial activities. He set about his task with energy, making clear that his *Kempeitai* was the only body permitted for law enforcement. At the same time, he found that his job, which made him responsible for all aspects of security, was capable of wide interpretation. In his red-brick headquarters he compiled comprehensive dossiers on the public and private activities of all who might be suspected of activities dangerous to established authority. None of this meant that Tojo consciously set up a secret police apparatus on the lines of Himmler's in Germany; but in army-run Manchuria, where intrigue was a way of life, and in an atmosphere where a preoccupation with security was obsessional, the development of the *Kempeitai* into a police-state type arm was almost inevitable. Unhappily, as events in Tokyo were building up to demonstrate, the conditions for the same kind of power and functions to be extended to the *Kempeitai* in Japan were not far off.

In 1936 those who deplored alien influences in Japan probably found comfort in the crowds, young and old, who still flocked to see the traditional *kabuki* plays, a highly stylized blend of the aural, visual and terpsichorean arts whose origins dated back to the sixteenth century. They must have been particularly reassured by those who sat through the eleven long acts of *Chushingura—the Forty-Seven Exemplary Loyal Subjects.* Based, like many of these dramas, on actual incidents which occurred in the Tokugawa period, *Chushingura,* one of the eighteen standard classics of the *kabuki* theatre, tells in gruesome detail the story of the forty-seven warrior retainers who served the *daimyo* Asano, Lord of Ako. Their graves at the temple of Sengakuji near Tokyo are to this day a place of pilgrimage for the Japanese. To know something of their story is to comprehend, as far as any westerner can ever do, something of *bushido,* the medieval code of the warrior which the youth and fighting men of twentieth-century Japan were exhorted to follow. Of *Chushingura,* one of the contemporary authorities on the cult wrote in the 1930s that it exemplified "an artistic embodiment of *bushido* in its purest form, fostered and tempered in the troublous days of old and handed down as a living flame which teaches a Japanese what he should be."[1]

The tale, spun out with subplots and counterplots, is one of assassination and revenge. In 1701 the *daimyo* Asano was provoked by a trick into drawing his sword while in the Tokugawa ruler's palace, wounding Kira, another nobleman. For this act of *lèse majesté* his possessions were confiscated and he was condemned to death. By reason of his warrior rank he was permitted to accomplish his own death by *hara-kiri.* His retainers, who by his death had become *ronin,* or masterless *samurai,* immediately began to plan revenge upon Kira.

Knowing that he would be expecting this and knowing that it was imperative to lull him into a sense of false security, the band scattered, degrading themselves by becoming laborers and tradesmen. Oishi, their leader, took up a life of debauchery and drunkenness, abandoning his wife and children and taking a prostitute to live with him, all to the end of deceiving Kira. For three years they played their roles. Then, on the night of the 14th of December, 1703, under cover of a heavy snowstorm, the forty-seven *ronin,* casting off pretense, assembled secretly, attacked the stronghold of the now unsuspecting Kira and cut him down. Laying his head on the grave of their late master in the temple at Sengakuji, honor satisfied, all forty-seven committed *hara-kiri.*

This, as dramatized, was the story over which members of the audience often had to go out and wring their tear-soaked *tenugui,* or facecloth, dry. The applause for the half-hour-long scene of the ceremonial suicide of Oishi, the *samurai* leader, as interpreted by one of the foremost *kabuki* actors, was frequently so prolonged and enthusiastic as to call for the whole scene to be repeated as an encore. This was the philosophy of loyalty and death before dishonor, implacable vengeance, and the end justifying the means—no matter what the degradation or deception, or sacrifice of self or family—that was held to be the model for all Japanese.

Tragically and bloodily, the extent to which medieval violence and fanaticism lived on was revealed on the early morning of the 26th of February, 1936. In almost a recreation of the night of the forty-seven *ronin,* groups of soldiers, many from Tojo's former unit, the First Infantry Regiment, which had been ordered overseas following the Nagata killing, suddenly set out in a murderous bid to take over the government.

Led by young officers, none higher in rank than captain, the soldiers hunted down their victims just before daylight. Assassination squads, cutting down or shooting servants, policemen, and anyone else who stood in their way, killed Viscount Saito, the lord privy seal, Mr. Takahashi, the minister of finance, and Colonel Watanabe, the inspector general of military training. They attacked the official residence of the aged prime minister, Admiral Okawa, and murdered his brother-in-law, apparently mistaking him for the premier, who hid in a cupboard and later escaped by a back entrance. Admiral Suzuki, the grand chamberlain, was severely wounded and, although left to die, recovered later.

Also on the killers' death list were Count Makino, a former privy seal, and even the revered Prince Saionji, the last surviving member of the *genro,* the elder statesmen who had advised on all important state decisions during the reign of the Emperor Meiji. Members of Makino's household staff and police guard sacrificed their lives to enable the Count to make his escape, and by the time that the assassins, intent on the murder of the eighty-year-old Saionji, arrived at his villa in the suburb of Okitsu, the old man had been taken away by police to a secret place of safety.

Before day broke, the mutineers had occupied the War Ministry, the Prime Minister's residence, the police headquarters, law courts, Diet building, army and navy headquarters, and newspaper offices. Setting up armed camps around the Imperial palace and calling themselves the "Loyalist Army," their leaders sent signals urging other troops to join them. They issued a proclamation calling for the abolition of parliamentary government and denounced elder statesmen, politicians, and big business. These, they declared, were responsible for the ills besetting Japan and for holding back the achievement of Japan's destiny. Such men had misled the Emperor and they, the soldiers, were doing their duty to His Majesty by taking direct action to rid him of these "insincere advisers."

Since their declared aims were almost identical with those openly stated by many of the commanding generals, the young officers, having successfully initiated the military coup, confidently expected that their army superiors would take it from there. At their headquarters set up at Tokyo's downtown Sanno hotel from which guests, including several foreigners, had been suddenly but courteously ejected, the ringleaders of the mutiny waited. And they waited in vain.

If any of their seniors had any thought of joining them, they were given pause. Emperor Hirohito, faced with open insurrection and the paralysis of government, its surviving members sheltered behind the barbed wire and cordon of obedient troops shielding the Imperial palace, made one of his rare interventions in public affairs. Summoning his minister of war, he pronounced that the self-styled loyalists were rebels and must be crushed. This was decisive.

Troops were swiftly brought in from outside garrisons, and naval landing parties from warships in Tokyo Bay took up battle stations sealing off the rebel-occupied areas. Pamphlets were dropped on them by naval aircraft and calls for surrender were displayed from advertising balloons flown overhead. Senior officers went to the barricades manned by the rebels and argued and exhorted for three days. It was agreed that their leaders should have the privilege of the defeated *samurai* of committing *hara-kiri* and eighteen coffins and swords were solemnly supplied to them for the purpose.

When the rebellion collapsed on the 29th of February, two of the rebel ringleaders had claimed their ancient right of suicide. The remainder, realizing that the support they had anticipated was not coming, capitulated. Many of the leaders were undoubtedly convinced that although the coup had failed, something might be achieved in the great capital, both emotional and political, which would be made of their sincerity and patriotism when they stood before their court martials. Even this consolation was to be denied them.

The trials, when they took place, were in secret and details were censored from the press and radio. Thirteen of the leaders were executed. Eighteen other officers were imprisoned for long terms; other leading participants, including many NCOs, were also sent to prison. Twenty officers were cashiered and others were posted overseas to Manchuria, where they were given something of a hero's reception from the men of the Kwangtung Army.

Eleven

In the Kwangtung Army and among the civilians in Manchuria, excitement and confusion had been intense as the first reports of the army rising in Tokyo reached them. A signal inviting the Kwangtung soldiers to join the mutiny had been sent to Manchuria army headquarters as it had been to other army groups and had placed General Itagaki in something of a dilemma. With his own history of plotting and direct action, he might well have been expected to have been one of the first to place his forces on the side of the rebels. The powerful support he could have given would very probably have tipped the scale in their favor, encouraging other senior officers and army units in Japan to declare themselves.

If he had so decided, a key figure would have been the chief of his now tightly organized internal security force. Indeed, the *Kempeitai* commander's cooperation would have been virtually indispensable. It would have been revealing to have seen how Tojo, with his narrow textbook approach to his duties, would have reacted to orders from his superior in the field to support the rebel cause. In this event, he was spared from having to make any agonized decision.

Itagaki appeared genuinely to have been taken by surprise. He showed no sign of wanting to get involved in anything so desperate as a half-baked direct and violent attempt by junior officers at an overthrow of the government. At the same time, whatever his own reservations were, he was in no position to ignore the situation. He was well aware that there were many among his own young officers—and some not so junior—who could very easily be persuaded to take their own independent action. Proclaiming a state of emergency, Itagaki told Tojo to take all steps he thought fit to maintain order.

Tojo's measures were swift and thorough. Working from the dossiers compiled and held in the *Kempeitai* headquarters and supplemented by information obtained from interrogation of suspects, police spies, and the interception of mail, his military police swooped. Within hours all soldiers and civilians likely to take any significant part in supporting the Tokyo mutineers were rounded up. Manchuria was firmly under control, and a crisis that would have been as dangerous nationally as locally was averted.

All of this Hideki Tojo carried out as a duty, even before news of the Emperor's condemnation of the mutineers as rebels had reached Manchuria. Publicly he was entirely resolute about his task, but in private he was shaken. Involved in the uprising in Tokyo were men who had been his subordinates, men he had known well from former days and whom he had exhorted not to be led into rash actions. It was a great tragedy, he confided to his wife who, with five of their children, was in Manchuria with him, that such men should have been made to feel that they had no other recourse than rebellion.[1] Nevertheless, like the Nagata killing, their violence had a significant influence on his career.

The army high command, shocked by the mutiny, lost no time in showing their appreciation of Tojo, whose loyalty and record as a hard-working and efficient administrator was beginning to mark him out. At the beginning of 1937, Hideki Tojo was gazetted to the rank of Lieutenant General and replaced Itagaki as Chief of Staff of the Kwangtung Army.

Those who chose Tojo for this important post on the basis of his reliability and dedication as a soldier and the premise that he was apparently uncommitted politically were amply justified by the meticulous standards of discipline and efficiency he imposed in the Kwangtung Army. What might have been overlooked or underestimated were the facts of life in Manchuria which made it impossible for one in his position to be concerned with military affairs alone. In a country more or less permanently on a war footing, there was a military aspect to every activity. The military commander there was automatically involved in all kinds of day-to-day and long-term decisions. Tojo, as conscientious as ever, extended himself to include among his professional contacts the kind of civilian with whom it was necessary to work in order to run the country. Notably among these were Nobusuke Kishi, an economics chief in the Manchukuo government, and Yosuke Matsuoka, then president of the South Manchurian Railway Company but who, a few years earlier, had led the Japanese delegation in its public walk-out from the League of Nations Assembly when the Japanese seizure of Manchuria had been condemned. Each in his way was to play an important part in the years that lay ahead, and as with Tojo, the attitudes formed in their Manchurian days, characterized by civilian deference to soldier, evidently persisted.

Also in Manchuria, where a great deal of his work as the army chief of staff was aimed at keeping his forces in a constant state of readiness against possible attack, Tojo's "Russia *delenda est"* fixation revived. More immediately, however, he was closely concerned with developments in China, where the Japanese had established the same kind of unwelcome and uneasy presence in the north as they had done in Manchuria in the days just before they finally took it over.

While it was true that militarily Tojo regarded a settlement with the Chinese as mostly a tactical step in relation to an ultimate battle with the Soviet Union for mastery in the Far East, the Kwangtung Army existed as much as anything else to support the China-based troops in case of trouble. The time was rapidly approaching when this was exactly what it would have to do.

Men who as colonels had been deeply involved in the army's independent move six years before—Itagaki and Doihara among them—were now serving with the Japanese forces in north China and were preparing to take direct action again. And, in Japan, civilian government which had shown itself impotent to control its soldiery overseas was well on the way to losing control to the army altogether, as the army's campaign for a one-party government stepped up.

Twelve

For liberal-minded Japanese—and there were still many—who saw in the collapse of the military rebellion in February a defeat for the extremists, relief was to be short-lived. One of those quickly disillusioned was Shigeru Yoshida, a member of the Foreign Office.

With the fall of Premier Okada, whose cabinet had resigned in the midst of the uprising, Koki Hirota, a former foreign minister and career diplomat, was asked to form a cabinet. Hirota was scarcely the man to lead a revival of liberal government. He was a protégé of Toyama of the Black Dragons, and was himself a member of the Society. This background may well have recommended the military to accept his nomination. Nevertheless, once nominated he proposed to include in his cabinet some experienced men known to be moderates, and Yoshida was talked of as prospective foreign minister. The army lost no time in making known how they felt about this and in showing the extent to which they were now interfering directly in political affairs.

General Terauchi, who had been selected as war minister, together with General Yamashita and other members of the army general staff, suddenly appeared at a meeting where the formation of the new cabinet was being discussed. Bluntly they told Hirota and his advisers that they had heard that men "out of sympathy with the political situation" were being considered for cabinet posts. If this were true, the army protested strongly. Yoshida, in his post-war *Memoirs*, observed wryly: "It was clear that I was among those to whom the Army objected, and I at once made it clear that I was unavailable for office."[1]

The Hirota government, when it was finally formed, included only men who were approved by General Terauchi and the general staff, and under Hirota more than half the national budget was devoted to preparation for war. Even more serious, what amounted to a right to veto any measures with which the services did not agree was ensured when Hirota acceded to restoring the requirement, dropped at the end of the Meiji era, that the positions of war and navy ministers should go to officers on the active list.

Direct participation in government by the armed services had been bad in principle, even in the days when the strong-minded Emperor Meiji and his advisers firmly controlled the military. The possibilities for mischief were infinitely greater now. Emperor Hirohito, studious and retiring and by nature the reverse of an autocrat, had been carefully reared to rule as a constitutional monarch. It was the policy of the aged Prince Saionji, who had been adviser to his grandfather, and other senior statesmen who now advised the Emperor to keep him—as the expression was—"above the clouds," in dignified detachment from the rough-and-tumble of parliamentary government.

The Imperial wish, traditionally expressed in indirect terms and in the convoluted semantics of Japanese court language, had become more than ever a matter of individual interpretation by extremists who in the last resort claimed, as the mutineers of 1936 had done, that the Emperor was "misled by insincere advisers." It represented little check now on service ministers, generals and admirals who were active members of the military establishment.

Under Hirota, in December 1936, Japan took another positive step into the anti-democratic camp by signing the Anti-Comintern Pact with Germany. The generals had made up their minds that this pact would help to protect Japan's advance into China from Russian intervention, and one of them, Major General Oshima, while military attaché in Germany, had established direct contact with Ribbentrop, Hitler's diplomatic henchman. Oshima, like Japanese military attachés in other capitals, reported directly back to his army superiors in Tokyo. He virtually took over foreign relations between Japan and Germany and later was made ambassador. He certainly had more hand in forging the new Tokyo-Berlin link than either the then Japanese ambassador, the foreign minister, or Hirota himself.

The army soon found that the ultranationalist Hirota was not patriot enough for them. The crunch came when, in January 1937, the war minister, Terauchi, was challenged in the Diet to deny that he was opposed to normal constitutional government. The challenger, a representative named Hamada, in the heated exchange which followed, suggested that the war minister should commit *hara-kiri* if the questioner was right. The choleric Terauchi, who not long before had pointed out the new Diet building to the British military attaché and asked if he did not agree that the money would have been better spent on two new army divisions,[2] reacted in a way that showed only too clearly that Hamada had not accused him lightly. The war minister demanded of the premier that the House of Representatives should be dissolved to make way for a one-party government capable of looking after "national defense."

No one, and least of all Hirota, had any illusion that this was just the general's own idea or that it had been recently conceived following what was now celebrated as the *"hara-kiri* incident."* "National defense" had become one of the double-talk phrases that meant anything the army wanted it to and was generally synonymous with expansion and military adventures overseas. Hirota, though far from being against these, was not ready for anything as drastic as changing the form of government to facilitate them. He temporized even though Terauchi declared threateningly that he could not serve in a government in which the army had no confidence and under which military discipline might not be maintained. When Hirota still would not agree, the war minister resigned and thereby compelled the premier and the remainder of his cabinet to do the same.

To replace Hirota, Prince Saionji, the adviser to the Throne, recommended the retired General Ugaki who, he recalled, had in the 1920s been strong enough as war minister to push through the much resented outs in the forces. But memories in the army were equally long. As Ugaki's car approached the Palace on his way to answer the Emperor's summons, it was stopped by the commanding officer of the *Kempeitai*, General Nakajima. The *Kempeitai* man informed Ugaki that before he saw the Emperor he should know that the army's feeling was that he should not accept the premiership. Ugaki, who had been looking forward to taking political office and who was not lacking in either tenacity or courage, ignored this warning, but in the following days the army chiefs declined to nominate a war minister to serve with the General. Ugaki, unable to form a cabinet without one, was obliged to report his failure to the Throne.

In 1937 the post of Japanese prime minister was becoming the most short-lived as well as what veteran journalist Kimpei Sheba described as "the most dangerous job in the world."[3] The dangers of political office were emphasized even more dramatically by Hugh Byas in his much-quoted description "government by assassination,"[4] and personal risk was always there as the unhappy toll of political murders only too clearly witnessed. Yet overemphasis on the bloody work of the lunatic and homicidal elements in the Japan of the 1930s can be misleading. Unlike the German racists and malcontents, the Japanese extremists never coalesced into a tightly organized, single political movement under one leader. Their real significance was that they were urging noisily and violently what most Japanese believed to be true—that Japan was both destined and fitted for the leadership of Asia. Only in the extent and the methods by which it was to be achieved did the great majority really differ, whether they were Black Dragons, army colonels, or liberal politicians.

Very few Japanese, even genuine moderates, doubted that the East Asia Co-prosperity Sphere, which was becoming the much touted keystone of Japanese policy, was in every way as benevolent and just in concept as many British in those days still believed their Empire to be. Fewer could see how Britain and the other colonial powers could equate colonial possessions of their own—which they showed no disposition to give up—with opposition to Japanese attempts to expand. Nor, after Mussolini's brutal conquest of Abyssinia and with Hitler's predatory hand threatening his smaller neighbors, did the argument that the days of territorial expansion were over carry much weight.

Even so, there were still men in Japan well fitted to take political office who were unconvinced that the way of the European dictators with their use of or threat of naked force was, in the long term, going to prevail. Men like Yoshida and Shigemitsu had a realistic approach to the art of what was internationally possible and would have sought to fulfill this without resort to military aggression. And even if the hazards of political office had been as severe as they were assumed by some western onlookers to be, such men would have been undeterred if this had been the only consideration.

It was not fear of death but what was for most Japanese the greater fear of humiliation that prompted Shigeru Yoshida to be "unavailable" for the post of foreign minister in the Hirota cabinet. A stubborn and brave man, he was later to survive arrest by the *Kempeitai* to become one of Japan's outstanding postwar prime ministers. Rather it was the frustrating knowledge—after the generals had indicated that he was unacceptable to them—that they could and undoubtedly would have inflicted on him the humiliating procedure of having been put up for and rejected for office.

The real danger to government was always rooted in the ability of the generals, quite legally under the Constitution, to prevent the formation of or to bring down, as Terauchi had done, any cabinet of whose members and leaders they did not approve. There was, then, the increasing necessity for the elder statesmen who acted for the Emperor to somehow find a prime minister and cabinet members who would not, at the first pretext, be toppled by the resignation of the war minister. It was this which had led to the premiership being filled by a succession of superannuated generals and admirals or politicians with ultranationalist sympathies—in the hope that control over the armed services could be maintained through them.

In June 1937 the advisers to the Throne turned to Prince Fumimaro Konoye, a member of the ancient Fujiwara line of court nobility. Konoye was, in truth, a man who aspired politically to be all things to all men. With close ties to the Throne, he was an intellectual who had a considerable, if dilettante, interest in politics and international affairs. His father had been a friend of Mitsuru Toyama of the Black Dragons. This and Konoye's own reverence for Japan's ancient institutions gave him some sympathy with the patriotic motives of the ultranationalists, although it could be said that it was not that he loved them so much but that he feared communism more. With all of this he combined an apparently genuine desire for friendship with the United States. When he took office in June 1937 he was, at this particular hour in his country's affairs, to all appearances a good choice. Those close to the Throne considered that he had the stature to exercise the kind of restraint over the military which, it had now become obvious, they were no longer prepared to accept from any ordinary civilian politician.

Konoye's policy was intended to have been on the lines of that advocated by Mamoru Shigemitsu of the Foreign Office for negotiating with the Chinese: that Manchuria should remain a separate border state but that Japanese troops would be withdrawn from other Chinese territory. How much chance this would ever have had of being considered by the Chinese is doubtful. The Japanese army in China, either because they suspected or had been informed that some such move was in the offing, made sure that no one would ever know. On the 7th of July, 1937, a Japanese detachment carrying out night exercises near the Marco Polo Bridge around Peking in north China was fired on, it was alleged, by Chinese troops.

It was widely represented and believed abroad at the time that the incident had been manufactured by Japanese commanders in the area. This was certainly true inasmuch as the maneuvers were being carried out on Chinese soil under an ancient treaty right exacted from the Chinese government after the crushing of the Boxer Rebellion in 1900. Whether the shots were fired by Chinese troops or if they were ever fired at all was in any case academic. The Japanese army there struck violently at Chinese government forces in a general attack that showed every sign, like the attack in Manchuria in 1931, of having been planned in advance and on a scale which ruled out any possibility that the action was merely retaliatory.

The Chinese fought back with spirit and unprecedented tenacity, and within a few weeks of Prince Konoye's installation as prime minister, China and Japan were locked in full-scale conflict. As in April 1931, the generals in the field had acted without reference to their government in Tokyo. The Japanese army had brought the scourge of war to the people of China, and the stench of death was to hang heavy over the land for long years to come.

Thirteen

It was never proven and, indeed, it was most improbable that Hideki Tojo took any part in or was privy to any military conspiracy behind the Marco Polo Bridge incident. At the same time, during his term of office as Chief of Staff of the Kwangtung Army, Tojo had quite definitely come to the conclusion that the Chiang Kai-shek regime in China must be eliminated. Shortly before the outbreak of the fighting, he had recommended to the war office in Tokyo that this essential preliminary to successful operations against the Soviet should be considered as a matter of urgency. He undoubtedly shared the common illusion that it could be done quickly and relatively easily. He must also then have shared the annoyance of the other generals at the resistance now being put up by the Chinese.

The Chinese soldiers were showing that they could no longer be dismissed with almost contemptuous ease as in the past. Instead of making the customary token opposition before withdrawing, the Nanking armies were standing and fighting with an entirely new and unexpected spirit. Five full divisions had to be rushed from Japan, and from Tokyo, War Minister Sugiyama—arguing military necessity and ignoring his cabinet colleagues and the prime minister who tried to get the fighting limited—ordered Tojo to send supporting forces from his Kwangtung Army. Having done this, Tojo, acting on his own initiative, personally led another

Kwangtung group to outflank Chinese forces which threatened Japanese in the Peking area.

In this, his first and only experience of commanding troops in combat, he thrust deep into China, carrying out with textbook precision an operation that secured the whole of Inner Mongolia. He spent no more time in the field than was necessary to accomplish the rôle allotted to his troops, and then returned to his Manchurian headquarters to be ready for any Russian intervention. He took no further part in the fighting in China, where stubborn resistance continued despite the fact that over 150,000 Japanese soldiers were now committed against adversaries far more numerous but infinitely inferior in leadership, equipment, and training.

In Japan hysterical war propaganda whipped up public feeling. Newspapers carried dramatic reports of gallantry and sacrifice; headlines blazoned victories and radio news programs were interrupted to tell of new ones. While the world outside read of the carnage among the Chinese civilian population and became grimly familiar with press and newsreel pictures of the pitiful victims of war in tormented China, the Japanese were told in harrowing detail of the atrocities committed against their side. Anti-Chinese sentiment flared high at reports of the killing of Japanese officers whose Chinese militia rose against them and, later, of the massacre of over two hundred Japanese subjects, including women and children.

Konoye and his cabinet, in a frantic effort to regain the initiative, were forced to show that they were no less filled with patriotic feeling than the army. Government spokesmen called for a final reckoning with China, declaring that she must be taught a lesson. Konoye spoke of a New Order in Asia, using for the first time the sinister phrase coined by Hitler in Europe. A "National Spiritual Mobilization Movement" was inaugurated; the activities of the *Kempeitai* were extended; the "dangerous thoughts" law was evoked with increasing frequency; widespread arrests were made of members of the socialist-leaning People's Popular Front Party. The hunt for Communists, whose overt actions had ceased when their leaders were jailed in 1928, was stepped up.

If the government in Tokyo imagined that by these measures they were exercising any kind of control over events in

China, the soldiers on the spot left war correspondents and other foreign nationals there in no doubt as to who were the masters. British subjects in particular were singled out for annoying and often humiliating treatment by the Japanese army. At Tientsin, under Japanese-imposed security regulations, they were searched and stripped on passing through military check points. If the Tientsin incidents provoked anger in Britain, and condemnation somewhat disproportionate to the severer indignities and brutalities suffered by the Chinese in the city and to the wider savageries of the war, they did, nevertheless, fairly accurately deduce that the action of the military at Tientsin was part of a deliberate policy to humble the proud white races in the eyes of orientals.

At a press conference the local commander, General Homma, blandly commented that he could see no particular cause for complaint. In Japan, he observed, there was nothing particularly shameful in uncovering the body in the presence of others of either sex. More pertinent was his remark to a British far-eastern correspondent when the latter presented his Japanese foreign office credentials at Homma's headquarters in Tientsin. Dropping them in the wastepaper basket, the commander told him, "We are running things here, not Tokyo."[1]

On other occasions it appeared for a time that the military had gone too far. British and United States gunboats patrolling the Yangtze River were attacked by Japanese artillery and warplanes. The gunboat, U.S.S. "Panay," was sunk and several of its complement killed. The British ambassador traveling in his official car, plainly marked on the roof with the Union Jack, was machine-gunned from the air and the ambassador gravely wounded. The Chamberlain government, hag-ridden by the Nazi threat in Europe, protested. The American government, under powerful pressure at home to keep out of this war or any other war, did the same. From Tokyo, the harassed Konoye government apologized repeatedly and offered compensation. The British prime minister, Neville Chamberlain, was to explain later that "in the presence even of these insults and injuries which have been inflicted on British subjects in China by the Japanese we must remember what are the limits of what we can do in this particular time to help our people there. At the present moment we have not in the Far East a fleet superior to the Japanese."

For the gunboat incidents and the air attack on the British ambassador, some responsible Japanese officers were recalled from China. Among them was Colonel Hashimoto whose troops had carried out the attacks on the gunboats. He arrived back in Japan quite unrepentant but now only one, if one of the most vociferous, of a growing number of army officers who were openly advocating that it was against the deteriorating power of the western colonial nations in southeast Asia rather than Soviet Russia that Japan's strength should be turned.

As the war spread, farewells to departing soldier members of the family, reservists and conscripts, became a familiar sight at railway stations in every town and village in the country. These were given wide press and newsfilm coverage as were the scenes—commonplace as casualties mounted—of wives and mothers receiving white-covered boxes containing the ashes of husbands and sons back from the battlefield.

Then, as the Japanese army fought on, striking out from Peking and Tientsin and further into north China, all hope of localizing the trouble there was lost as fighting flared up suddenly many miles south of the main battle area. Overnight the war had spread to the international city of Shanghai in a move by the Japanese navy that was to change the whole character of not only the present conflict in China but the greater one yet to come.

Fourteen

While the navy had never exerted the same kind of pressure on government as the army had, the admirals who took office in the cabinet inevitably found themselves in competition with the generals for a larger share of the national budget. This had not become serious until the Kwangtung Army's Manchuria action in 1931. The soldiers' success had not been without effect in arousing ambition and dissatisfaction among naval officers. This was especially evident with the young fliers of the relatively new naval air arm, where the traditional conservatism of the service was not so strong.

For many years, too, there had been resentment of the naval treaty at Washington in 1922. Coinciding, through American pressure, with the ending by Britain of the old and valued Anglo-Japanese alliance, the naval treaty actually permitted the Japanese navy to become the most powerful in the Pacific. It was, however, widely regarded in Japan as a western-imposed instrument to keep Japan's naval strength below that of Britain and America and, in the navy, as a curb not shared by the army. Senior naval leaders, among them dedicated naval expansionists like Admirals Nagano and Yamamoto, had consistently pressed for the Washington limit to be ended, as it was finally when Nagano, as the Japanese delegate to a further conference in London in 1935, walked out.

This did not mean that the navy leaders as a whole were as belligerent as those in the army or that they wanted war with the western powers. Generally, thinking was, as tends to be natural in all navies, still strongly influenced by older officers, such men as Admirals Suzuki, Oikawa, Yonai, and Okada who saw Japan as a naval power comparable with Britain rather than a military one like Germany. The role of their service they conceived to be similar to that of the British navy which had enabled the British from their small island to achieve world position and influence out of all proportion to their numbers.

The sailors had no faith in and were deeply apprehensive of the army's "northward advance" policy. This, if pursued, would lead to Japan's eighty millions being eventually mired down in a continental war of attrition against two great land powers, both of them with a population several times greater than Japan's. There were those in the navy as well as in the government (and many of the admirals had served in both) who remembered how, behind the victories and gallantry of the Russo-Japanese War, the nation's strength had been drained almost completely, and who recalled its cost in Japanese lives, the specter of which had haunted General Nogi for the rest of his days.

As the generals dragged Japan deeper into north China and to the brink of a collision with Soviet Russia, there developed in naval circles a determination that if Japan had to risk war, it must be in a direction in which she stood the most chance of success and in which her character as an island power with a strong navy would be exploited to the full. Out of this was formulated the navy's own "southward advance" policy.

Since Japan was now committed to dominating the Chinese mainland, the logical way to bring this about, as the admirals saw it, was by the employment of superior naval power along China's seaboard. As Britain had done in Europe for centuries—and in Asia, too—a relatively small army could then be used flexibly and most effectively against the numerically greater Chinese in combined military and naval operations. In this area the possibility of a head-on clash with other nations would be much reduced. The western countries would not lightly challenge physically a first-rate naval power—an Asian one operating in its home waters—over China where, apart from Hong Kong and one or two other small concessions, they held no territories and had no clearly defined spheres of interest.

Moreover, the presence of the Japanese navy, thus

extended in southeast Asia, would give meaningful support to Japanese diplomatic and commercial efforts there, particularly in respect to the oil-rich Dutch East Indies. There the Japanese had been for some time trying to increase their trade and influence, and it was those islands that the admirals had begun to regard, as the actions of the army in China incurred increasing hostility on the international scene, as an area vital to them. Viscount Inoue, a member of the Japanese House of Peers, on a visit to London in 1937, might have been speaking especially for the Japanese navy when he drew attention to his country's almost total lack of raw materials within her own borders and compared Japan's situation with Britain. "You have no oil," Inoue pointed out, "but you have secured political and economic control over oil-producing countries in various parts of the world. . . . Not only do we possess no oil supplies but this is true of very many other materials without which today a nation is helpless in wartime. To secure assured supply of raw materials has become a problem of greatly increased importance. The very life of Japan as a first-class power is dependent on this question."

As early as 1932, following the outbreak of the war in Manchuria, a Japanese naval landing party had got involved in fighting Chinese troops in the international city of Shanghai, and it had been necessary for them to be rescued by army units. Since then, there had been clear enough signs that this had been more than just an unfortunate and temporary involvement of the Navy in a side-issue of the fighting in the north. On navy insistence, an admiral had been appointed as governor-general of the island of Formosa to counterbalance the army's governor-general in Korea. In Formosa the Navy had established its own Kwangtung-style headquarters, working directly with consulates on the mainland of China and with a newly formed and Navy-sponsored Asia Development Board. All signs pointed in 1937 to the Japanese navy having taken advantage of a local incident in Shanghai to get in on the war and implement its "southward advance" policy.

The action was touched off by the murder of a Japanese naval lieutenant on the outskirts of the city. Immediately afterwards Japanese navy landing parties were engaged in fighting a crack Chinese division and had very quickly to be supported by Japanese troops. The fierce fighting that followed made necessary the landing of a complete Japanese expeditionary force south of Shanghai, which outflanked the Chinese defenders still doggedly holding out against Japanese army and naval units already engaged there and compelled the Chinese to retire from the city. The Japanese force drove on into the interior, taking the Kuomintang capital of Nanking and subjecting its citizens to a four-day orgy of looting, murder, and rape. But behind the shock reports and the headlines which made the Nanking atrocity known to the world was hidden the fact that the Japanese navy had achieved its aim of involving the army in the southward advance. Both services were now committed together in China, and it was from the navy-administered island of Formosa that the large-scale landings and operations against southern China took place soon afterwards.

By early 1938, Prince Konoye was a very discouraged man. An early end to the fighting in China was as far off as ever. He had failed to play off the navy against the army. He was, in fact, no longer so sure that the navy was a moderating factor as some of its members, even those in government, were making noises as reckless as those from the army officers. Admiral Suetsugi, the minister of the interior, had been quoted as speaking of Japan's task to drive the white races out of Asia and saying that Chinese resistance had to be broken even at the risk of war with Britain. And now the hopelessness of his own attempts to keep control by trying to show that he was at least as nationalist as the generals was exposed, as once more they revealed that they would always be one step ahead of him.

Through General Sugiyama, the war minister, it was conveyed to him that the army considered that a government more fitted to deal with the "national emergency" was required. Offering his own resignation, Sugiyama suggested that the rest of the cabinet should do the same to make way for such a government. Konoye, still anxious to keep command, accepted the general's resignation and called for those of his cabinet colleagues. Retaining his premier's office, he set about forming a new cabinet acceptable to the army. Its membership, when the army finally consented to nominate a war minister to serve with the cabinet, was significantly martial.

General Araki, an ultranationalist and a leading "Imperial Way" advocate, was made minister of education. A general and an admiral filled the foreign and home affairs posts. The almost entirely military composition of the new cabinet was not much affected because a civilian, Seihin Ikeda, was chosen as finance minister. Ikeda was from the massive Mitsui *zaibatsu* industrial combine and his appointment represented no more than the extent to which big business and industry were now harnessed to the military chariot.

Men of the Kwangtung Army who had figured in the Manchurian takeover and the Marco Polo Bridge attack which had set off the war in China were now well represented in the army general staff in Tokyo. For the key position of war minister, the generals selected one of the foremost of the Kwangtung clique, General Itagaki. Konoye appears to have favored Itagaki because he seemed pliable and easy going—an apparent contradiction in view of the latter's record of independent action in Manchuria, but explicable in that such a man would conceivably have been swayed by stronger and subtler characters. For a conscientious and capable vice-minister to assist the new war minister, the army named the one who had served Itagaki so well as chief of the *Kempeitai* in Manchuria and who, Konoye thought, from his reputation for having a methodical mind, would be a good complementary choice.

Two days after the formation of the new Konoye cabinet, Lieutenant General Hideki Tojo handed over his command of the Kwangtung Army and, boarding a plane for Tokyo, headed toward his first experience of political office.

Fifteen

When Hideki Tojo arrived back in Tokyo in May 1938, the war against the Chinese was going less than ever as expected. Generalissimo Chiang Kai-shek had not given up when his capital of Nanking had fallen. Withdrawing to Chungking, a small provincial city deep in the interior of China, he had set up his war headquarters.

In Japan this had been turned to the advantage of the militarists. Effectively exploited by army propagandists and the ultranationalist societies, the "national emergency" had served to create a climate of public opinion that was generally resigned to the imposition of wartime measures. By playing upon the pride and the latent chauvinism of the Japanese people, they had aroused antiwestern feeling, blaming American and British support of Chiang Kai-shek for the latter's stubborn refusal to "show sincerity"—standard Japanese extremist parlance for accepting their point of view. With all of this the vacillating Konoye was made the more vulnerable to pressure from the army general staff.

Nevertheless, the fact remained that when the fighting in China had started a year before, the generals had boasted that they would finish off the China incident in a brief four months. Then, shortly after Tojo took up his new duties in Tokyo, another rebuff to Japanese arms gave more cause for anxious reappraisal.

In the summer months there occurred an outbreak of

fighting that developed into a pitched battle between Japanese and Soviet troops on the Manchurian border in the area of Chang-kufeng. The stalemate which ended it signified different things to the Japanese and to the Russians. To the Japanese it seemed that while the Russians would react very positively if challenged in the area they had shown themselves not anxious to get into a full-scale war in the Far East.

On their part, the Russians had some assurance that the danger of an all-out Japanese aggression against them was receding, and their information came from a source very close to the Japanese premier himself. Ironically, Konoye, who was almost pathologically fearful of Communism, had on his staff as a member of his personal brains trust one Hozumi Ozaki, secretly a Communist and working with Richard Sorge, a top Soviet secret agent planted in the German embassy in Tokyo.

Tojo's chief, Itagaki, as war minister, had to take the responsibility for the border-fighting which had made him the recipient of an almost unprecedented personal rebuke from the Emperor. The ruler characterized some of the actions of the army in the past as "abominable" and angrily told the army chief of staff and Itagaki that in the future "not one soldier" was to be moved without his permission.

Even in a matter as serious as this, the Emperor was unlikely to have intervened, however much he might personally have wanted to, unless requested either formally or informally. It is probable that Konoye, supported by the navy minister, had some hand in this, impelled by his chronic nightmare of a full-scale war with Russia. But Itagaki himself was having second thoughts about the desirability of this, as were many on the army general staff who up to now had been convinced of its inevitability. For those not obsessed with resuming the Russo-Japanese war of 1904–5, it was becoming clear that events in Europe over the last few years had created an entirely new situation.

Britain was preoccupied with the near threat of Nazi Germany and Fascist Italy, and in a few weeks British Prime Minister Chamberlain was to make his journey of appeasement to Hitler and Mussolini in Munich in the company of the French premier. Britain's weakness at home was reflected in her lack of positive reaction to Japanese action in China, and it was obvious that the ability of Britain, France, and Holland to defend their other Far Eastern interests had been considerably reduced.

America had continued to make no secret of her displeasure at Japanese aggression in China, but apart from the known fact that sentiment there was still strongly isolationist, the Japanese had now achieved naval superiority over the U.S. Pacific fleet. This fact, which was known to the Americans, would not make them more ready to contemplate measures stronger than the protests to which the Japanese were becoming inured. The south, therefore, was beginning to appear far more attractive in its possibilities than the forbidding wastes of the north and the probability of another bloody nose from the Russians.

If other high-ranking officers serving on the army general staff and in the government were changing their views, Hideki Tojo soon revealed himself as a man who had, apparently, learned nothing and forgotten nothing. Major General Piggott, who had spent many years in Japan as a language officer and who was now the British military attaché in Tokyo, recalled him as being an exception among the senior army officers with whom he had often formed cordial relationships, a tradition of friendly association which, as he said, "can hardly be said to have been maintained when General Tojo held the post of Vice-Minister of War. . . ." Tojo was, General Piggott said

. . . one of the very few army officers with whom I failed to establish any relations other than formal. On the occasion of my first interview it was obvious from his references to the effect on Japan of such matters as the German seizure of Tsingtao in 1898, the Russian aggression in Manchuria of 1903, the abrogation of the Anglo–Japanese Alliance in 1921, and the American Immigration Act of 1924, that he regarded most foreigners with some suspicion, if not dislike. General Tojo gave me the impression of a strong man badly disillusioned, who intended to pursue his path unhindered by any interest other than Japanese; he never showed any sign of sociability.[1]

Nor was the British military attaché the only one to observe Tojo's lack of charm and narrow preoccupation with the past. His attitude was, in fact, to make his first venture into the political field short-lived.

In the face of the major change of outlook among his

own army colleagues, Tojo called together a group of leading industrialists to set out the current situation as he saw it and to indicate the lines on which they would be required to work. Barking at them "as if he were laying down the law to a company of new recruits"[2] he told them that continued opposition from the Chinese and support for them by the British who intended to defend their colonial and commercial interests must be expected. So must America's unrealistic and hostile attempts to hamper Japan. But the main danger was Soviet Russia, whose policy it was to have the Japanese dissipate their strength in China while it prepared for war with Japan. This was the conflict Japan must be ready to face and for those who placed profit before national interest "the Army would find means of seeing that they toed the line in the future."[3]

The furore that broke out after the red-faced industrialists had dispersed brought to an end Tojo's first and brief tenure in political office. His name made the news headlines, not only in Japan but internationally, where his prediction of war with Russia was widely quoted. The industrialists still counted enough to make their indignation at his high-handed treatment of them felt. In the Diet, Tojo's chief, Itagaki, was closely questioned by members who, even if most of them were by this time conditioned to the slide toward war, could still express their alarm at the prospect of taking on Britain, the United States, and Russia all at once.

In the following month (December 1938) Tojo was removed quietly to the nonpolitical post of Inspector General of the Air Forces. In this he had an opportunity to reflect that the manners and methods of browbeating civilians in army-run Manchuria were not yet appropriate in the imperial capital where politicians—even generals—were still expected to pay at least lip service to constitutional processes. More important for him was that the new job gave him the chance of living down his gaffe with the industrialists. He set vigorously about the task of boosting military aircraft production and reorganizing the forces with emphasis on co-operation with the naval and military arms.

Konoye, declaring the "the China incident had entered a new stage" and that he felt he "lacked the ability to cope with the new situation," resigned in January 1939 and was succeeded as premier by Baron Hiranuma. Hiranuma was another ultranationalist who had once held the post of minister of justice. One of his special interests had been the combatting of leftist tendencies among students and he had been a prime mover in setting up *Kokuhon-sha,* one of the leading ultra-nationalistic organizations. He made clear his attitude on China when he told the Diet that he hoped "the intention of Japan will be understood by the Chinese so that they may co-operate with us. As for those who fail to understand we have no other alternative but to exterminate them."

To mark his installation, the navy took another step in the direction of southeast Asia by moving into the Chinese island of Hainan, strategically situated so that its possession could be considered a direct threat to the French colony of Indochina. Neither Hiranuma nor any of his government were informed of this in advance, although grave international issues were implicit in the move.

The Hiranuma government was dealt another blow when in August 1939 a short-lived nonaggression pact was signed between Germany and Russia. Its conclusion severely shocked and angered the military and was seen as an act of betrayal by Germany since Japan's own Anti-Comintern Pact with Germany was designed to exploit the German threat to Russia, inhibiting the latter's freedom of action in the Far East. For those in the army who still believed that war must come with Russia, the pact was a double blow.

In May, despite Emperor Hirohito's earlier prohibition, renewed fighting had broken out between detachments of the Kwangtung Army and Russian troops on the borders of Manchuria and Outer Mongolia and was still going on. This was no skirmish but a small war in which tanks, artillery, and aircraft were used. The result, when the fighting ended in September 1939, was once again hardly salutary for the Japanese. Their losses of over 50,000 in battle exceeded those of the Russians by more than five to one. The Russians had proved superior in firepower and had shown that they kept forces in the Far East fully capable of fighting off an attack even as large-scale and as protracted as this one had been.

The resignation of the seven-months-old Hiranuma government signified a retreat by the most extreme proponents of expansion and was an indication of the state of indecision and confusion into which recent events had thrown them. The choice of a general as Hiranuma's successor was no more than a face-saving concession to the army. General Abe, who became the new premier, was on the retired list and his only experience of political life had been on the rarefied level of Governor General of Korea.

On the 3rd of September, 1939, a little more than a week after Abe had taken office, war in Europe broke out with Hitler's attack on Poland. Influenced by distrust of Germany and by second thoughts about Britain, now that she had taken up arms at last, the Abe government declared that its course would be a "middle way," predicated on keeping Japan out of the war in the west.

In the ensuing months Hitler made no further move after his conquest and division of Poland with Stalin, and the adversaries in Europe settled down to a long period of inaction. General Abe's government resigned to make way for one headed by a retired naval man, Admiral Yonai, a staunch advocate of the traditional naval outlook of cautious national advance. His foreign minister, Hachiro Arita, a liberal statesman of great experience, lost no time in making it known that Yonai's government intended to keep out of the European conflict. Moreover, he declared in the Diet in February 1940 that Japan had no territorial designs in southeast Asia. Her interests there were exclusively economic and she was willing to conclude nonaggression pacts with any other powers with interests in the area.

Both Yonai's government and the "middle way" policy were, unfortunately, early casualties when, after the German occupations of Denmark and Norway, Hitler launched his *blitzkrieg* in May 1940 and ended the so-called "phony war" in Europe. As the apparently invincible Nazi armies in a few weeks overran France, Belgium, and Holland and expelled the British from the continent, the Japanese militarists and superpatriots, their confidence regained and reinforced, put on pressure again.

The rich Far Eastern colonies of defeated France and Holland appeared more than ever ripe for the taking. Britain was alone, awaiting invasion, and Churchill's defiant proclamation that his nation would fight on, while quoted with some admiration in Japan, seemed to bear little relation to the realities of his nation's position in Europe, even if he was reluctantly facing them in the Far East. In June, the British prime minister had announced that Britain was acceding to a Japanese request to close the Burma road, China's last remaining land link with the west. The British government, he said, "could not ignore the dominant fact that we ourselves are engaged in a life and death struggle." Two days after he had spoken, Japanese troops moved into positions around Hong Kong, completely blockading the colony from the land. America, still on the sidelines, was the big question mark for Japan. The Americans' displeasure was evident, but nothing they had yet done indicated that they had the will to prevent Japan from availing herself of the prospects, all too tempting, which were now held out to the Japanese nation. Indeed, any argument against them was branded as traitorous.

Once again murder was planned to remove leading men reputed to be anti-Axis, among them the Imperial Household Minister, Marquis Matsudaira, and the premier, Admiral Yonai. The police, alerted in the nick of time, seized thirty-eight young officers taking part, but the ubiquitous and compulsive plotter, Colonel Hashimoto, widely believed to be the ringleader in this as in previous conspiracies, remained free, enjoying his customary apparent immunity from arrest and punishment. The army high command was, in any case, about to remove Yonai from power by a less dramatic but by now routine method.

In mid-July 1940, General Hata, the war minister, informed Premier Yonai that the army "desired a renovation of the internal structure in order to cope with the international situation" and that he now found it necessary to show his "firm determination" by resigning to bring this about. At the same time it was made clear to Yonai that the army general staff would not feel able to nominate another war minister to serve with him. Two days later, since the cabinet could not legally exist without a war minister, Yonai resigned together with his cabinet.

The kind of renovation called for by General Hata had, by what would appear to be more than a coincidence, only recently been proposed. Three weeks before Prince Konoye, who as an ex-premier was a member of the emperor's privy council, had announced that he was forming "a new political structure." Avoiding the word "party," he indicated that it would be, rather, a unification of existing parties under the guidance of the Imperial Rule Assistance Association, which he had sponsored earlier in March.

Obviously inspired by General Araki's *Kodo-ha* movement, the declared object of the Association was to unite the nation by reviving the virtues and mystic spirit of old Japan. Fundamental to it was the study of *Shin Taisei*—the ancient arts and folklore. Its principles were propagated through the *tonari-gumi*, the neighborhood associations that were the basic unit of communal life in towns and villages. Through their intimate knowledge of members of the families and with a police box within each group, the *tonari-gumi* later became knit into a nationwide complex of control almost Orwellian in scope. Army officers were urged to join the Imperial Rule Assistance Association to be its "propelling force," and government officials were encouraged to adopt its "spiritual and nonpolitical" aims. Shortly after the Association's formation, the foreign office announced that in future the training of its personnel would include, in addition to protocol and treaty-making, tuition in the *samurai* skills of *kendo* (sword-fighting) and *judo*.

There is good reason to believe that the prince's role in forming the Imperial Rule Assistance Association represented, as much as his own authoritarian and traditionalist outlook, another attempt by those close to the Throne to keep control. The army was determined to have a one-party state in Japan and, by the wrecking tactics of its ministers in the cabinet, was obviously going to continue to bring down any government that opposed it. If this had to be, then it was best that the elder statesmen, privy councillors, and ex-premiers who advised the Emperor should take the initiative themselves through Konoye so that the direction of such a concentration of power would be kept in responsible hands.

When Prince Konoye took the office of premier for the second time on the 18th of July, 1940, it was to head a one-party government, dedicated, as he announced, to national unity, the successful conclusion of the China incident, and strengthened relations with Germany and Italy. For the post of foreign minister he brought in Yosuke Matsuoka, who two years before had been helping General Tojo to run things in Manchuria.

Meanwhile, the army general staff and the outgoing war minister, General Hata, were considering very carefully who should be their man in the new cabinet. Realistically, Konoye had foregone the formality of requesting the army general staff to submit names for his approval. Instead he had asked Hata to name his own successor, specifying only that he should be someone who —repeating the well-worn incantation—could control the army. Disposed at this time to look with favor on Konoye, it seems probable that Hata and his colleagues decided on one who by now had a proven record for maintaining discipline but, at the same time, would yield to no one in seeing that the army's point of view was always observed.

Tojo, who was touring army air-force installations in Manchuria at the time, was suddenly summoned to return to Tokyo by air. On his arrival he was immediately received in private by General Hata. At this meeting he was thoroughly briefed on the events leading to the overthrow of the Yonai government and told that he had been nominated by the general staff to be the new minister of war.

Sixteen

Very soon after Konoye took over he made it plain not only to the army but to the Japanese nation and the rest of the world that whatever else he stood for, he was no believer in democracy. It was, he declared in a radio speech five days after he became premier, equally with liberalism and socialism, one of the evils of party politics which were "not agreeable to the national ideas of Japan."

Nevertheless, those close to the Throne who had chosen him, while leaving him to deal with the China incident in any way he thought fit, had also required that he avoid escalation into war beyond it. This coincided almost entirely with his own wishes. His fear and dislike of Soviet ideology had not blinded him to the knowledge that a conflict which drew Japanese armies deep into the vast land mass of eastern Russia was the very worst kind of war to fight. He was as determined for other reasons, more complex and not unmixed with personal reluctance, to avert war with the United States. In this, although he was destined for historic failure, he persisted in genuine efforts which ceased only when, deprived of support and worn down by a man more obdurate than himself, he hopelessly abandoned the premiership.

Yet, in his early encounters with Hideki Tojo, the prince was encouraged to believe that the aim of getting the army to accept control within the one-party state might be achieved. Despite Tojo's unfortunate hectoring of the industrialists when he last held office, the premier and his war minister were surprisingly in accord. At their first meeting the General accepted that the China incident must be satisfactorily concluded; agreed that discipline must be maintained in the armed forces, endorsed the need for co-ordination between the army and navy high commands, and indicated his belief that the authority of the office of premier should be restored.

It would be difficult to say exactly when Tojo began to see Konoye as being inadequate to exercise this authority, but as the prince drifted, irresolute and vacillating, and as his policy of playing one interest off against the other collapsed, something much like contempt replaced the war minister's early attitude toward his cabinet chief.

In the foreign office the fast-talking, mercurial Yosuke Matsuoka was setting that conservative establishment on its ear. It was very clear that he was convinced that Germany was winning the war and that he was set on Japan getting a share of the spoils.

Two weeks after he took office he declared that the mission of Japan was to "proclaim and demonstrate *Kodo,* the Imperial Way, throughout the world." This, he went on to explain, meant enabling "all nations and races to find their proper place in the world." His concept of Japan's proper place in relation to other nations was indicated by his claim that the Dutch East Indies and French Indochina were part of "Greater East Asia" which, as a foreign office spokesman explained later at a press conference, were regarded by the Konoye government as within Japan's sphere of influence. The spokesman went even further than Matsuoka. This sphere, he said, "definitely includes other places in the South Seas in addition to the East Indies." Asked by an American correspondent to define the exact area and to say if it included the Philippines, he refused to commit himself. In the Diet, later Matsuoka declared that if the United States persisted in opposing these Japanese aims, Japan would retaliate even if it meant entering the European war.

In Germany, where the consideration was how Japan's ambitions could best serve German interest, Matsuoka's threat that he might embroil his nation in the European conflict was received with no enthusiasm at all. In the European mainland, where they were in firm control, the Nazis required no assistance. Hitler had now abandoned his plans for invasion of Britain. Britain, it was true, was still in the fight but as a direct military threat to Germany was regarded as of little more than gadfly value.

The British navy was another thing and the more of it the Japanese could tie up in the Pacific the better. At the same time the Japanese could render valuable service in continuing to divert America's attention from Europe. More important, since Hitler was now hurrying forward preparations for an all-out surprise assault on Russia, it was essential that the Russians should not feel it safe to move westward any of the substantial forces they maintained in the Far East. In Tokyo, Nazi envoys hastened to explain that Germany put more store on Japan's power in Asia, where Japan could take advantage of an almost clear field.

In the meetings with Konoye and Matsuoka, War Minister Tojo heard the German point of view with its implications for Japan put with great persuasiveness and eloquence by the foreign minister. He was apparently convinced of the immediate prospects in southeast Asia even to the point of being prepared to put off a settlement with Russia, which he expected to fall "like a ripe persimmon."

In early 1941, Matsuoka hurried to Berlin and Rome, where he ratified the Triple Alliance signed between the two Axis powers and Japan in September of the previous year. In Berlin he declared that Japan stood by Germany "in joy and sorrow" and, before finally departing in April, wished the Nazis "good luck and success" in their invasion of the Balkans.

Returning to Japan through the Soviet Union, Matsuoka signed a Treaty of Neutrality with Stalin's government, with the idea of ensuring against Russian intervention in the Greater East Asia design. A joint statement issued after the formal signature declared that Soviet Russia would respect the integrity and inviolability of Manchukuo; Japan on her part undertook to respect that of Outer Mongolia. On his departure from Moscow, Matsuoka was seen off personally by Stalin, the first time that the Soviet leader had so honored a visiting dignitary. It was typical of Matsuoka that despite this when, on his return to Japan, Germany attacked Russia on the 22nd of June, 1941, he immediately advocated joining Germany by invading Russia from the East.

The German invasion of Russia, in fact, caused frantic rethinking in Tokyo among others besides Matsuoka. For one thing it was clear that Britain, relieved of the threat of invasion, would be freer to defend British interests in the Far East. With the early and sweeping German successes in Russia, too, it appeared that a quick German victory would not merely balk Japan of a seat at the victor's table but might even face her with an entirely new threat—that of a triumphant and mighty German military presence in the Far East.

Hitler's boast that he would take Moscow in three weeks and the rest of Russia in as many months was taken seriously enough by War Minister Tojo for him to order the Japanese army to be built up by mobilization to its greatest strength ever. Particularly, the Kwangtung Army—whose staff officers were now planning hastily and hopefully a military government for occupied areas of Siberia if word came for the attack on Russia—was doubled in numbers to 600,000 men. For some weeks they stood ready to assault and partition Russia as Stalin had already divided Poland with Hitler earlier in the war. As Hitler's armies were stalled before Moscow, the Kwangtung reinforcements, much to the relief of the naval chiefs and Prince Konoye, were brought south where, in an almost automatic countermove, the navy had taken the initiative again.

Following their envelopment of virtually all of the south China coastal areas and the occupation of Hainan island, the Japanese had in 1940 taken early advantage of France's defeat by the Germans to make their first tentative move beyond China. Maintaining that important supplies were reaching the Chiang Kai-shek government through French Indochina, they insisted that to cut these off, the northern border with China must be controlled by Japanese forces. By a combination of German pressure on the Pétain government in France and Japanese threats on the spot, the Vichy-appointed governor of the colony was compelled to agree, and Japanese navy transports swiftly disembarked troops who occupied northern Indochina.

Once they were installed there further pressure was brought on the colony's governor to accept the extension of Japanese "protection" to the whole of Indochina, against the alleged threat of a British invasion linked with a possible Gaullist take-over. The governor, having very little choice, consented, and in July 1941 Japanese army and navy forces entered the southern half of the colony. There, from the eight airfields and three naval bases available to them, Japanese sea and air arms were within striking distance of Manila and Singapore, and on land Japanese troops were well placed for further advances into Siam, which lay between them and the entire Malayan peninsula. Immediately the Siamese government was invited to "imitate the example of Indo-china and be protected by Tokyo."

The decision to enter southern Indochina had been taken on the 2nd of July, 1941, at a council before the Throne. While Japan was to continue to be ready to attack the Soviet Union if the German war against that country achieved a decisive success, there was to be no intervention until, as Tojo had for-merly put it, the persimmon was really ripe and ready to fall. At the insistence of Tojo and the service ministers and representa-tives, the decision to occupy southern Indochina was coupled with the resolve that "if need be, we accept war with Britain and the United States." To Konoye, who never had any intention of ac-cepting war with the United States, the declaration, momentous though it was, would not have appeared as death-defying as it sounded. His earlier fears of a clash with the United States over China had now abated.

On record, too, was his new government's intention of "advancing the national fortune by taking a farsighted view of the international situation." It must have appeared to him that in ex-ploiting the French defeat in Europe with the agreement—however unwillingly given—of the Vichy French government, Japan was doing no more than this. Moreover, harassed by Matsuoka's ad-vocacy of an immediate attack on Russia and fearful that Tojo's massive reinforcement of the Kwangtung Army might at any moment lead to this, the occupation of Indochina represented to him by far the lesser of the two evils.

He had, in the meantime, relieved himself of the em-barrassing presence in his government of Matsuoka, whose volatile temperament and changes of mind, particularly in his urging for an attack on Russia, had by this time made Tojo, who was suspicious of civilian attempts to influence the course of military operations, distrust him.

It is likely that with things appearing to be going his way, the prince was over-confident and unaware, at the time, of the full extent to which the Japanese supreme command was already preparing for war. Special troops were being trained for jungle fighting; combined military and naval operations were being perfected; occupation currency was being printed by order of the ministry of finance. From airfields in northern Indochina Japanese reconnaissance planes had flown over Malaya taking aerial photographs of suitable landing areas. Intelligence was being gathered on U.S. fleet movements from secret agents in the Panama Canal Zone and a variety of other sources. As Japanese troops were disembarking in southern Indochina at the end of July 1941, American naval patrols seized seventeen Japanese small craft ostensibly fishing in Hawaiian waters. All were found to be fully equipped with radio transmitters, cameras, and navigational charts. Each carried, posing as a fisherman, an officer of the Japanese navy. In Japan, on the top-secret order of Admiral Yamamoto, chief of the combined fleet, detailed plans for an attack on the American Pacific fleet were being drawn up.

Konoye had correctly guessed that neither Britain nor America was prepared to go to war to recover Indochina for the French. What he had entirely underestimated was the alarm and anger which the arrival of powerful Japanese forces in this critical and strategic area of southeast Asia would arouse. Neither had he comprehended the impossibility of convincing America or Britain that this new move by a nation with a long history of aggression would, if unchallenged, stop at Indochina.

Within forty-eight hours of the first Japanese landings in July, the United States, Britain, and Holland simultaneously imposed trade embargoes on Japan and froze all Japanese assets. A week later, as Japanese forces completed their occupation of the French colony and the press and radio in Tokyo stepped up the war of nerves on Siam, came the body blow which showed how grievously Konoye had miscalculated. Still short of war, it was nevertheless aimed to hit where Japan was most vulnerable. On the 1st of August, the United States banned all further shipments of oil to Japan, and Holland followed by halting supplies from the oil fields in the Dutch East Indies.

Japan was now confronted with a tight economic blockade which, if not soon lifted or broken, could result in slow but sure strangulation. And, for the navy, the southward advance policy became overnight a matter of life and death. The danger now was no longer just the possibility of defeat in a war with the United States. Denied oil, Japan could be brought down without a single blow being struck. Unless the Americans relented, the stranglehold could be broken only by seizing the oil fields of the Dutch East Indies and the resources, including vital rubber and tin, of Malaya.

With sufficient stocks of oil to keep it operational for a few months, the question for the Japanese navy was not so much if they must be seized but how much time was left to do it.

Seventeen

Konoye's shocked surprise at the unexpected severity of the Allied reprisals may have been naïve, but it was real enough. It was not allayed by the reaction of the navy chiefs whose dismay appeared to exceed his own. The response of the army general staff, conveyed to him through his war minister, Tojo, had been prompt and predictably belligerent. They would give him until November to resolve the deadlock by diplomatic means. While the premier was still grappling with the implications of the army ultimatum which gave him very little time as it was, he was shaken again by an urgent message from the naval staff. The navy, he was told, could not wait until November. October was their deadline for war or peace.

With the Damoclean sword of the navy's decision hanging over him and the nation, Konoye redoubled his efforts to get some understanding with the United States. In Washington, Japanese Ambassador Nomura, an admiral grappling hopelessly with diplomatic problems far beyond his experience as a sailor, was having little success with Cordell Hull, the American Secretary of State. The negotiations there—although important British and Dutch interests were at stake—were an all American affair.

The Americans were now insisting on not only the evacuation of Japanese forces from Indochina but a general withdrawal from China. To the Japanese, this undoubtedly represented an unreasonable increase in pressure. They were taking the narrow view that since the allied action had been in retaliation for their occupation of southern Indochina, the latter was the point at issue. The fact was that Cordell Hull believed that the time had come to get tough with Japan, and with the memory of the humiliation and failure of the British at Munich fresh in his mind, appeasement had become a dirty word with him. During the course of the negotiations, he was to come under what he described as "hysterical" attack from Chiang Kai-shek when, at one stage, he was considering a *modus vivendi* with the Japanese which, in return for withdrawal from southern Indochina and a promise to desist from further moves, would have left them *vis-à-vis* the United States and China in a position very similar to the one they had held before completing their occupation of the French colony. But Konoye's patent anxiety to get a settlement certainly influenced Hull and other American statesmen in believing that with the effect of economic sanctions and the buildup of Anglo-American forces in the Far East, time was on the Allied side.

There was, in addition, unfortunate wishful thinking in America and the west generally that Japan had been drained of strength in China. This was fed by exaggerated reports put out by the Chiang Kai-shek government of the scale of Chinese resistance and of Japanese losses there. From Chungking it had recently been claimed that the Japanese had lost more than a million and a half killed and wounded in China since the Sino–Japanese war started in 1937, a figure considerably in excess of the total Japanese forces ever engaged there. The truth—which came as such an unpleasant shock at the time of Pearl Harbor and in the Allied reverses which followed—was that Japan, having been on a war footing for years, was by mid–1941 approaching her full formidable potential in military strength. Of this, only a fraction had been committed in China.

Matsuoka, when foreign minister, had expressed something of the exasperation the Japanese now felt toward the Americans. If America believed, he declared, that Japan had exhausted her power and, therefore, stiffened her attitude, she "must be shown that such was not the case." The United States accused Japan of wanting to dominate the western Pacific although Japan had "constantly stated that her aims were to create a peaceful and prosperous Greater East Asia, free from conquest, exploitation and oppression." He did not see, he said, "how Mr. Hull could possibly object to that." And what if Japan had such dark designs as Mr. Hull implied? How could America criticize her? Hadn't the United States by the Monroe Doctrine exercised a dominating influence over the Western Hemisphere?

That the Monroe declaration of 1823, by which the United States had aimed at forbidding outside interference when the South American dominions of Spain were fighting a war of liberation against their colonial masters, should have been invoked by Matsuoka was a breathtaking piece of sophistry. American intervention in the affairs of her neighbors had not been entirely free of the guilt of armed intervention or self-interest in the past. But except in the Philippines, the United States had never aspired to supplant Spain as the ruling power; the interests of other powers in the area had been respected; and never at any time had their intervention approached in scale and brutality that of Japan in China.

Nevertheless, with the Dutch and French defeated in Europe and the British an almost naked emperor in the Far East, the Americans now constituted the main and much resented stumbling block to Japan's ambitions in Asia and the Pacific. Once again, they were obstinately trying to hold back what was held to be a natural order of events by Japan's leaders and, by thousands of Japanese, even a supernatural one.

The hardening of the American attitude was made unpleasantly clear to Konoye when he took the extraordinary step of proposing through American Ambassador Joseph Grew in Tokyo a meeting between himself and President Franklin Roosevelt in Hawaii. The navy minister, Admiral Oikawa, readily gave his approval. Tojo was critical, on the grounds that such a meeting would upset the Germans. How serious an objection this was is open to doubt. The Germans were already put out by the sudden removal of Matsuoka, in whose ouster Tojo had connived by agreeing to resign with the entire cabinet so that Konoye could reform it with a different foreign minister. And although the Germans were known to have taken a jaundiced view of the fact that Japan had entered into negotiations with the Americans without prior consultation with them, Tojo had himself been quick to observe at the time that Hitler had attacked Russia without bothering to consult his Japanese ally. Tojo did not, however, forbid the projected visit. The army was not necessarily in disagreement, he told Konoye "if it is your intention to uphold Japan's plans and, if you fail to get the Americans to understand Japan's true intentions, you will not resign but will return prepared to lead the country in war."

What hopes Konoye may have held for such a summit type confrontation were killed when, after a period in which there seemed a chance that it might take place, the American government turned down the proposal. Their reply, which came on the 3rd of September, stipulated that before such a meeting could be considered there must be some preliminary and substantial measure of agreement between the United States and Japanese governments.

As Konoye received the American note, he learned from the Japanese supreme command that the navy deadline of October had been agreed upon. On the 5th of September, the day before a full-dress Imperial Conference had been scheduled, Emperor Hirohito summoned Konoye, together with army and navy chiefs of staff, General Sugiyama and Admiral Nagano. How long, the Emperor demanded, would it take for the planned southern advance to be accomplished? When Sugiyama replied that it had been estimated at three months, the Emperor remarked that the same kind of estimate had been made about China. Both Sugiyama and Nagano protested that the situation was entirely different and Nagano held that Japan's whole situation required the drastic surgery of war. "Something must be done quickly," he told the ruler. "If things go on as they are, we are steadily losing the game."

At the Imperial Conference the next day, the navy deadline was reaffirmed in the presence of the Emperor, who could do no more than take formal note of the decision of his cabinet. At this conference, according to Tojo, a general plan of national policy was agreed on. Determined efforts were to be made to reach agreement with the United States no later than the first ten days in October. If that failed, preparations for war were to be completed no later than the last ten days of that month "in order to ensure Japan's self defense and self-preservation." Before the conference closed the Emperor earnestly desired of those present that every possible diplomatic endeavor should be made in the meantime.

On the part of the navy minister, Admiral Oikawa, there was some disposition to support Konoye in his efforts to break the deadlock by negotiations, both from his own conviction and from personal relationship with the Emperor whom he had served as an aide in the latter's years as crown prince. To War Minister Tojo and those on the army side of the supreme command, however, the Imperial Conference of the 6th of September plainly constituted the Emperor's sanction for the October deadline.

Before the end of the month, what remained of Konoye's resolution and nerve sustained a double shock. On the 18th of September, as he was entering his car on the way from his official residence to the office, four would-be assassins armed with daggers and swords rushed at him. Armed guards, who now constantly attended the premier, thwarted the attempt and Konoye went on his way, physically unhurt but shaken. A few days later came the second blow. From the supreme command he heard that he had until the 15th of October, another three weeks, for the crisis to be resolved, one way or the other.

Hurriedly he consulted with his cabinet. Tojo insisted that this deadline was in line with the Imperial Conference decision and was not, therefore, a subject for discussion. Privately, Navy Minister Oikawa undertook to sound out naval opinion, which might not prove as adamant as in the army. Clutching at this straw, Konoye in a resumed conversation with Tojo said that he would persevere in negotiations with the Americans until the very last moment. Tojo's reply was short and uncompromising. The premier should certainly continue to negotiate, but he should bear in mind that the last moment, as far as Tojo and the army were concerned, was the 15th of October.

If Konoye had much hope of a dramatic reversal by the navy from Navy Minister Oikawa's soundings, the latter's report soon dampened it. The navy view, as represented by Admiral Nagano, the navy chief of staff, was that time was rapidly running out. Considerations of fuel stocks, weather, the need for setting up operational bases, and the progress of the buildup of the American Pacific fleet all combined to leave the navy with little choice. Tojo was more blunt. Showing impatience with Konoye, he reiterated that the Imperial assent to the supreme command had been given and the hour for argument had passed. He knew the dangers, but there came a time when the plunge had to be taken regardless of risks. America was rich and strong but lacked Japan's fighting spirit. The Americans were keeping the negotiations going because delay was a weapon in their hands.

On the 11th of October, the day before a meeting Konoye had called at his villa at Ogikubu, for a "final conference" as he had termed it, the premier was visited by an emissary of Admiral Oikawa, the navy minister. Possibly with the object of warning Konoye that at the meeting he would be, so to speak, on his own, Oikawa's message repeated that many senior officers of the navy—the "brains" as he described them—were against going to war with America. But, he stressed, he could not in his official capacity come out and say that the navy lacked confidence for fear of the effect it would have on both the public and the army.

The meeting next day was attended by Admiral Oikawa, General Suzuki, President of the Planning Board, Admiral Toyoda, who was serving as foreign minister, and Tojo. As he now expected, Konoye was given qualified support from Oikawa, who said that the issue of peace or war was for the premier to decide and that the navy would uphold his decision. Konoye promptly said that if that were so, his own wish would be to continue talking with the Americans. Tojo's rejoinder was that the premier was going too fast. The matter was not one that Konoye alone could decide, and before they lost the country the chance of prosecuting a successful war through what he described as "palavering," there must be an assurance that it was going to be worth it.

The foreign minister, Toyoda, pointed out that as things stood, only one major issue blocked the hope of reaching an agreement with the United States and this was the question of the stationing of Japanese troops in China. If the army would make some concessions, if only in principle, on that score, diplomacy might succeed. On this, Tojo was adamant. The army could not yield, he said, on this matter of life or death. Japanese soldiers were essential in China if Japan was to retain Manchuria and Korea, keep China stable, and stop communism from spreading over Asia. He implied that the army had already shown great moderation in that Japan was quite entitled to annex Chinese territory but had not and was not proposing to do so out of respect for Konoye's policy. But if, after its efforts and sacrifice, the army was compelled to pull out, morale would be broken and the consequences for the nation would be disastrous. If the Americans refused to understand this, then there was not much point in talking to them and no alternative to war. Then, said Konoye, "if the Minister of War insists, as he does, it is not a question of whether there is any hope . . . There is none."

On the day before the deadline expired, the premier —in the excruciating position of having the entire decision for war or peace virtually left an issue between himself and Tojo by the Pilate-like attitude of the navy minister—made a final effort to get Tojo to reconsider. Konoye's approach on this occasion was that they might contemplate a complete reappraisal of relations with the United States. They might take a lesson from the days of the Russo-Japanese war of 1904–5, when the good offices of the United States had been enlisted to end matters. Probably, with Tojo's own biased memory of those times, he could have used no worse analogy.

Tojo repeated that he could not give way. America wanted mastery over the Far East herself. Konoye even hinted that Japan need only pretend to agree with the withdrawal of her troops from China to satisfy the Americans. If Japan made one concession to America, Tojo said, others would be demanded. Konoye attempted to justify his wish to avoid war by reference to Japan's comparatively unfavorable position in taking on formidable new enemies while still deeply committed in China. As he understood it, he said, Japan could be involved in a war of up to ten years "once the arrow had left the bow."

Angrily Tojo told him that he was too concerned with dangers and exclaimed that there must be a difference between his and Konoye's characters. He repeated this and more, excitedly and forcefully, at a cabinet meeting later in the day during which Tojo was, as Konoye unhappily noted, the "absolute master." He made no attempt to conceal that his patience was at an end, or his antipathy to the prince who, in his eyes, was guilty of indecision and, possibly, the even more unforgivable failing of lack of courage. Contemptuously, after the meeting, he suggested that he and Konoye should avoid personal contact in the future since he doubted if he could refrain from losing his temper with him. That night he sent a note to Konoye telling him that if the Cabinet could not decide on war, it should resign. If a new cabinet should decide against war, he said, that *may* appear to settle it. But, he added ominously, "the army is straining at the leash."

Konoye, at the end of this tether, handed in the resignations of himself and his cabinet. He had, as he expressed it, "no choice but to withdraw," and was merely anticipating by a few days the certain overthrow of his government by Tojo through the now established method of forcing it by resignation of the war minister.

In the consultations which now took place, the lord privy seal, Marquis Kido, emerged as a leading figure. In 1940, upon the death of Prince Saionji at the age of ninety-two, Kido had inherited the function of chief adviser to the Emperor. The post was onerous and carried with it not merely the responsibility of keeping the Emperor fully informed of all that went on politically but of referring to the ruler matters grave enough to warrant Imperial intervention. With long experience of political and cabinet posts he was well qualified, and from 1930 onward had been involved with the problem of what to do about the Kwangtung Army's independent actions and the generals' persistent activities to establish a one-party state.

It was said of Kido that he was too smart for his own good and that in receiving a sentence of life imprisonment as a war criminal after the surrender he paid the penalty of his own deviousness. It is fair also to say that he was a victim of, as well as a devout believer in, the policy of keeping the Emperor above politics, which he had inherited from his illustrious predecessor, Saionji.

Probably Kido's ultimate error in the issue of war and peace in the last fatal days before Pearl Harbor had been his decision that the situation was too far gone for the only resort left that might have kept Japan from going to war—a request to the Emperor for his outright intervention. The risk that the army would have disregarded it was great; against it was that of the enormous calamity war would bring to the people of Japan. But, to

Kido, the possibility the soldiers might disobey a direct command from their Emperor, thus showing disrespect for the sacred Imperial line, transcended all other considerations. It was a gamble he was unwilling to take—or, it would be more correct to say, was incapable of taking.

Nowhere was his influence more damaging in the long run than in accepting and recommending for his ruler's approval the successive expedients aimed at controlling the generals—always turning out to be yet another concession to them. Kido had personally intervened in 1940 on learning that the army had decided to oust the allegedly pro-western prime minister, Admiral Yonai, and had persuaded Konoye to head the new one-party state. Now that Konoye had thrown in his hand, the Marquis, in the eternal search for one strong enough to contain the turbulence in the army, took upon himself the main role in choosing the next premier.

If he had achieved nothing else, Konoye, even in his downfall, had bought a little time. The 15th of October deadline had passed and negotiations were still going on in Washington. The problem was to replace the prince with a strong successor who could break the deadlock. Tojo's own suggestion had been another member of the royal house, Prince Higashikuni. The prince, although little more than a figurehead militarily, had served in China and, as a general officer, had some standing with the army. But to this the privy seal was absolutely opposed. Konoye's own dismal record did not suggest that royal status assured control; rather it had exposed the Imperial house to the danger of decreased respect. Nor was martial rank, *per se,* sufficient. What was called for was someone who understood the critical situation and had a chance of wielding the kind of authority it called for.

The choice, it was depressingly evident, was not a wide one and it quickly narrowed down to two men in the cabinet. Navy minister Oikawa's long association with the Emperor, his reputation for moderation, and familiarity with the intimate details of the crisis and its background strongly recommended him. But it was the army, throughout, which had exerted the most extreme pressure, and the question was if an admiral would at this stage be able to hold the army. On the other hand, the tough disciplinarian General Tojo was a man of proven ability, and there was no reason to doubt his fundamental loyalty. Even his resistance to Konoye had been rooted in a literal interpretation of the Imperial Conference decision of the 6th of September. The big question in the privy seal's mind was whether Tojo's stand on this was as irrevocable as it appeared.

On the 16th of October, Kido called Tojo to his official residence to sound him out. Prince Konoye, the privy seal pointed out, had resigned because he had felt unable to carry out the Imperial Conference decision. Did he think a new premier should be bound by it? Tojo told him that the whole matter turned on knowing exactly where the navy stood. As he understood it, Konoye's reason for not wanting to go to war had been based on his belief that the navy was undecided. On the other hand, Admiral Nagano, chief of the naval general staff, had said it was. The navy must say where it stood. If it was true that it had reservations, he agreed that reconsideration of the decision for war was inevitable. The new prime minister must be a man who understood this.

For Kido, who was already more than half convinced that Tojo was the man, this apparently was enough. He noted in his diary that "respect for Imperial wishes was common to all soldiers, but it was stronger in Tojo. . . . If it was commanded by the Emperor to scrap the [September 6] decision of the Imperial Conference in question, and review the situation on a fresh basis, I had sincere confidence that Tojo would change his policy in pursuance of Imperial wishes."

On the following day, Hideki Tojo was summoned to the Imperial Palace. At the residence of the war minister, Mrs. Tojo helped him put on his decorations and her husband, serious and uncommunicative as ever, left in the official car. On arrival at the palace he was immediately received by Emperor Hirohito and, to his genuine surprise, was told that he had been chosen for the highest political post in the land. He asked royal indulgence for time to reflect on whether he was indeed worthy of the honor and was given permission to withdraw to an anteroom. Then, after a suitably modest period had passed, the fifty-seven-year-old general returned to tell his ruler that, with great humility, he was prepared to become prime minister of Japan.

Eighteen

When General Hideki Tojo became prime minister of Japan on the 17th of October, 1941, there was almost universal acceptance that this meant that the chances that Japan would not go to war in the Far East—balanced on a knife-edge since Hitler's bloody subjugation of Europe had started two years before—had all but disappeared.

In America—save for initial guarded and what now appears to have been absurdly hopeful comment in some quarters that the General's emergence to power was a sign of victory for "moderate nationalism" in Japan—he was seen as a "typical officer of the Kwangtung Army clique," a "Manchurian continentalist," "smart, hardboiled, resourceful, contemptuous of theories, sentiments and negotiations." In the British press much play was made of his nickname, "Razor." To one of the tabloids he was a "son of Satan" getting on with the job of "unleashing all hell on the Far East." More conservatively, the image was that capsuled by a military correspondent of "a swashbuckling soldier-premier who does what the army tells him." And with this description was coupled the warning that it was dangerous to underrate such a man.

In Germany, the Nazi press hailed Tojo as "a man charged with energy, thinking clearly and with a single purpose—a man for whom the old military adage 'duty is duty' might have been expressly coined." With unconscious irony, the writer observed that the former premier, Prince Konoye, "would not have been able to steer so steady a course" if Hideki Tojo, as his war minister, with his "high-pitched, penetrating voice," had not "sometimes with noteworthy energy trimmed the sails for him."

Japanese commentators—no more free than their German counterparts to voice anything but the officially inspired line—gave little enough support to the theory that there was anything moderate in the nationalism which the new premier represented. Tojo's aim was to build Japan into a "high-degree defense state . . . established on a military economy." General Tojo believed that "the whole nation should move as one cannonball of fiery resolution" and "his decisive leadership was a signal for the nation to rise and administer a great shock to the anti-Axis powers." Domei, the official news agency, declared that Tojo's government was "vested with powers to direct the country towards peace or war" and spoke of "fifty days of double-dealing" by the United States. How greatly the chances were loaded against peace was revealed by the *Japan Times and Advertiser,* the leading propaganda mouthpiece for the government. Japan, it declared, was "imperiled by the encirclement of hostile powers" and General Tojo, the soldier-premier, was a logical choice at such a time.

With every allowance made for the extravagance of phrase in the mood of the times and for the need for dispassionate historical judgment, any suggestion that Hideki Tojo did not become premier in order to lead Japan into war seems overmeticulous. Mamoru Shigemitsu who, at the time, had just returned from his ambassador's post in Britain, was sure that Japan was heading straight for war and had little doubt that Tojo was leading her there. Arrested himself after the Japanese surrender in 1945 as a war criminal and writing his memoirs in Sugamo prison, he recalled how the General, as war minister, had made it impossible for Prince Konoye, the former premier, to continue negotiations with the American government in the crucial days before the Japanese attack on Pearl Harbor in December 1941. Was there ever any real hope, Shigemitsu commented, that these could now succeed under what was essentially a war cabinet headed by General Tojo? Certainly Tojo by his subsequent words and actions gave none.

Tojo was not, it was true, a flamboyant adventurer like Mussolini or a moody tyrant like Hitler. He personally adhered to no particular ideology. Nor was he the leader of a military revolt as General Franco was. It was equally true that he was as authoritarian in outlook as could be expected from a man of his character and professional background. He believed unreservedly that Japan must dominate in the Far East and was as convinced as any of the European dictators in his belief that force or the threat of it was the instrument to achieve this. And, while the checks and balances in the Japanese system of government provided by the weight of the Emperor and his advisers made personal dictatorship theoretically impossible, the unhappy fact was that at the time that Tojo achieved office these were ineffectual.

The military party, of which Tojo was the representative, had through its foothold in government and by relentless assault and intrigue destroyed all but the trappings of constitutional rule. The same army officers who, unsanctioned by their Emperor or government, had gone to war against neighboring China back in 1931, shouting *"Tenno Hei-ka Banzai!"*—"May His Glorious Majesty Live Ten Thousand Years!"—had seen to it that the Emperor, revered though he still might be by his subjects as the Son of Heaven, had retained little power on earth.

Their man, General Tojo, holding the key posts which gave him control of government, the police, and the judiciary, wielded an unprecedented concentration of power that was for all practical purposes absolute, excluding, of course, the armed services. Even so, it had been reported from China that high army officers there did not necessarily regard him as their final choice. It was suggested that Tojo's cabinet might only be another care-taker government, likely to last a few months. His period in office would be used to strengthen military control in Japan while negotiations went on with the United States and Russia to gain time to prepare for a conflict in the Pacific that was regarded as inevitable.

Had he known of it, Tojo might have been strongly at variance with their view that he was a temporary expedient. But what is certain is that if he had not shared their belief in the inevitability of war he would very soon have been removed for someone who did. The inescapable conclusion remains that in the case of Hideki Tojo, this was never necessary.

Nineteen

After he had accepted the Imperial mandate to form a government on the 17th of October, Tojo went straight from the palace to offer homage at the Tokyo shrine to the Emperor Meiji. He then paid his respects at the memorial to the Russo–Japanese war hero, Admiral Togo, going on from there to the great Yasukuni shrine dedicated to General Nogi and Japan's war dead. On the following morning, the day on which it was announced that the new premier had been promoted to the rank of full general, he made known his choice of cabinet ministers.

The navy minister went, of course, to a serving naval officer, Admiral Shimada, who had commanded the China Fleet in 1940. General Suzuki, like Tojo a former member of the army's military affairs bureau and something of an all-purpose soldier cum administrator, retained his Konoye cabinet post of planning chief and was also made minister without portfolio. In charge of foreign affairs Tojo nominated Shigenori Togo, an Axis career diplomat who had first met him when they were both serving in Europe after the First World War. Although pro-Axis, Togo had a good understanding of Soviet affairs from his tenure as ambassador to Moscow during 1939 and 1940. He subsequently insisted that Tojo's cabinet was not dedicated to going to war and claimed that, before he would accept office, he had some assurance from Tojo that the army would not maintain its obstinate stand over the question of the withdrawal of troops from China. He did, however, continue in office for long after this matter had become academic, and until the middle of 1942, when he quit in protest against Tojo's plan to take the handling of Japanese-occupied territories out of the hands of the Foreign Office.

Two other former acquaintances—civilians who had helped the General run Manchuria in his Kwangtung Army days—were brought in. Naoki Hoshino, who was later to say of Tojo that his chief "actually was not quite up to the premiership," became chief cabinet secretary. He came nearer perhaps than any other non-military person to having Tojo's confidence and was able to say that the general was "a very easy man to work under," an opinion not commonly held by those who had. Hoshino was one of the few people from whom Tojo would brook a certain amount of criticism. "He can say things to me," Tojo once said to his wife, "because he is trying to protect me and he is to be trusted." Nobusuke Kishi took over the ministry of commerce and industry. (Kishi was to prove a politician with a remarkable gift for not merely surviving but also emerging from vicissitudes more successful and secure than before. After the war, having served a substantial sentence as a major war criminal, he then brought off the improbable feat of becoming prime minister of a staunchly pro-American administration.) Tojo himself took the home and war ministries to ensure direct control of internal security and military affairs. He was later to hold that he took the Home Ministry as a precaution against the possibility of there being peace rather than war, when internal confusion would follow and he would have to be responsible for dealing with it.

That afternoon, after his ceremonial investiture, Premier Tojo made his first speech to the nation over the radio, a cliché-replete exhortation calling for unity and trust and proclaiming Japan's "determination to contribute to world peace" by settling the "China affair" and establishing the Greater East Asia Co-Prosperity Sphere. He then left for the Imperial shrine to report to the Sun Goddess at Ise, traditionally the first of a number of sacred places where he was required to give homage to Japan's *shinto* deities. There, after he had completed his ritual dedication and prayers, he spoke of his "awe and trepidation at his own limited abilities."

Neither of these emotions was evident a few days later on the 26th of October when he went on to the industrial heartland of Japan to report to the gods of the Kansai shrine at Osaka. In a harangue after the ceremony he told two hundred senior officials that Japan's policies were "immutable and irrevocable." "We cannot tell what lies in store for us," he said, "but we must go on to develop in ever-expanding progression. . . . Naturally, difficulties arise, but if one hundred million people merge into one in iron solidarity and go forward, nothing can stop us. . . . Wars can be fought with ease." In an interview afterwards he declared that the nation must show the same confidence in the government as "a person trusts a driver when he is taking a taxicab." The analogy, if prophetic, seems to have been ill-chosen for the occasion to any who have experienced the Japanese taxi driver's notorious recklessness and inexact knowledge of where he is going.

If the Hitlerian ring of Hideki Tojo's public utterance led those with whom his envoys in Washington were still negotiating and Churchill's government in Britain to believe that the General who had taken over government in Japan was another dictator in the totalitarian mold, they could scarcely be blamed. To a world long assailed by the hoarse, strident voice from Berlin claiming "living space," a "new order," and "master-race" status for the Germans, there was a sickening familiarity in Tojo's ranting demands for a "Greater East Asia Co-Prosperity Sphere," "ever-expanding progression," and in his shrill assertions of Japan's mystic destiny to lead. Nor, to nations with recent and bitter memory of humiliating failure to appease Hitler, was there any comfort in speculating if Tojo would peacefully settle for less than the whole of Asia.

The creation of the Imperial Rule Assistance Association under Konoye had already effectively made the country into a one-party state. Much of the apparatus of authoritarianism, oppressive and petty, was established. Measures like price fixing, gasoline rationing, censorship, and the peculiarly Japanese law forbidding "dangerous thoughts" were in force. Military conscription, which had operated since the Meiji era, had been extended by the drafting of civilians into mines and armament factories.

Western fashions for men adopted from Meiji times

were not much affected at first, but a utility military-style jacket was being increasingly worn. For women, frivolous manifestations of western-type feminine emancipation such as permanent waves, thought to detract from the traditional modesty of Japanese womanhood, were banned outright. And in place of the elegant *kimono* and brocaded *obi* sash, the patriotic woman was expected to wear *mompei,* baggy trousers into which a short *kimono* could be tucked, thus saving cloth and providing more practical wear for work in field and factory.

The more basic womanly function of childbearing was not overlooked. In a land where pressure of population was one of the arguments advanced by the expansionists as justification for Japanese designs on the territories of other nations, a ten-year program to increase the birth rate had been inaugurated. Mrs. Tojo, as a leading member of one of the patriotic women's associations and a mother of seven children herself, was credited with having coined the slogan, "Having children is fun." At all hours "groups of tired women clad in white aprons and sashes which proclaimed their membership in the Women's Patriotic Association waited on passing troop trains and send-off parties. . . . Cleaning shrine compounds, collecting subscriptions, pushing savings drives, attending spiritual mobilization meetings, the people of Japan were all at the beck and call of this form of patriotic blackmail."[1] Western contacts were more than ever suspect and anti-western feeling was fanned by such propaganda devices as posters depicting "sinister foreigners . . . dressed in a Sherlock Holmes rigout with curly pipe and deerstalker hat."[2] Less comic were the activities of the *Kempeitai.* These had already led to tragic consequences in the previous year when eleven prominent Britishers, including M. J. Cox, the Reuters correspondent, were arrested in Tokyo. The arrests, which the Japanese government in answer to British official protests insisted "could not be described as unfriendly," were justified on the grounds of alleged "increasing activities of foreign organs of espionage and conspiracy." According to an announcement made by the ministries of war and the interior later, Cox "committed suicide" after two days of interrogation by "throwing himself" from the third floor of the *Kempeitai* headquarters building.

Press and radio attacks on British oppression and

exploitation of Asians were constant; also attacked were color prejudice and lynching in the United States. Golf, one of the favorite diversions of Prince Konoye and through which game U.S. Ambassador Joseph Grew had maintained contact with top Japanese more effectively than through diplomatic channels, was frowned on. The ancient *shinto* worship was the official state religion and, as in Tokugawa times, priests of all sects were paid servants of the government.

In the school, respect for the Emperor had been thoroughly subverted to the ends of nationalism and the legend of his divine descent solemnly implanted into impressionable young minds. The day's teaching started with a ceremonial dedication before the ruler's portrait, taken each morning from a specially consecrated Emperor Room and displayed before the assembled company of teachers and students.

Indoctrination in ultranationalist principles became part of all school curricula. All the myths of Japan from its miraculous creation by the Sun Goddess two thousand years before were taught as historical fact. *Hakko ichiu*—the injunction of the god-ancestors that the eight corners of the world must be united by Japan "under one roof"—was inculcated as an article of faith. Pupils, from toddlers armed with miniature rifles, were trained by regular or retired noncommissioned officers of the army and navy.

The thunderous cries of *"Banzai"* from the well-manipulated crowds who now flocked to patriotic rallies all over the land testified, as Mamoru Shigemitsu observed, how much war fever was already on the nation. This was somberly reflected when Tojo reconvened the Diet a few weeks after he became prime minister.

In the place of representatives of the caliber of the courageous Hamada, who had defied war minister Terauchi just before parliament had last met as an independent body in 1937, there were men like Seigo Nakano, leader of the fascist Tohokai Party. Nakano called for Japan to "blast a way through Singapore to the Persian Gulf" to join hands with Germany. In a later session, Toshio Shimada, a former minister, declared that it was clear that "the fundamental motivating force for the present conflict between the Axis powers and the British, American, and Soviet nations is the inordinate desire of the United States for world hegemony." There was a limit, he said, to "our patience and self-restraint." The cancer in the Pacific in the minds of "arrogant American leaders who are seeking world domination and are meddling even in Europe by assisting Britain" must be removed by Japan "wielding the big knife." If the Americans refused to acknowledge that Japan was engaged in a holy war, there were "other ways of making such a party understand." So aggressive were the Diet members, a western correspondent observed, that the government appeared moderate in comparison.

On the day of Tojo's appointment to the premiership, both Emperor Hirohito and the lord privy seal made it as clear as possible within the straitjacket of court protocol and tradition, which forbade a direct Imperial command, that he was to start with a clean slate. Konoye before his resignation had reported to the ruler that the navy did not want war but could not say so in view of the Conference. In his personal interview with Tojo the Emperor enjoined him, therefore, to ensure close co-operation between army and navy. He added pointedly that he intended to summon Oikawa, the outgoing navy minister, and repeat this injunction. Kido, after the royal audience, explicitly conveyed to Tojo the Emperor's wish that he should take an entirely new look at the situation confronting the nation, uninhibited by the 6th of September decision.

Tojo could claim that in the days that followed, he had met the Imperial wish. Co-operation with the navy was close in the tense deliberations which occupied the rest of the month of October. Unhappily Oikawa, in his new post of Supreme War Councillor, had little say in naval affairs compared with Admiral Yamamoto, the truculent Chief of the Combined Fleet, and Admiral Nagano, the Chief of Naval Staff, who was literally counting the days left for a decision in terms of diminishing oil stocks.

With the Emperor's wish that he should not be bound by the terms of the Imperial Conference of the 6th of September, Tojo would have held that he complied, too, in the sense that he accepted that the plan based on the original deadline of the 15th of October must be re-examined and, if necessary, amended or recast. He allowed negotiations in Washington to proceed and the deadline was, in the meantime, extended to the 30th of October.

Any suggestion that this represented any drawing back from war on Tojo's part can hardly be sustained. Japan, he declared, was being driven to war and must be prepared for the worst. He was, as his wife observed at the time, an angry man. The use of American economic power to threaten another country's right to live by cutting off vital supplies was, he said, an outrage.[3] There was no doubt in his mind that the American action was aimed at forcing a Japanese withdrawal from China. On this—though he might conceivably have parleyed on other issues—Tojo was immovable.

The provisional data of the 30th of October passed with no final decision taken. That this was more indicative of the state of readiness of the supreme command's plans for action than of second thoughts was emphasized when the premier addressed the nation on the following day. He declared that Japan was faced with "an unprecedented crisis."

The "honor" had been conferred on Japan of "shouldering the responsibility of a New Order in East Asia" and, he admonished, "the road is not strewn with roses." Japan was "confronted with obstacles thrown across our path by hostile countries." On the same day British foreign office officials in Shanghai gave a final warning to British subjects in Japanese-occupied China to leave. Those who did not register to leave in twelve days "must be prepared to remain," the official announcement said ominously, "irrespective of the future course of events. No similar opportunity is likely to recur." Similar urgent advice had already been given to American nationals in China by the government of the United States.

At a liaison meeting of the members of the armed services high commands and leading cabinet ministers, which went on until early in the morning of the 2nd of November, Togo, the foreign minister, and Kaya, the finance minister, questioned whether Japan should not wait before going to war, even if the Washington talks broke down, to see if the international situation developed more favorably. Nagano, the navy chief of staff, replied that unless Japan went to war before the end of November it was possible that she would have to surrender without fighting. He was confident of initial success against Britain and America. The representatives of the army were even more definite in insisting the hostilities should begin without further delay and before Britain and America could build up their strength in the Far East. Tojo summed up the feeling of the armed forces. "Rather than waiting for extinction with folded hands," he declared, "it is better to face death by breaking through the encircling ring to find a way for existence." The next day he reported to Emperor Hirohito that a final try at negotiations with the Americans was going to be made, but if this had no success, Japan would be compelled to go to war. The Emperor, according to Tojo, told him that if the situation was as he described there appeared to be no alternative, but while proceeding with preparations for war, all possible means to overcome the difficulties with the American talks should be explored.

On the 5th of November, Saburo Kurusu, an experienced foreign office man, was suddenly flown to Washington. He was sent there ostensibly to assist Admiral Nomura, the Japanese ambassador who had, a couple of weeks earlier, cabled his third request to be relieved of the post and was staying on only because it was thought inappropriate for him to leave at this crucial stage lest it should be misconstrued both abroad and at home. Kurusu's dispatch just a few weeks before the strike on Pearl Harbor was later to be angrily denounced by the Americans as an act of almost unbelievable treachery by Tojo's government. If it was, in fact, a piece of calculated deception by the Japanese, it is strange that the Americans should have fallen for such a plot so completely. Joseph Grew, their ambassador in Tokyo since 1932, had reported to the President in December, 1940 that "sooner or later, unless we are prepared . . . to withdraw bag and baggage from the entire sphere of 'Greater East Asia including the South Seas' (which God forbid), we are bound eventually to come to a head-on clash with Japan."[4] More specifically he had reported back to Secretary of State Cordell Hull a month later that "my Peruvian colleague told a member of my staff that he had heard from many sources including a Japanese source that the Japanese military forces planned, in the event of trouble with the United States, to attempt a surprise mass attack on Pearl Harbor using all of their military facilities." He added that "although the project seemed fantastic the fact that he had heard it from many sources prompted him to pass on the information."[5] And they had even more substantial warning than ambassadorial dispatches.

American intelligence men had brought off the remarkable feat of breaking the Japanese naval code in use between the Tokyo foreign office and its embassies abroad and were regularly intercepting messages. This had enabled the Americans in July, 1941 to warn the Churchill government that Japan was preparing a move south against the British. And about the time that Kurusu arrived in Washington, the Americans already knew from an intercepted signal to Ambassador Nomura that the Japanese government intended to break off negotiations, and on what date.

Whether primarily intended to deceive or not, on the same day that Kurusu left Japan, Tojo, at a conference before the Throne on the 5th of November, had confirmed that Japan was going to war on or very shortly after the 30th of that month. Orders for the Japanese navy to take up battle stations for an attack on the United States, Britain, and Holland were given immediately after the Imperial Conference by Admiral Yamamoto, the Chief of the Combined Fleet. And, while Kurusu was in special audience with President Roosevelt in Washington five days later on the 10th of November, the Japanese task force assigned for the attack on the American Pacific Fleet at its Hawaiian base of Pearl Harbor was already formed and in an advanced state of readiness to sail.

Twenty

In November 1940 fliers of the British fleet air arm had accomplished a feat unique in naval history and unsurpassed in courage. Two waves of ten slow-moving old "Swordfish" biplanes, launched from the aircraft carrier "Illustrious," had made a surprise attack on the main Italian fleet in its base at Taranto. Pressing home their attack in the face of frantic and murderous fire, they had sunk or crippled more than half the enemy battleships. For the loss of only two planes, the Italian navy had been dealt a blow from which it never fully recovered, and in the space of a little more than an hour, the entire balance of naval power in the Mediterranean had been altered in favor of Britain.

For Admiral Yamamoto, a proponent of naval carrier warfare, the Taranto victory was the subject of more than just earnest study. In January 1941—the month in which U.S. Ambassador Grew had warned his government of rumors of a surprise attack by the Japanese—Yamamoto issued a top-secret memorandum to certain of his staff officers calling for an operational plan to be prepared for the destruction of the U.S. Pacific fleet at its Hawaiian base of Pearl Harbor. Moreover, he stipulated it must be accomplished in one blow.

The reasons were both physical and psychological, he explained. Japanese combined operations planned against the Philippines, Malaya, and the Dutch East Indies could not be freely carried out as long as the U.S. fleet threatened from the rear. At the same time a long war would in the navy's view be ruinous for Japan. Therefore, the Americans must be so overawed from the start as to cause them to shrink from continuing the war. Faced with an enemy capable of destroying their entire Pacific fleet in a single assault delivered at a range of over three thousand miles, they would be forced to consider what chance there would be of beating this same enemy that held an impregnable ring of defensive positions with interior lines of communication and a complete command of the air and sea.

In April, Yamamoto had approved his staff's plans and ordered the formation of a special attack force for the operation. His planners had already worked out the strike in much detail. The force would set out from a base in the remote Kurile Islands in the north, and taking a circuitous northern route, avoiding common shipping routes, would sweep down to within two hundred and thirty miles of Hawaii. From this point, the carrier planes would take off. It had been estimated that 360 planes would be needed and that bombs of over three times the usual weight would be required to pierce the deck armor of the American capital ships. To minimize the risk of heavy losses to the Japanese force on its long return voyage, when it would be vulnerable to retaliatory attack, there was to be an element of complete surprise. In other words, this first act of war must take place without warning.

On a large-scale model of Pearl Harbor and the units of the U.S. fleet in the Imperial Naval College in Tokyo, commanders of the force spent long hours familiarizing themselves with every aspect of their objective. And the same accurate intelligence from Japanese agents in Hawaii which had enabled the model to be constructed, even to the harbor soundings at the U.S. base, provided the planners with their biggest headache, one which was to plague them right until almost the last moment. Theoretically, in an aerial assault, it was impossible at Pearl Harbor to use the most deadly and effective weapon against warships, the torpedo. Launched conventionally from a plane, they required five times the depth of water that existed there.

With a little less than three weeks to go before the date of the attack, this problem was finally solved. By dint of unremitting experiment and practice in the bay of Kagoshima in the southern island of Kyushu, picked because of its similarity to the area of Pearl Harbor, the carrier pilots of the force found a technique to overcome the problem. By flying in almost at sea level, releasing their torpedoes—fitted with special fins—low over the water, and banking steeply immediately afterward to clear their targets, they were able to score a high percentage of strikes. On the 17th of November, when Admiral Yamamoto gave his final address to the commanders of the attack force on the battleship "Nagato," he knew that when the Japanese torpedoes were launched at Pearl Harbor, there was a good chance that at least eight out of every ten would find their mark.

As the task force sailed north for its secret rendezvous at Hitokappu bay in the Kuriles, and Japanese units and supplies were embarked on troopships at inland sea ports for the invasion of the southern areas, Tojo spoke on the 17th of November at a plenary session of the Diet which lasted a brief nine minutes. In an address broadcast to the nation he said that Japan was "at the crossroads of her two thousand years of existence." Third powers were not to "obstruct the successful conclusion of the China Affair" and economic blockade, "which constituted a measure little less hostile than armed warfare" had to cease. He extended "sincere felicitations" on the accomplishments of Germany and Italy, hoping that they would, together with the Japanese empire, establish a new world order "based on justice." Two days later, Japanese embassies in Washington and London were warned to stand by and were given the code signal (to be included in one of the regular daily short-wave overseas programs from Tokyo) ordering them to burn their ciphers and confidential documents.

On the 20th of November, the day on which the Pearl Harbor task force signaled back to supreme command headquarters in Tokyo that it was in position and ready to sail, Kurusu and Nomura presented Japan's final offer to U.S. Secretary of State Cordell Hull. In the last resort, Japan would withdraw from southern Indochina. In return for this, she must be assured of free access to the raw materials and oil of the Dutch East Indies and of the resumption of substantial American oil deliveries. Japanese forces would remain in north Indochina and in China, but the rest of southeast Asia and the south Pacific was to be a neutral zone respected by both countries. Again it was insisted that American support for China's Generalissimo Chiang Kai-shek must stop.

On the 25th of November, the day before the American reply to Japan's note was delivered, Henry Stimson, the U.S. Secretary of War, noted in his diary that at a White House meeting that day President Roosevelt had spoken of an imminent attack by the Japanese, perhaps within a week. As reported by Stimson, the President posed the question of "how we should maneuver them into the position of firing the first shot." It is, however, extremely doubtful that this statement, even if accurately represented, was a decision to precipitate war by deliberately provoking Japan.

Roosevelt personally was unquestionably and wholeheartedly against the aggressor nations and dedicated to sustaining those who opposed them, as were a very great number of Americans. And if he was, in his own way, also dedicated to the liquidation of the European colonial empires, it was never with any intention that they should be divided out between Japan and the other Axis powers. But Roosevelt the politician had to take into account other factors. Noninterventionist sentiment as voiced by the press of William Randolph Hearst and by senators like Taft and Gillette was powerful and persuasive. And, by the strangest of ironies, whereas Shigemitsu, Japan's ambassador to the Court of St. James, never believed that Britain would be defeated, Roosevelt's own ambassador to Britain, Joseph Kennedy, had come back to Washington impressed by German might and supporting the isolationists by his expressed opinion that America should keep out of a war Britain could not win.

In the United States in general, sympathy with the victims of the aggressor powers was widespread and deep, and the very great majority of Americans shared Roosevelt's own detestation of totalitarian ideology and his desire to help those countries who still fought against it. But in 1941 only a handful of volunteers in the Canadian Army, the RAF's "Eagle Squadron," and Chennault's "Flying Tigers" in China, were personally committed to fight along with them. The average American was no more spoiling for war than the average Briton or Frenchman had been until it was impelled upon him.

In the meantime, America was buying "precious months," as the President acknowledged after Pearl Harbor, by supplying arms to Britain, China, and Russia. In November 1941 the U.S. military and naval chiefs of staff, General Marshall and Admiral Stark, were asking for more time and had advised Roosevelt that war should be avoided for as long as possible to gain it. At no stage in the negotiations in Washington had Japan been challenged by the certainty of war with the United States, and it had never been made clear to the British and Dutch that a Japanese attack on their Far Eastern possessions would automatically involve America.

All of this would appear to support the American contention that their reply to Japan's note, delivered by Cordell Hull to Nomura and Kurusu on the 26th of November, was not an ultimatum as the Japanese alleged it to be. Quite clearly it conveyed Hull's own uncompromising attitude. Far from making any concessions to meet Japan's final proposals, it reiterated that Japanese withdrawal from Indochina and the whole of China (and —as the Japanese understood it—the Americans included Manchuria as part of China) was a prerequisite to the lifting of sanctions. It is one thing to argue in western terms that since it set no time limit, this could not be called an ultimatum. How it appeared to the Japanese in the highly charged days of 1941 was another matter. It is not without significance that Justice Pal of India, an oriental member of the Far East War Crime Tribunal who often dissented from his western colleagues, was quoted as saying that, "even Monaco or Luxembourg would have opened war against the United States if they had received the same memorandum the U.S. State Department sent to the Japanese government prior to Pearl Harbor." As interpreted by the Japanese, it meant that whereas they had been prepared to make a military withdrawal to the position they had held in July 1941, the Americans required them to retreat to where they stood before January 1931.

For the ultranationalists and those of the military who were already set on a collision course with the west, no further proof was needed that in all the months of negotiations the Americans had never had any real intention of relaxing the stranglehold on Japan. And the raising of the Manchurian issue was calculated to bring those who wavered into line. Their assertion that Manchuria was a border state colonized by the Chinese and to which China had no greater moral claim than any other conqueror, had by constant repetition become accepted as fact. Its seizure by the army in 1931 had long become merged in the Japanese consciousness as the completion of an historical process which began with the heroic victories over Tsarist Russia in 1904.

Tojo held that the Hull note demonstrated that the Americans were "insincere" and showed "no spirit of reconciliation whatever." Ironically, he was now being criticized for appearing less than resolute. In the Diet the fascist representative Nakano had called on him to "heed the true voice of the people." Letters were sent to him urging war. People called by telephone or at his house demanding to know what he was going to do. One of the latter, a major general and a former classmate of Tojo, came direct from a meeting of army officers to see Mrs. Tojo. Excitedly he told her that he had been trying to see Tojo but had been put off on the excuse that the premier was too busy. He wanted Mrs. Tojo to let her husband know of their anger that he had not yet made a decision. At Waseda University students taunted Tojo's nephew, a student there, saying that he should get his uncle to make up his mind.[1]

On the 26th of November, at an extraordinary session of the Diet, Premier Tojo approached the raised dais where Emperor Hirohito sat in the full uniform and regalia of a generalissimo. Holding a scroll in his hand, he "advanced to the throne chair, and, keeping his head bowed, awkwardly hobbled up the steps by advancing only with his right foot and dragging his left after him in exaggerated respect. With an almost impatient gesture, the Emperor stretched out his hand, and taking the scroll"[2] read a brief message formally empowering the passing of various laws to meet the emergency situation. Tojo, in a speech that followed, asserted that the "haughty attitude taken by the United States was beyond words" and accused the Americans, British, Dutch, and Chinese of conspiring to encircle the Japanese and threatening Japan's existence.

That night, as darkness fell on their mist-enshrouded base in the Kuriles, the Pearl Harbor task force, a fleet of six aircraft carriers, two battleships, and escorting craft, had begun their stealthy approach across the Pacific towards their objective, the U.S. Pacific fleet based in Hawaii.

Tojo was to claim later that he knew nothing of this.

Whether he did or not, a few days later, on the occasion of the celebration of the anniversary of the signing of the Anti-Comintern Pact, he gave a strong impression that some Japanese action was imminent. In a speech which, bellicose as it sounded, was apparently mild by comparison with others made at the time by officers of the Imperial Rule Assistance Association, he declared that Britain and America had been "fishing in the troubled waters of East Asia" and turning Asians against each other. Japan, he said, must "purge this sort of practice from the Far East with a vengeance." American press agency reports of the speech brought President Roosevelt hastening back to Washington from a brief holiday in Georgia. He was not much reassured by an explanation from the Japanese embassy that Tojo's words, as originally translated and released by the official Japanese Domei agency, had appeared more menacing than they really were.

In the following days Emperor Hirohito, within the strictly circumscribed limits available to him, went to some lengths to discover if there was not, even at this late stage, some way out. A meeting was called at the Imperial Palace on the 29th of November so that his advisory council of ex-premiers, the *jushin,* which included Prince Konoye, could question Tojo on the crisis. Although present, the Emperor took no part in the discussion, but several of the ex-premiers expressed reservations that might well have been the Emperor's own. Could Japan fight an extended war? Was war necessary at all? Konoye asked if, even though negotiations had to be broken off with the Americans, war necessarily had to follow?

Tojo, speaking for the cabinet and the supreme command, told them with scarcely concealed impatience that it must if Japan's existence was to be assured. It was not a question of whether America was strong or if Japan was fully prepared. Japan had been challenged in such a manner that she had to fight whatever the state of her military preparedness. There was no other way. It had all been gone over, he said, "until it makes my head ache, but the conclusion always is that war is unavoidable."[3] In any case, the chances were better than doubters might think. Expounding the supreme command's strategy as Admiral Yamamoto had laid it down to his planning staff months before, Tojo said that by knocking out the American Pacific Fleet and seizing all the resources of south-east Asia, Japan would hold a self-contained area in Asia, strongly defended in depth. The Americans would be forced to see the hopelessness of continuing to fight. The conflict might then be ended relatively quickly and this was what Japan aimed to do. At the right time, peace talks could be initiated, perhaps through the Soviet Union or the Vatican. But if there had to be a long war, it had to be faced. Looking straight at Konoye he added with heavy sarcasm that if anyone else had any more brilliant ideas, he was prepared to listen. Clearly none of those present knew enough of the military's plans or resources to dispute on that level. No one did, and if one of the *jushin* had been so minded, Tojo's manner, described by foreign minister Togo as "curt and brusque," was certainly not encouraging.

Emperor Hirohito might still have been able to use his Imperial right to intervene. By tradition, as always, this could be exercised only indirectly, on his being called upon to arbitrate where there was disagreement on some vital issue in the Cabinet. It was probably with the slender chance that such disagreement existed that he privately called Admiral Shimada, the navy minister, with Admiral Nagano, the chief of naval staff, into private audience the day before a full-dress Imperial Conference scheduled for the 1st of December. He had heard, he told them, that the navy was not entirely confident of the chances of success in a war against the United States and asked them if this were true. If they sensed the meaning implicit in the ruler's question, the navy chiefs, more anxious to retain the navy's initiative in the conflict that now seemed inevitable than they were hopeful of averting it, gave him no help. The navy, they assured him, was "reasonably confident."

The ubiquitous secret police, if no one else, would have reported to Tojo their visit to the Emperor, and there is no doubt that the premier would have had a fairly accurate guess at the reasons behind the summons. The quizzing by the Emperor's advisory council of ex-premiers had given him a good idea that there were those behind the Throne who still sought to avoid war. It is likely, too, that the navy minister himself, having evaded the Emperor's unspoken question, informed Tojo of what had been said, letting the premier draw his own conclusions and, more to the point, putting the responsibility for war on to him as the navy had left it to Konoye before.

At the Imperial Conference the next day, Tojo opened with a brisk and no-nonsense statement of the situation as he saw it and, he made it clear, he was determined that the meeting would see it.

With His Majesty's permission, I shall manage today's proceedings. On the basis of the Imperial Conference decision of the 5th of November, our army and navy have devoted themselves to completion of preparations for their operations, while the government has made all possible efforts to readjust diplomatic relations with the United States. The United States, however, not only does not recede a step from its former contentions, but has now demanded unilateral concessions by us, in adding such requirements as unconditional and wholesale military evacuation from China, withdrawal of recognition of the Nanking government, and abrogation of the Japan-Germany-Italy Tripartite Pact. If we submit to these demands, not only will the honor of the Empire be lost and any prospect for successful conclusion of the China Affair vanish, but our very existence will be threatened. It is clear we cannot gain our contentions by diplomatic means. On the other hand, the United States, Great Britain, the Netherlands and China have recently increased their economic and military pressure on us. . . . Things having reached this point we have no recourse but to go to war against the United States, Great Britain and the Netherlands. . . .[4]

However regrettable it was that His Majesty should have cause for concern, war was absolutely and urgently necessary. Every aspect had been considered, and in national morale and material strength, Japan would never be in a better position to win than she was now. He assured the Emperor that in the unlikely event that the Americans should decide to give way, he was prepared right up to the last moment to cancel the order to attack. His foreign minister, Togo, confirmed that in his opinion diplomacy could go no further. The service chiefs said that the nation's soldiers and sailors were "burning with desire to give their lives" and awaited the Emperor's command. Emperor Hirohito, accepting the unanimous decision of his government, withdrew and the conference was over.

Twenty-one

Sunday the 8th of December—the 7th by American time—was the day chosen by the supreme command for the opening act of hostilities, the planned strike on Pearl Harbor. The Sabbath day, it was reasoned, would catch the greatest number of American warcraft in the base and its personnel at their maximum state of unreadiness. On the 2nd of December, the Imperial assent having been formally given, Admiral Yamamoto signaled the attack date to the strike force: "Ascend Mount Niitaka. 1208." On the same day smoke from the Japanese embassy in Washington indicated that the embassy staff were burning their code books and papers.

Emperor Hirohito now became concerned that no reply had yet been sent to the Hull note. Summoning Tojo, he reminded him that negotiations with the Americans must be officially broken off before the first act of war took place. Tojo instructed his foreign minister that this should be done, and it was agreed with the supreme command that the breaking off of negotiations should serve as a declaration of war.

Since it had been decided from the inception of planning the assault on Pearl Harbor that complete surprise was essential both for the success of the attack and for the safe withdrawal of the task force, the supreme command insisted that the notification to the American government should be delayed until the very last moment. Evidently it was intended that this should be handed to the U.S. Secretary of State at a time coinciding with the opening of hostilities. But because no one outside of the supreme command, not even Tojo, knew the exact time of the assault and because of the confusion reigning in their embassy in Washington, the Japanese were laid open to yet more charges of deceit. Kurusu and Nomura did not hand their government's note to Cordell Hull until one o'clock in the afternoon of Sunday, the 7th of December. Tojo, when he heard from his foreign minister that it had been delayed, was apparently astonished and suggested that, possibly for propaganda purposes, the American government had themselves held the cable up.

In any case, by the time it was delivered to Hull, there was no need for him to read it. At Pearl Harbor, five hours earlier, Japanese warplanes had delivered their own lethal message, the "brutal answer," as Churchill described it later, to a personal message sent by President Roosevelt directly to the Emperor of Japan only the day before.

Although ignorant of the blow about to fall on them, the Americans' suspicion that Japan was about to take hostile action—not necessarily against them but probably against the British and Dutch—had been confirmed into certainty as reports began to come in from intelligence sources of powerful units of the Japanese navy under way in southeast Asian waters. On Saturday, the 6th of December, it was announced in Washington that President Roosevelt had sent a note to the Emperor of Japan. It asked, as a matter of urgency, for an explanation of the purpose for which Japanese armed forces were concentrated in Indochina. The President was, in fact, repeating a similar request for information made by U.S. Secretary of War Stimson to Nomura and Kurusu a few days before.

At the central telegraph bureau in Tokyo, on "advice" from the army general staff, the censorship section was delaying all incoming foreign cables. The interception of cables by the military had been regular practice for some time. Togo, the foreign minister, had heard how Tojo, when he had been minister of war, "had a pile of telegrams from the Foreign Office" waiting on his desk every morning, each one of which he read and "if any number was missing, demanded that it should be supplied."[1] No exception was made for such a high-level communication as this, and it is likely that the holdup was longer than normal since those of obvious interest to the army were first passed to army intelligence. The President's message was not delivered to Ambassador Grew until past ten o'clock that night, ten hours after its arrival in Tokyo.

The ambassador, as soon as the cable had been deciphered, hurried to Togo and asked for an urgent audience with the Emperor. The minister consulted with Premier Tojo who asked if it contained any concessions by the Americans. When informed it did not, Tojo told the foreign minister that he had no objection to Grew handing it to the Emperor. He remarked that it was a good thing it had arrived late. Had it been received "a day or two earlier we would have had more of a to do."[2] It was, as he implied, too late anyway.

It was close to three o'clock on Sunday morning before Grew was received at the Palace to present the President's note to Emperor Hirohito, about two hours after the Japanese attack force making for Pearl Harbor had crossed the point of no return. One o'clock in the morning had been the hour specified as the last moment at which the force's commander, Admiral Nagumo, might receive a signal ordering him to turn back.

Just before dawn, with the moon still intermittently concealed by clouds, the carriers were in position and poised for attack. Day broke and at six o'clock the battle flag of the Rising Sun was hoisted and the carrier planes revved up on the decks ready for takeoff. Officers and men on the ships gave three ceremonial shouts of *"Banzai"* as the leading plane, piloted by Commander Fuchida who was heading the attack, skimmed off the flight deck, the shouts almost drowned out by the roar of the planes that followed him into the air, taking formation and rapidly disappearing into the distance.

As the first assault wave of high-flying aircraft arrived in sight of the emerald shape of the island of Oahu showing through breaks in the clouds, the American Pacific base was just awakening to another day of rest. At the extreme tip of the islands the pilots saw below them in the waters of the harbor, shimmering in the sun, the U.S. fleet lying at anchor. Commander Fuchida observed that it was "calm and peaceful" and wrote later of his amazement at the unsuspecting and almost perfect target the warships presented. "Had the Americans never heard of Port Arthur?" he asked himself.[3]

There was little activity on the American warships. Many of the crews were ashore for the Sunday, some at early morning church service. Others still on board were about to have breakfast or were taking it easy around the ship. Some of the men on duty were just preparing for the customary morning raising of the Stars and Stripes when the Japanese attackers swooped out of the sun.

The first bomb smashed into a seaplane ramp at 7:55 and, as the signal tower flashed the message: "We are under enemy aerial attack; this is not an exercise!" the battleship "Arizona" was hit by a torpedo. Almost immediately afterwards, another struck the "Oklahoma." Minutes after eight o'clock, the "California" was hit and started to keel over. A bomb tore through the deck of the "Arizona," blasting the magazine, followed by another which exploded in one of the stricken ship's stacks. As more waves of planes came in, the battleship "West Virginia" and the naval auxiliary vessel "Utah" were sunk and the battleship "Pennsylvania" was crippled. Two destroyers were pounded into hulks of twisted metal.

For an hour and a half the Japanese planes dived in, hardly disturbed by a few anti-aircraft guns the Americans had managed to get into action or by the ineffectual fire of rifles discharged by men on the ground more in helpless fury than with any hope of hitting their assailants. With little opposition to deal with, the escorting Japanese navy Zero fighters darted over the area, machine-gunning everything in sight. The sky was streaked with aircraft vapor trails and the pall of smoke thickened, as methodically and with terrible precision the hornet horde went about the work of destruction. The last plane soared off just after 9:30 in the morning.

Five battleships, two cruisers, three destroyers, and two other naval vessels were sunk. One cruiser and four other destroyers were badly damaged. One hundred and seventy-five planes lay wrecked or burnt out on Hickman Airfield. Hangars and installations were smoking ruins. Two and a half thousand were dead, over one thousand of them officers and men on the sunken "Arizona." When the attacking force landed back on the waiting carriers at 11 A.M., the Japanese airmen reported that they had carried out Admiral Yamamoto's command. With the loss of only twenty-eight Japanese planes, the U.S. Pacific Fleet had been eradicated in one blow.

When Nomura and Kurusu presented themselves that afternoon at the office of the American Secretary of State to hand over their government's note—a long recital of Japan's "sincere" efforts in China, American bad faith, and accusations that the United States' leaders had plotted to extend the European war to the Far East—the fact was that the two Japanese representatives still did not know that their country had taken up arms or how. Cordell Hull told them with glacial contempt and anger that in fifty years of public service he had never seen a document more crowded with infamous falsehoods and distortions. They were, he said, so huge that he had never imagined any government on the planet was capable of uttering them. Without allowing them to reply, he motioned the envoys to leave.

In Tokyo, Imperial headquarters announced that the Japanese army and navy had "entered into a state of war with American and British forces" and radios gave out the news of the victory at Pearl Harbor interspersed with the blare of patriotic marches. Crowds stood in the streets and sang the national anthem, "Kimigayo." Newspaper sellers ran through the streets sounding handbells and wooden clappers to announce special victory editions of the *Asahi, Nichi-nichi,* and *Yomiuri* dailies. Thousands made their way to the plaza of the Imperial Palace to bow and invoke the aid of the nation's divine ancestors.

Mrs. Tojo, who had been worrying about reports that extremists were plotting to assassinate her husband because he had not made a decision yet, heard the news on the radio with her family after her husband had left for his office. Womanlike, she felt a sense of relief, knowing that he would now return safely that night.[4] And General Tojo, uniformed and bemedalled, thankfully reported to the national shrines in Tokyo and to the spirit of his late father this auspicious opening of the Japanese bid to take over the Far East.

Part Two

THE GARDENS OF BATTLE

"The young men depart
For the gardens of battle
In our fields
Old men alone"

From a poem
by the
EMPEROR MEIJI
(1852-1912)

Twenty-two

It was some eight hours after the Pearl Harbor attack that an Imperial Rescript was published, officially and formally declaring that the nation was engaged in the greatest gamble in its history:

We, by the grace of Heaven, Emperor of Japan, seated on the throne of a line unbroken for ages eternal, enjoin upon our loyal and brave subjects: We hereby declare war on the United States of America and the British Empire. . . . Eager for the realization of their inordinate ambition to dominate the Orient . . . both America and Britain . . . obstructed by every means our peaceful commerce and finally resorted to direct severance. . . . The situation being such as it is, Our Empire for its existence and self-defence has no other recourse but to appeal to arms. . . .

The Imperial Rescripts issued on great and significant occasions did not necessarily represent the Emperor's own thoughts or feelings any more than the king's Speech read at the opening of Parliament does those of the British sovereign. There was, nevertheless, inserted in this momentous rescript a statement which, it was said, had been included at Emperor Hirohito's express wish:

Now, unfortunately, it has come—truly unavoidable and far from Our Wishes—that Our Empire has to cross swords with America and Britain.

In America, President Roosevelt, reporting to Congress the next day, told of the "unprovoked and dastardly attack" which had taken place on a "date that will live in infamy." It was a thoroughly dishonorable deed, "but," the President said grimly, "we must face the fact that modern warfare, as conducted in the Nazi manner, is a dirty business. We don't like it, we didn't want to get into it. But we are in it, and we are going to fight with everything we have got."

Winston Churchill addressed the House of Commons in similar vein. "Every circumstance of calculated and characteristic Japanese treachery was employed," he declared, but "we must count ourselves very fortunate . . . that we were not attacked alone by Japan in our period of weakness after Dunkirk or at any time in 1940."

Hitler, at a special meeting of the Reichstag, accused the "mentally insane" Roosevelt of provoking Japan into war. His Asian ally had struck a blow, he held, against the "American forger" who had violated "the rules of decency." And from his balcony on the Palazzo Venezia, the Italian dictator put in an appearance on "this day of solemn decision in the history of Italy" which was now united with "heroic Japan." The successful assault in the Pacific, Mussolini told the cheering hundreds in the plaza below him, had demonstrated the spirit of the soldiers of the Rising Sun and it was "a privilege to fight alongside them."

Shortly after the Imperial Rescript had been published, Tojo spoke on the radio from Tokyo. Echoing the general theme of the royal document, he claimed that Japan had done her utmost to prevent war. But Japan had never lost a war in the 2600 years of its history and, he proclaimed, "I promise you final victory."

Although the nation had been well aware from newspapers and radio for some time that a crisis was approaching between Japan and the United States, the sudden attack on Pearl Harbor was as much of a surprise and shock to the ordinary Japanese as it was to his American counterpart. Initially, something like stunned acceptance had greeted the news. This very quickly changed as confirmation of the apparent complete and devastating success of this first act of war was followed by news of the irresistible progress of Japanese arms in southeast Asia.

On the radio, breathless and excited bulletins telling of the latest glorious achievement in the onrush of the country's soldiers and sailors were interspersed with music and song calculated to set the mood for greater heights of patriotic fervor. As well as songs revived from the Meiji era which had stirred the nation in the heroic days of the Russo–Japanese war, Nippon's balladeers contributed such contemporary items as *"Boku no Tojo"* ("Our Tojo"). These were lustily taken up at rallies, in factories, and in schools all over the land. Enthusiasm and pride were universal and boundless.

The *Japan Times* exulted that the United States, which had been reduced in one morning to a third-class naval power, was "trembling in her shoes." Broken-down old Britain now held America in the same "deathly" embrace which had preceded the fall of Britain's other erstwhile allies: Czechoslovakia, Poland, Belgium, Holland, and France. What had happened to them was a clear indication of what lay ahead for America. Captain Hirade, a spokesman at the Imperial Navy headquarters who, just before the war, had announced that the navy was "itching for action," delivered during the course of a radio interview the prediction that the United States would be forced to capitulate on the steps of the White House. In the weeks that followed, their confidence must have seemed not unjustified.

Within forty-eight hours of the Pearl Harbor assault, Japanese forces carried out simultaneous attacks on Hong Kong, Malaya, the Philippines, and U.S. island bases in the Pacific. All of the long and careful planning paid off in almost perfectly executed operations. Nothing, it appeared, could stop the warriors of the Rising Sun.

Hong Kong, recently reinforced by Indian and Canadian troops, was attacked on the 8th of December. Troops from the Japanese army in China rapidly overran Kowloon, leased territory on the mainland, and crossed the short stretch of water to Hong Kong Island. On the 25th of December, two days after Tokyo Radio had paid tribute to the "gallant but unavailing fight" being put up by the defenders, the Colony's governor, advised by his naval and military commanders that no further effective resistance was possible, surrendered the island with its garrison.

On Wake Island, in the Pacific, on the 22nd of December, the two American fighters that had survived the destruction on the ground of the outpost's original twelve planes, took to the air in a last gallant sortie. They accounted for several planes of the Japanese invading force before they were themselves shot down and Japanese troops landed. The four-hundred-strong garrison of U.S. marines was finally overcome that day after withstanding fourteen days of unabated air and naval pounding.

Japanese troops began landings in Malaya in the early morning of the 8th of December. Early in the attack the two most modern and formidable British naval ships in the Far East, the battleships "Prince of Wales" and "Repulse," were moved in to attack enemy transports and landing craft. With no aircraft available to cover their movements, they relied on clouds to mask them. A rift in the clouds, similar to an earlier one through which a Japanese reconnaissance plane had spotted them, enabled Japanese torpedo planes called up from an Indochina base four hundred miles away to sink the warships by repeated blows delivered with great accuracy and determination.

The loss laid bare the whole Malaya coastline to virtually unimpeded amphibious assaults, constantly outflanking the hard-pressed defenders who never succeeded in establishing a firm defensive line which they could hold. The enemy, in combined operations with close air support, drove them inexorably down the length of the peninsula to their last stand on Singapore Island. The Battle of Malaya, announced the British General Officer Commanding, Lieutenant-General Percival, had come to an end and the Battle of Singapore had started. "Our task," he told his British, Australian, Indian, and Malayan troops, "is to hold this fortress until help comes—as it assuredly will come."

By the 1st of February, the island was under bomber and artillery attack from the mainland, much of it concentrated on planes that were still operational. At the same time, leaflets from the air gave spurious reports that the Americans had asked for peace while others demanded of British soldiers why they put up with the "intolerable torture of malarial mosquitoes merely to pamper the British aristocrat?"

A week later the Japanese crossed the narrow Johore straits and with picked troops, including a unit of the elite Imperial Guards, pressed on with complete disregard for losses. On the

15th of February, a little more than two months since the Malaya fighting had started, and a month less than the Japanese supreme command had estimated for the campaign, General Percival surrendered his garrison of 60,000 men. Many of them were reinforcements who had been arriving right up to the time that Malaya was attacked. Britain's greatest base in the Far East, its defenses predicated on a threat from the sea that never materialized, had fallen to land assault from the rear, its great shore guns silent to the last and still pointing futile defiance in the wrong direction.

Winston Churchill, speaking to a hushed House of Commons "under the shadow of a heavy and far-reaching defeat" told its members, "Tonight the Japanese are triumphant." In the Japanese parliament, Tojo led a wildly excited assembly of Diet representatives in three jubilant roars of *"Banzai!"* and declared that with the capture of Singapore, all important bases for "the encroachment of Britain and America in southeast Asia" were in the hands of Japan. The following day, he told them, would be proclaimed "Singapore Victory Day."

The newspaper *Kokumin,* reporting the capture of the city, claimed that to stop there would be to give up halfway. Japan must go on, the commentator declared, "to the prospect of economic and military contact with our European allies." It did indeed seem, as Mamoru Shigemitsu observed, that in an incredibly short time since Japan had gone to war, the Swastika of Nazi Germany and the Rising Sun of Japan "were destined to meet at the Persian Gulf."[1] And Australia and New Zealand were to accept the inevitable. No reliance, Tojo told them, could be placed on the British and Americans for protection. The future happiness of their peoples, he warned, now depended entirely on whether their governments understood Japan's "real intentions."

Japan, it was announced, would henceforward be known as *"Dai Nippon"* ("Great Land of the Rising Sun"), and as with Singapore, which had been renamed *"Shonan"* (Light of the South), all conquered territories having European names were to have the stigma of the colonial past and occidental domination removed by being given suitable Japanese names. In the homeland the use of English words—of which more than a thousand had been incorporated into the Japanese language over the last fifty years—was banned as unpatriotic and undignified.

Japan had not bothered to declare war on the Dutch until the end of January. This was intended to give the Dutch colonial governor of the East Indies, whose home country was itself now no more than a province of Nazi Germany, a chance to submit to the realities of his situation as the governor of French Indochina had done. There would have been very obvious advantages if the oil of the area—now more vital to the Japanese than ever—could have been secured without the cost of fighting for it and at the same time avoiding the risk of action to deny it to them by extensive sabotage. As the Dutch colonial rulers refused to yield, not only declaring themselves at war with Japan but actually taking their declaration seriously by having their naval and air forces fight alongside the British in defense of Malaya, the Japanese supreme command acted.

Landings had already been made in British and Dutch Borneo when, on the 27th of February, the Dutch admiral, Doorman, commanding a composite fleet of British, Australian, American, and Dutch warships and charged with guarding the main East Indies islands, sighted a large Japanese invasion armada in the Java sea. Battered in previous fighting, outnumbered and heavily outgunned by the enemy ships that were escorting a flock of nearly one hundred troopships, Doorman nevertheless went into action. Without a single fighter plane to attack the Japanese aircraft that circled above, spotting for the Japanese gunners and torpedo-men, Doorman's fleet was destroyed in a desperate two-and-a-half-day fight. The coasts clear, Japanese troops were landed and soon overran the East Indies islands, where their airborne troops had been dropped, and were almost entirely successful in preventing major damage being done to the oil installations.

The second Victory Day held in Japan on the 12th of March was a double event to celebrate, as well as the capture of the Dutch East Indies, the fall of the Burmese capital of Rangoon. Burma had been invaded from Thailand, whose rulers had philosophically accepted Japanese protection, declared war on the Allies, and awarded General Tojo the highest Thai decoration of the White Elephant. The invaders, in many cases welcomed by the xenophobic Burmese, pushed swiftly on, cutting China's sole remaining land-link with the west at the terminal of the Burma Road despite an ineffectual intervention by Chinese troops commanded by the American general, "Vinegar Joe" Stilwell. Rangoon was entered unopposed on the 8th of March.

With the arrival on the Burma front of General Alexander, who was to emerge later in the Middle East and Italy as one of Britain's most brilliant and consistently successful commanders, the Japanese found the going stiffer. It was not until the 6th of May that they took Mandalay, when the city was reported by Tokyo to be in "smoldering ruins." Fears that the Japanese would sweep on through to India eased as they halted at a line on the borders of Assam, partly because they were being handled more severely but mostly because they had outrun their lines of communication while those of the British and Indian defenders were now relatively short. Time was needed to consolidate and build up reserves, and there was a British Far Eastern fleet based on Ceylon to be disposed of by the navy before such a vast operation as the invasion of India could be seriously contemplated.

Even so, Burma had been conquered, and as Tojo had boasted to the Diet, the last land supply route to Chiang Kai-shek had been cut off. He could scarcely have foreseen that the Allies would, by an unprecedented American organization of air supply, regularly lift more material aid over the "Hump" of the Himalayas than had ever been carried over the winding miles of the old trading road.

In the Philippines, the Japanese, after the first shock of their assault, had not been having things their own way. Their campaign there, unlike the Malayan one, was taking much longer than they had planned and General Yamashita—now dubbed "The Tiger of Malaya"—had been sent to take over. Three and a half months since the first Japanese landings and in spite of the arrival of reinforcements Yamashita had called for, General MacArthur's American and Filipino defenders were still holding out on the island of Corregidor, in the forts at the entrance of Manila Bay, and on the Bataan Peninsula. Ordered to go to Australia, MacArthur slipped out of Bataan by motor torpedo boat at night accompanied by his wife and young son and some of his staff officers, but the garrison he left behind under General Wainwright fought on for twenty-eight more days. It was not until almost a month later than this that those on Corregidor and in the Manila forts succumbed to overwhelming Japanese attacks spearheaded by special shock troops and using armored assault craft.

On the front pages of the newspapers in Japan, on which the Imperial Rescript declaring war was reprinted daily, victory after victory was reported in ecstatic prose. The *Japan Times* told of Japan's undisputed sway over vast areas where "the land has rumbled to the tread of Japan's legions or the skies have thundered to the roar of Japan's winged knights of the air." Nor was allegory all that far from fact. Japan's conquests were, by any measure, enormous. With their subsequent occupations of various Pacific islands including the Solomons, New Britain, and the greater part of New Guinea, they had taken all the territory enclosed in a line stretching from northern Burma, through the west Burma port of Akyab, the Indian Andaman Islands, the whole of Dutch and the northern part of Australian New Guinea, the Solomon, Gilbert and Marshall islands, through Wake Island and, later, to the Aleutians, a few miles from the Alaskan mainland.

These gains had only to be consolidated and their resources exploited to make Japan unassailable and rich. The only question in the minds of the Japanese leaders now was where they should go from there?

Twenty-three

When President Roosevelt had told Congress of the attack on Pearl Harbor, he had paid the Japanese the bitter compliment of performing a "brilliant feat of deception—perfectly timed and executed with great skill." Early in the Philippines fighting, too, U.S. Secretary of War Stimson had been impelled to contradict reports that Japanese troops there were poorly trained and using inferior weapons. The enemy, he said, "was disciplined, well armed, and the work of Japanese staff officers was of a high order."

It says something for the durability of the myths and wishful thinking about the Japanese so long current in the West that this still needed to be said. And varied and fanciful these myths were. The Japanese could not shoot straight or fly planes and some of the reasons for these disabilities, advanced in all seriousness, had less scientific basis than many an old wives' tale. The oriental could not close one eye; the Japanese all had bad eyesight—a combined result of their rice diet and close study of their complicated written language; they suffered from vertigo from being strapped to their mothers' backs as children. There was the conclusion by those who had forgotten or had never heard of the Russo–Japanese war that the Japanese might be successful enough in pushing poorly armed and poorly led Chinese around (who, after all, were only orientals like the Japanese), but they would meet more than their match if they came up against western soldiery.

The danger now was that another myth was in the making—that of the invincibility of the Japanese. The troops who had fought them, shaken by their unexpected efficiency and fanatic courage, told of their ferocity, and the tales grew with the telling. The Japanese could survive and fight in the jungle as no white man could. They had inhuman powers of endurance and could subsist on a handful of rice a day.

For a time something akin to superstitious awe of the new *samurai* prevailed, driving those who commanded the Allied soldiers into making fatuous attempts at reassurance. General Wavell declared that once the Japanese lost their "superior mobility" they would soon lose courage. "Vinegar Joe" Stilwell asserted that they fought better in attack than defense, a curiously misleading statement since he had at that time no more experience or opportunity, unfortunately, than any other Allied commander of putting the Japanese soldier on the defensive. His remark might have been recalled with some bitterness by those American and other Allied soldiers who later were to have, at tragic cost to themselves, the bloody task of burning and blasting out the suicidal Japanese defenders of places like Buna, Mandalay, Saipan, and Iwo Jima.

The illusion of an overwhelming enemy horde swarming over outnumbered defenders was nourished by official British military bulletins like the one issued during the course of the fighting in Malaya which spoke of "an increasingly unfavorable ratio" of forces. Japanese air and naval superiority was, of course, decisive, but in numbers actually committed on the ground the Japanese were relatively few, though well led and trained to a hair for their operational tasks. General Wavell admitted after the fall of Rangoon that the British "were always behind the clock . . . and the Japanese moved quicker than we hoped."

The British prime minister, Winston Churchill, telling his countrymen of the fall of Singapore, was even blunter. "We must," he said, "no longer underrate the efficiency of the Japanese fighting machine." And he found it necessary to add a grim warning of another aspect of the Japanese soldier. "They have proved themselves," Churchill said, "formidable, deadly and—I am sorry to say—barbarous antagonists."

Twenty-four

In February 1942, as his triumphant divisions swept through Malaya and were poised before Singapore, leaflets containing a personal message from the Japanese commander in chief, General Yamashita, were dropped over the city. In this he advised "the immediate surrender of the British forces from the standpoint of *bushido* and promised to treat them as "soldiers-in-arms."

Only a month later Foreign Secretary Anthony Eden described *bushido* as "nauseating hypocrisy." When Hong Kong capitulated, he said, the Japanese army "perpetrated against their helpless military prisoners and civil population . . . the same kind of barbarities which aroused the horror of the civilized world at the time of the Nanking massacre of 1937. . . . It is known that women both Asiatic and European were raped and murdered and that one entire Chinese district was declared a brothel . . . fifty officers and men of the British army were bound hand and foot and then bayoneted to death. . . . The Japanese government has refused to consent to a visit to Hong Kong of a representative of the protecting power."

It was to be the first of a series of protests made by the Allied powers in a vain effort to get the Japanese government headed by Hideki Tojo to observe international conventions in the treatment of those who were unfortunate enough to fall into the hands of its soldiers. Two years later, Eden spoke again to the

House of Commons on the estimated 140,000 British Common-wealth prisoners taken by the Japanese and described the tropical jungle conditions in which thousands, many reduced to "skin and bone, unshaven with long matted hair, and half-naked," were existing and forced to work—often when sick and, with terrible frequency, to their deaths.

The case against Hideki Tojo and those who sat in the dock of the International Military Tribunal after the war was to a great extent concerned with atrocities that were, unhappily, only too well documented and authenticated to be disputed. Out of an estimated more than a million deaths due to brutality and neglect between 1931 and 1945, allied lawyers listed 302,000 specific cases. According to the indictment, torture, murder, rape, and other cruelties "of the most inhuman and barbarous character" were freely practiced by the Japanese army and navy "on a scale so vast and on so common a pattern that the only conclusion possible was that they were either secretly ordered or willfully permitted by the Japanese government or by the leaders of the armed forces. . . . Prisoners were regarded as disgraced and entitled to live only by the tolerance of their captors." Apart from massacres such as those in Nanking, sadistic individual killings had been carried out "apparently for no other purpose than to gratify the cruel instincts of the perpetrators." Vivisection had been carried out on living captives, and toward the end of the war, even cannibalism had been authorized and practiced.

Much of the ill-treatment was, indeed, little more than could have been expected from men who were indoctrinated in the belief that soldiers who permitted themselves to fall captive were without honor; who were commanded to fight to the death and did so almost invariably with a fanaticism that was scarcely human. The number of Japanese troops taken alive throughout the whole course of the Pacific fighting was infinitesimal in relation to the total numbers involved. Those who did not die by enemy action more often than not killed themselves when further resistance was impossible, usually with a grenade but sometimes even biting off their own tongues rather than suffer the disgrace of yielding.

Examples of the ferocity and desperation which characterized their resistance to the last in hopeless situations were grimly recorded by all who fought them. Australians who had trapped Japanese troops on a beachhead in New Guinea noticed that many of the enemy were wearing gasmasks, and it was not until all were wiped out that Australians found the reason. The Japanese were not burying their dead but using them as defense parapets, as they had done years before in assaulting Port Arthur. On other Pacific islands, U.S. marines were frequently shot at by wounded Japanese they were trying to help. The mere 450 Japanese prisoners taken in the entire course of the Solomons fighting later in the war all said they had expected to be killed and many declared they never wanted to return to Japan. This wish had nothing to do with any sense of revulsion against their own country. Rather it was because they now considered themselves, by the act of falling into enemy hands alive, to be dishonored and therefore unfit to return.

Nevertheless, while fanatic courage was no new thing in Japanese soldiers the treatment accorded to their prisoners was in complete contrast to the great chivalry shown by Japanese to captured opponents in the Russo–Japanese and the First World War. In these Japan had demonstrated, as Anthony Eden pointed out, that she knew well "the obligations of a civilized power to safeguard the life and health of prisoners who have fallen into their hands." And the change in attitude since then had been so distinct as apparently to justify the charge of the Allied lawyers after the war that the "ill-treatment of prisoners was a deliberate policy."

It was in the fighting against the Chinese in the 1930s that the Japanese soldiery had first shown, on any large scale, ominous signs that they were no longer the chivalrous opponents of General Nogi's day. Then, Japan had been an aspirant great power and was fighting with the approbation of Britain and other western nations. In China the Kwangtung Army's attack in 1931 and its actions thereafter had branded Japan as an outlaw, and as each subsequent aggression revealed the apparent impotence of those who protested against them to do more than protest, the army showed increasingly less regard for what the westerners thought.

It is not without significance that, even in the days of the Russo–Japanese war, the Japanese did not necessarily extend the consideration observed toward the Russians to their fellow orientals. In the days when the fall of Port Arthur seemed imminent, the besieging Japanese army openly threatened that no Chinese "who has in any way assisted the Russians to defend the place will be given quarter."[1] In the fighting in China in the 1930s the Japanese brought to the battle, not only this ambivalence in attitude, but also something of the violent mixture of alarm and fury that the strong often exhibit to the weak who dare to stand up to them.

In China, too, for all the modern weapons, the barbarity of the middle ages was brutally evident, as was shockingly demonstrated at Nanking. And if Japanese protestations over the relatively minor and less publicized atrocities perpetrated on occasions against their nationals by the Chinese might have appeared hypocritical and played up for propaganda purposes, it must be acknowledged that this fighting between orientals had its own special character of cruelty on both sides and had scant regard for western conventions of warfare. By 1941, the Japanese officer, NCO, or common soldier with previous combat experience in China was unlikely to be better behaved towards a white enemy who, he had been conditioned to think, he had more reason to hate and humiliate than his fellow Asiatics.

In the very early stages of the war, in 1942, Tojo himself made it clear that his government did not propose to be inhibited by western concepts of warfare. "We have," Tojo was quoted as saying in instructions circulated to commandants of prisoner-of-war camps, "our own ideology concerning prisoners of war which should naturally make their treatment more or less different from that in Europe and America." At about the same time, on the 20th of March, 1942, his navy minister and faithful henchman Admiral Shimada announced at a cabinet meeting that Japan would not recognize the international convention of 1909 on prisoners of war. The reason, he explained, was that Britain had waged "extreme warfare based on retaliation and hatred" making it necessary for Japan to revise her own rules of war.

The real reasons were, needless to say, rather different and more convoluted. There was, for example, the desire to destroy the mystique of the white races. This led General Itagaki, then in charge of the army in Korea, to ask for a number of British and American war prisoners taken in various theaters to be brought to Korea. After arriving in very poor shape, which no attempt was made to alleviate, they were paraded through the streets of Korean cities to make Koreans, as Itagaki put it, "realize positively the true might of our Empire as well as to contribute psychological propaganda work for stamping out any ideas of the worship of Europe and America."

The desire to humble the white man in front of orientals and the kind of brutality begotten by the sustained harshness of treatment endured by the Japanese soldier himself were perhaps mixed in the attitudes that brought about the "death march" from Bataan. On the surrender of the fortress at the end of the Philippines fighting, American and Filipino survivors, many of them sick and wounded, were herded together and forced to march in extreme heat to prison quarters seventy-five miles away. Already weak from lack of food before surrendering, they were kept short of food and water, beaten and kicked to keep them going. Those who dropped out were shot or bayoneted. An estimated eight thousand died, almost a thousand for every day of their march.

Tojo admitted to knowing of this and other inhuman incidents involving Allied prisoners and actually made inquiries about it when he visited General Homma in the Philippines later. His explanation of the fact that he took no action against those responsible was that in the Japanese army an officer was given a mission but had an almost completely free hand in its performance. Generals Homma and Yamashita, when the time came for them to face the consequences of this and other criminal excesses carried out by their troops, offered a similar explanation for their own failure to prevent them.

In the early part of 1942, Field Marshal Terauchi, who was now commanding the Japanese Southern Army in the Indochina–Malaya area, had been instructed to provide labor and services for the building of a two-hundred-and-fifty-mile railway line through Thailand to Burma, a project estimated in the normal way to take five or six years but which, it was ordered, must be completed in eighteen months. To accomplish this, Tojo agreed that in addition to locally impressed coolie labor, Allied prisoners of war could be used. Forty-six thousand were brought from camps all over southeast Asia. They were worked—almost a third of them literally to death—and kept in almost indescribable conditions. "Each mile of the 'Railroad of Death' was paid for with the lives of sixty-four Allied prisoners of war and two hundred and forty coolie slaves."[2]

Tojo's admission of only limited responsibility for the treatment of prisoners of war because of his inability to control the actions of field commanders was, unfortunately for him, countered by his own words, in a directive issued to one of them in May 1942. "The present condition of affairs in this country does not," he wrote, "permit anyone to lie idle, doing nothing, but eating freely. . . . In dealing with prisoners, I hope you will see that they are usefully employed." He could still have protested that these words did not constitute, *per se,* any kind of permission to work and beat sick and ill-fed prisoners to death. But he failed almost utterly to do anything when it had been made known to him that his injunction was being implemented in the camps as a "no work —no food" order. Later, under the persuasion of Mamoru Shigemitsu, when the latter became his foreign minister, he ordered an investigation of persistent reports and complaints from the Allies on the conduct of camps on the Siam railway. This was carried out by a senior member of the Imperial general staff who confirmed that the prisoners were in poor physical condition, improperly fed, and suffering a very high death rate. The report, Tojo afterwards maintained, was passed to the appropriate military authority to be dealt with. His own and only step was to order the court-martial of a company commander, a measure which the judgment of the International Military Tribunal found to be "so insignificant and inadequate" as to amount to condonation.

In the much condemned treatment of the captured American fliers who carried out the first air raid on Japan, fear and anger played a major part, the kind revealed when it took place on the 18th of April, 1942. On that date, in bright sunny weather at midday, sixteen American bombers from a U.S. carrier carried out a low-level raid lasting several hours. It was the more effective because such an attack had been thought impossible. The fliers, led by Brigadier General Doolittle, had flown conventional B25 twin-engined bombers with a range greater than the normal carrier plane. This range they further extended by planning to fly on to relatively close airfields in China instead of returning to the carrier "Hornet" from which they had been launched. Of the eighty air crewmen who took part in the attack, sixty-four baled out over China. There, although they landed in Japanese-occupied territory, sympathetic Chinese got most of them to safety. Eight, however, were either betrayed or fell into the hands of Japanese patrols.

The intention of the Americans had been to demonstrate to the Japanese at the earliest possible moment in the war their vulnerability to air attack. In this they entirely succeeded, as was disclosed by the fury touched off by the unexpected assault. The commanders of Japanese home defense units, it was announced by Tokyo radio, were to be court-martialed for failing in their duty to prevent the attacks. The Japanese communiqué, while acknowledging that industrial targets had been blasted, spoke of strikes on "schools, hospitals, in residential districts . . . houses and cinemas" and of "machine-gun attacks on farming villages." Describing the raid as "criminal and inhuman" with the victims exclusively civilian—"children and hospital patients"— Tokyo Radio proclaimed that the United States no longer had "any idea of humanity in warfare."

Particularly enraged was chief of the army general staff, General Sugiyama. The general, at the Imperial Conference that had decided for war, had assured those assembled in the presence of the Emperor that if all went according to plan in the first stages of the war, there would be no danger of Japan suffering from air attack. Sugiyama now went personally to Tojo and insisted that the captured fliers were not to be treated as war prisoners, but that they should be tried under military law. Tojo agreed and, in order to permit it, introduced new regulations carrying the death penalty, with retroactive effect. These were sent to General Hata commanding the armies in China where the American airmen were held.

On the 19th of October, 1942, Domei, the official news agency, announced in Tokyo that American airmen captured after the 18th of April attack had been tried in Shanghai and "punished according to military law." They had "confessed under examination" (the nature of which can be imagined) that they had "only bombed hospitals, schools, and civilian homes." Five of the eight airmen who were thus given death sentences had them commuted by Tojo to life imprisonment. The remaining three, who were held responsible for the deaths of school children, were executed. On the day the executions were revealed an official high command announcement threatened that any other fliers who committed "inhuman and atrocious acts" in the course of raids on Japan or Japanese-occupied territory would be subject to the same penalty.

Mamoru Shigemitsu, writing after the war, deplored the "many wrongful acts involving inhumanity" which came to light. He argued that a great deal of this was the result of administrative breakdowns, war conditions, and shortage of food, but admitted that hatred was whipped up, much of it by wartime propaganda. Reports, he wrote, "were current of inhuman handling and of lynching of Japanese in the United States. Specious conversations were retailed imputing malicious treatment of repatriated Japanese when their ship called at British Indian ports. Great indignation was caused by the Doolittle air raid which had no military significance but in which small schoolchildren were killed and wounded. Presently there appeared reproductions from American magazines showing toys made of human bones, and caricaturing Japanese war heroes, which had a great vogue in the United States."[3]

If anyone should be tempted to accuse Shigemitsu of being either brazen or naïve when he went on to ask if, despite all the evidence, it could fairly be said of his countrymen that they were "cruel monsters" whose common characteristic was to commit atrocities, it is as well for the western reader to bear in mind that he was expressing a genuine point of view. No one who ever knew or met the late diplomat was ever in any doubt that, besides being an intense patriot, he was personally an intelligent and humane man. And no one who had lived for any period among the Japanese and experienced the great kindness and loyalty of which they are capable could ever agree that they are basically a race of cruel barbarians.

It has to be said that the record of Japan, deplorable as it was, nowhere approached in scope, numbers, or character the cold-blooded, scientific exterminations of several millions of souls by the Nazis. Unlike the Germans, the Japanese never had a Himmler, nor had they a specific policy of inhumanity and murder with a large and shockingly efficient complex of special units, installations, and apparatus entirely devoted to carrying it out. The treatment of war prisoners was, as John Morris said, "totally at variance with the very different treatment accorded to those who lived and worked in Japan before the war."[4]

Eric Linklater, writing of the Japanese during the period of the China Incident, observed that they were a "pleasing example of a psychologist's hypothesis," who "for centuries had been bullied, swindled, and humiliated." In civilization, he wrote, they had discovered

. . . the very weapons they needed, and had adopted along with it a modern code of ethics, imperialism, and revengeful efficiency. In their rapid progress they had scarcely time to reconcile some contradictions in their national character. They were, on the one side as clean and tidy and orderly, as fond of flowers and bright colours as the Dutch; on the other side they were apt to be hysterical, fanatical, and curiously addicted to suicide.[5]

Writing from his own study of the Japanese, D. J. Enright noted that it appeared that they "always had some kind of grudge against the 'merely human' " and that the "intolerably high standards which the Japanese have set for themselves are surely intimately connected with the thread of violence through their history."[6] Fosco Maraini has also observed that throughout Japanese literature and drama "there runs a constant thread of sublime sacrifice and horrid bloodshed"[7] and he quotes a contemporary western missionary who recorded during the days of the Tokugawa persecutions of the Japanese Christians that it was "necessary to keep the new Japanese Christian converts in check at times of persecution because they offered themselves for death as if it were a festival." And Reginald Hargreaves wrote of the Japanese soldier in the fighting at Port Arthur in 1905 that, for them, "success was an offering on the altar of patriotism . . . to die in the service of the Mikado and the Fatherland was both an ecstasy and a fulfilment."[8]

In time the Japanese were to show—particularly after the ending of the Allied military occupation—that they had their own recollections of brutalities committed against them, many of which were published in magazines or in book form. And most Japanese today regard, illogically or simply not from the western point of view, the holocaust of the atom-bombing of their population in the last stages of the war as an atrocity infinitely surpassing any attributed to them.

The kind of *tu quoque* argument here does the Japanese little service. Nor is it even relevant to their own wartime treatment of prisoners. Clumsily but more pertinently, Hideki Tojo hinted at the cause when he spoke of it as being due to the Japanese soldiers' psychology. There were irreconcilable differences in attitude between them and the western enemy they fought. It is interesting to note that Yuji Aida, a professor of history at Kyoto University who was a private in the Japanese Imperial Army in Burma and was captured by the British, held in his best-selling book *Prisoner of the British* that his captors were, in their own way, no less stupid and brutal than his own countrymen but in a subtler, cleverer way, having the ability to be cruel with detachment.

"It is true," Aida admits, "that the British did not beat prisoners up or kick them or butcher people alive. They committed almost none of what are usually termed atrocities. But this does not mean that they behaved according to humanitarian principles. On the contrary they often behaved with childish vindictiveness. And yet even the most vindictive act had a facade of reasonableness, and was carried out in such a way as to avoid any accusation being made against them. And British troops were always cool and collected and carried out these actions calmly, with great indifference. From one point of view they were certainly not cruel, but from another point of view I felt that their treatment reflected the cruellest attitude a man can have towards his fellowmen."[9]

Perhaps the most revealing piece written of the utterly different concepts which governed the two patterns of behavior is contained in Lewis Bush's account of an incident in the camp for British prisoners at Omori, near Tokyo, where Bush, then a naval officer but a long-time resident in Japan, was himself imprisoned. A British prisoner was caught stealing on a scale for which, Bush wrote,

he would probably be beheaded judging by the punishments we experienced at that time even for blinking an eye at roll call or failing to salute any Japanese, even civilians. But the Tommy was sentenced to special labour in the camp and to go around with a placard hanging around his neck which in English and Japanese announced, "I am a Thief". Quite unconcerned about a prisoner being beaten senseless *or one of their own comrades* being bashed with a rifle butt, yet this was too much for many of our guards who wagged their heads in sympathy that the poor fellow was thus humiliated by the placard which made him lose face. Soon he was thriving on delicacies, such as they were, from the Japanese cook house and his guards sacrificing their own food, to feed the delighted cockney, in order to alleviate what they seriously considered the barbarous treatment meted out to him.[10]

Fosco Maraini, who was himself a civilian internee in Japan and suffered considerably during the war, has given what might almost be considered the final judgment on Japanese war atrocities.

It was absurd of their leaders to imagine that in a mass army of conscripts, instincts of such terrible power, associated with archaic levels of the human personality, could be regulated with the rigor of a rite, of an etiquette of death, as they had been among small groups of *samurai* brought up from childhood to an extremely rigorous code.

Anthony Eden, later in the war, exhorted the Japanese government to "reflect in time that the record of their military authorities in this war will not be forgotten." But in the heady days of mid-1942, it is extremly doubtful if anyone in Japan—and least of all Hideki Tojo—could have imagined any circumstances in which they would be required to answer for, as members of a defeated nation, acts committed during the war.

Yet, hidden in the plethora of victories, Japan had already experienced at the end of May the first checks to her triumphal progress, and there were signs that it had reached its high-water mark. And on the 6th of June, 1942, Admiral Naguma, with what was left of his badly mauled force, was painfully withdrawing from a costly defeat at the hands of the American Pacific Fleet which, supposedly, had been eradicated by his audacious blow at Pearl Harbor a little less than seven months before.

Part **T**hree

THE SAIPAN MASK

*"On the model of
the false mask
of the Saipan shield"*

From a poem
by
KANEKO MITSUHARU
(1895-   )

Twenty-five

Long before the attack on Pearl Harbor, Admiral Yamamoto had foreseen that in any naval war in the Pacific the aircraft carrier would be queen of the battle. His considerable influence and ability had been largely devoted to and responsible for forging Japan's deadly naval air arm. "Battleships," he had once declared, "were like the *samurai* sword. Relics of the past, ornaments for the wealthy and useful only for prestige purposes." By his measure, then, the blow at Pearl Harbor, spectacular though it had been, was actually less than half a victory.

On the 7th of December, 1941, the day of the attack, none of the three aircraft carriers of the United States Pacific Fleet was at its Hawaiian base. The "Saratoga" was at an American west coast port; the "Lexington" and the "Enterprise" were away delivering planes to Pacific garrison islands. These three carriers—augmented shortly afterwards by the "Wasp" and the "Hornet"—were to become the cutting edge of the reconstituted American Far Eastern fleet. By his failure to seek out and destroy them immediately after the attack at Hawaii, Yamamoto's man, Admiral Nagumo, lost the war in the Pacific.

On the face of it, the Japanese navy, with eight carriers, still held an overwhelming superiority and in the first few months of the war Yamamoto's warships rampaged through the Pacific in an alarming manner. Nevertheless, after the completion of the inaugural carefully planned combined operations in southeast Asia and the south seas, the story was to be one first of frustration and finally disaster for Admiral Yamamoto.

The Java Sea battle was followed up with an attempt to put out of action the hurriedly assembled and obsolescent British Far Eastern fleet based on Ceylon and commanded by Admiral Sir James Somerville. This time there was no element of surprise. Although an initial heavy-carrier plane attack caused considerable damage to shipping and land installations at Colombo, the returning Japanese planes were jumped by RAF Hurricanes which shot down twenty-four of the enemy for the loss of fourteen of their own fighters. Two British cruisers, the "Dorsetshire" and "Cornwall," which set out to engage the Japanese, were sunk by dive bombers. Admiral Somerville thereupon made one of the few correct military decisions taken by the British in the early months of the Pacific war by declining Nagumo's challenge and withdrawing to the Maldive Islands.

Nagumo, bedeviled by not knowing the strength or position of the British fleet, trailed his coat for four more days during which time his planes attacked the British naval base at Trincomalee, sinking four more warships including a light aircraft carrier. When Somerville still refused to be drawn, Nagumo gave up and withdrew, concluding the first and last foray by the Japanese navy into the Indian Ocean. The conquest of India, if it was to take place now, would be entirely up to the Japanese army in Burma.

The long-standing rivalry between the army and navy was already beginning to have its effect on the conduct of the war. "The supreme command was divided between the army and navy," Tojo admitted after the war, "and they would not work in unison." Originally the plan had been to carry out combined operations for landing troops in northern Australia. This was now dropped because of the refusal of the army high command to provide the necessary number of divisions. The continental-minded generals had their quite independent strategy for the war on land—"taking walks" as the navy scornfully referred to their operations.

As a compromise it was decided that Port Moresby in the southern part of Australian New Guinea must be seized to bring northern Australia under attack. More important, its capture would remove a serious threat from Allied land-based aircraft there. In Japanese hands, Moresby would be the base from which Japanese naval units operating in the seas around could be supported and protected.

On the 1st of May, 1942, a Japanese task force sailing from Rabaul for an attack on Port Moresby was spotted by Allied aircraft and attacked. After days of grim blindman's buff, with planes from both sides vainly trying in bad weather to find the others' carriers, a long-distance battle fought by carrier planes against ships out of sight of each other was joined on the morning of the 8th of May. With three carriers in each fleet, the opponents were evenly matched, the Japanese having an edge in battle-tried pilots and the Americans with the advantage of radar. One Japanese carrier was sunk and another severely damaged; U.S. carrier "Lexington" was so severely damaged that the Americans torpedoed the ship themselves to prevent it falling into enemy hands, and the "Yorktown" suffered several hits.

When the action was broken off, on the 10th of May, both sides claimed victory. Militarily, it had been a draw, but strategically the Battle of the Coral Sea was a severe blow to Japan with results that went far beyond the failure of their main objective, the capture of Port Moresby from the sea. The "Yorktown," reported by Japanese fliers to have been left sinking, limped back to Hawaii for repairs. The Japanese loss of one small carrier, although a blow to their pride and a much needed morale-booster for the Allies, was in itself not severe. Far more damaging was the loss of trained and experienced naval air arm pilots. So many were lost and—an ominous pointer for the Japanese supreme command—so difficult was it to replace them that the surviving two carriers were unable to take part in the next and decisive naval action in the Pacific war, the Battle of Midway.

Midway, an island atoll, almost exactly the halfway mark to Hawaii, had started to be a place of bad omen for the Japanese even at the time of Pearl Harbor. The U.S. carriers "Lexington" and "Enterprise" had been delivering planes to Wake and Midway islands on the day of the attack and had therefore missed sharing the fate of the remainder of the U.S. Pacific Fleet. With the island now more strategically important than ever, the Americans had put more marines into Midway, heavily reinforcing anti-aircraft and coastal artillery and sending additional planes.

On the 27th of May, the day on which Japan was

celebrating the thirty-seventh anniversary of Admiral Togo's great naval victory over the Russians in the Tsushima straits, Premier Tojo was telling the members of the Japanese Diet of the "great victory" in the Coral Sea. It had, he said, "led to the disappearance of the naval forces defending Australia," which was now "the orphan of the Pacific," helplessly awaiting Japanese attack. With the "present favorable situation at home and abroad," he declared, "Japan will never sheathe her sword of righteousness until the influence of the Anglo–American powers with their dream of dominating the world has been completely uprooted."

It was on this same day that Admiral Yamamoto set sail with a powerful fleet. With it were transports carrying a brigade of picked Japanese troops for the conquest of Midway. At the same time a smaller diversionary force set out to occupy the Aleutian islands off the coast of Alaska. The inclusion of the four largest aircraft carriers in the Japanese navy was intended for more than just the invasion of the Midway atoll. Believing that the Americans were committed to keeping Midway, Yamamoto expected that they would be forced to use their aircraft carriers. In bringing them to battle, he confidently anticipated that the failure to destroy them on the 7th of December, which had been exercising him greatly, would be crushingly rectified.

Once again the Americans enjoyed the inestimable advantage of superior intelligence and, in battle, the use of radar. Through their monitoring and deciphering of the Japanese naval code signals, Admiral Nimitz had foreknowledge of the impending strike. As the attacking force neared Midway, U.S. planes kept the Japanese under constant surveillance, but Nimitz held off his flattops three hundred miles away in the early stages of the battle, which began on the 4th of June with Japanese aerial bombardment of the island. Land-based marine planes from Midway made the first attacks on the Japanese carriers. In the attacks the marine fliers suffered grievously, but these, although largely ineffectual, were invaluable in that they kept the invaders off balance and concentrated the attention of Admiral Nagumo, who was commanding the Japanese carriers, on destroying the land-based planes on Midway.

When Nimitz at last launched his carriers' torpedo aircraft, their attacks, though pressed home with superb courage, were also unsuccessful. But as the Japanese Zero fighters were engaged in fighting off the few American torpedo planes that had survived the storm of anti-aircraft fire, the American dive bombers, which had made their approach unnoticed at high altitude, tore down into the attack. Within a short time all four of the Japanese carriers had suffered mortal hits. Japanese planes sent to destroy the American carriers hit the "Yorktown" and, this time accurately, reported it sunk. But returning, they found their own mother ships blazing and, with nowhere to land, plunged one after the other into the sea as they ran out of gasoline. They were joined by hundreds of crewmen of the Japanese aircraft carriers who perished as the great ships, now burned-out hulks, disappeared beneath the waves, the commanders, lashed to the steering wheels, going down with their ships.

On the following day, with all his carriers—half the entire carrier strength of the Japanese fleet—lost, Admiral Yamamoto ordered the fleet to break off action. In the initial stages of the withdrawal, what was left of his armada was further mauled by pursuing American planes and submarines.

On the 5th of June, the day when Yamamoto's fleet was in full flight from the victorious American navy, Hideki Tojo addressed a delegation of international journalists in Tokyo. "Japan," he told the newsmen, "is prepared to fight for a hundred years until victory is won and our enemies are crushed. We are confident that militarily and politically and economically we can bring this sacred war to a successful conclusion." If the journalists found no hint in this that Japan had just suffered a defeat that was unparalleled in its history and was to mark the turn of the tide for the Pacific Allies, it was not because Tojo was purposely dissembling. In the headquarters of the naval supreme command, even high-ranking officers were kept in ignorance of the reports of the disaster at Midway that were just coming in.

Tojo, as premier, was considered no more to be taken into their confidence than any other politician and was beginning to suffer the consequences of a system he had always supported: the independence of the armed forces command from political control. It had not been a bad thing to conduct operations without political interference in Meiji times, he said. But from the day he had assumed the premiership he had begun to apprehend, as he admitted later, that in the delicate and complicated business of international affairs, the head of government must exercise control. "When the prime minister," he complained after the war, "has not the authority to participate in supreme decisions, it is not likely that the country will win a war. . . . I did not hear of the Midway defeat until more than a month after it occurred. Even now I do not know the details."

The Japanese naval supreme command had, in fact, gone to great lengths to make sure that no one knew the details. On their arrival back in their home bases, extraordinary security precautions were imposed to prevent the full extent of the defeat from becoming known. Casualties were taken ashore under cover of darkness and all, including Captain Fuchida, the flier who had led the Pearl Harbor attack and who was wounded in the Midway fighting, were kept incommunicado for some time after they were smuggled ashore from their hospital ships. Strict censorship of mail and published references, and even of official records of the battle, prevented the truth of the gravity of the losses and the heaviness of the defeat from becoming known to the Japanese people.

Nevertheless, against the background of the unalloyed triumph of the last few months, the first mention of the Midway battle, made on the 10th of June, held an unmistakably sober note. The official announcement, which truthfully stated that the Aleutian islands of Kiska and Attu had been occupied by Japanese forces, made the Midway battle out, in terms of losses, to be a Japanese victory. On the same day, a Japanese naval spokesman in an interview in the *Asahi* newspaper said, "one cannot always expect victories and we must be able to stand losses." Five days later, Tokyo radio referred to losses at Midway as being "not inconsiderable" and admitted that they were "the greatest suffered since the beginning of the war."

It was about this time that a report of an attack on Tojo himself reached the United States. In Washington the representative of the Sino–Korean People's League said that he had learned from underground sources of an attempt on the premier's life. This was alleged to have taken place at the entrance to the war ministry building in Tokyo, where a young Korean nationalist, a member of a Korean terrorist group, fired two shots, slightly wounding Tojo with the first and hitting the ex-premier Hirota with the second. Japanese police opened fire, killing the assailant and, in the confusion, also wounding a member of the Japanese air force who happened to be near. This was the story and, if true, it was censored even more completely than the first accounts of the Midway battle, for it was never repeated, confirmed, or even denied.

It was probably even more fanciful than some of the other stories now coming out of Japan, many of them based on hearsay and retailed by the first batch of American civilians exchanged for Japanese internees in August 1942. One of these told of a worker who, when Tojo was visiting a Tokyo factory, threw a spanner at the premier in protest against Tojo's failure to protect the factory during the Doolittle raid in which "one hundred workers were killed." Other accounts were given of Tojo's "almost defiant manner" to the Emperor, who was pictured as virtually a prisoner in the palace and allowed only to read censored newspapers, while Tojo consolidated his position as Japan's first modern *shogun*.

Tojo's picture, western readers were told, appeared almost every day in the newspapers "talking with young students, assisting old women across the road, and so on. When he makes speeches their trend is always that he, Tojo, is the 'man of the hour' who will lead Japan to victory."

This last accorded more nearly with the adulation publicly showered on the premier when Japanese military successes were at their highwater mark. For Tojo did not confine himself to the walls of his home and office. As much time as he could spare was spent in touring industrial and war plants, farming and fishing areas and addressing rallies, exhorting and encouraging. In publications of the day he was extolled as "The Lightning Premier" and as "The Man of Sincerity and Iron." In his infrequent and brief periods off duty he had the habit of exercising on his white military charger from the cavalry stables in Tokyo. On this the propagandists seized, dubbing him "The Premier on Horseback." And he was always ready to reiterate his personal creed of hard work. "In the fish market where supplies were scanty and the dealers complained of difficulties because of lack of gasoline for transport, he cried, 'Gasoline, gasoline. Never mind gasoline! Get up earlier!' "[1]

He even took time on at least one occasion to visit an allied prisoner of war camp at Omori. Lewis Bush recalled the occasion when, on a day in October 1943, Lieutenant Ichimura, a Japanese camp officer rushed into their bath house and called them to attention. As they all stood, some naked, just behind the officer came

a sturdy-looking gentleman attired in a gray tweed suit, a grey felt hat, and carrying a walking stick with an ivory handle which seemed to be shaped in the form of a dog or horse's head. At the camp officer's command we all bowed. And General Hideki Tojo raised his hat to us, smiled, and proceeded to ply the almost petrified Ichimura with questions. . . . Tojo visited all the huts. In one of them was the camp idiot . . . Tojo expressed much sympathy with this individual. The men, Bush noted, seemed quite impressed with Tojo, describing him afterwards as "not a bad old bugger" and a "fatherly sort of old cove," although one took issue with the term fatherly, "with all the muckin' trouble he's caused."[2]

A few weeks after the defeat at Midway, Japanese and Australian troops in New Guinea were locked in what was described by an American war correspondent as "the worst fighting in the war." Now having given up as hopeless the prospect of taking Port Moresby by naval action, a strong force of the Japanese army had advanced from Buna on the northwest coast along the Kokoda Trail over the Owen Stanley mountains. In the following month, on the 9th of August, 1942, Tokyo radio announced that a large-scale battle was in progress in the Solomons region between a Japanese naval task force and a combined fleet of American and Australian warships.

Three days later the Americans went into the offensive in the Pacific when U.S. marines landed on Guadalcanal, in the Solomon Islands. As the marines held firm in the face of desperate counter-attacks in the anxious weeks that followed, the Japanese in New Guinea—checked a few miles from their objective—were being forced painfully back over the Kokoda Trail by Australian troops, many of them veterans of the Middle East campaigns, on to a narrow beachhead at Buna. In the Solomons, the Americans lost an aircraft carrier—their fourth in the war—in carrying out successfully Admiral Halsey's command to stop at "whatever the cost" large Japanese naval forces attempting to reinforce their troops in Guadalcanal.

By November, soon after the decisive British victory over Rommel at El Alamein and the announcement of Allied landings in French North Africa, Japanese troops under Lieutenant General Horii were preparing to make their last stand on the strip of beach at Buna into which they had been driven by Australians who had now linked up with American troops. Before the month had ended, a last effort by the Japanese navy to retain Guadalcanal had ended in defeat on the 16th of November after fighting which, at one stage, had been so confused that Japanese ships were firing on one another.

In the light of our knowledge that these Axis defeats were the beginning of successful counter-attacks by the Allies which, from then on, were to be pressed on without serious check to overwhelming victory, there is something almost wistful in the telegram Tojo chose, on the 13th of December, to send to Adolf Hitler. "Today, when the knowledge is gaining ground among all right-thinking people that a better world can only be achieved by the complete victory of the three [Axis] nations, I should like again to proclaim to the whole world that our three nations have the unalterable will as well as the power jointly to achieve this victory."

Nevertheless, when he addressed the Japanese Diet on the 28th of December, 1942, he sounded, as he had every reason to be, significantly less confident than on previous occasions. "Fighting during the past half-year," he said, "has resolved itself into a persistent tug-of-war. . . . Close observation of the situation reveals that moves of the utmost strategic importance are lurking everywhere, giving the impression that the real war is starting now." Everything was going well, he declared, except for Guadalcanal where Japanese troops consisting of only a "nominal unit of the Japanese navy" were fighting under "adverse conditions." He went on: "I wish to state that the Japanese army, under our August Emperor and with the enthusiastic support of the 100 million subjects of the Japanese Empire, have definitely established a strategic foothold that will lead to eventual victory." Other army units were "engaged day and night in providing against air raids."

At the same session of the Diet, his navy minister,

Admiral Shimada, who a few months previously had dismissed American naval action in the Pacific as "occasional guerilla warfare," warned of sterner things to come. "The war has now entered on a decisive stage," he reported, "and the enemy relying upon his production capacity is expected to attempt counter-attacks." The year 1943, as Tojo told the Diet a month later, would be the "year of decisive battles."

Twenty-six

In January 1943 there were reports in the western press that the opening of the Diet had been postponed because of Tojo's ill health. These were denied by Tokyo Radio as wishful thinking. The premier, the bulletin announced, had "never looked more robust." He was, in fact, down with a high fever of unknown origin. He refused to eat solid food and kept himself going with apple juice that Mrs. Tojo got from his family home in Morioka. In spite of urging from his worried wife and two members of his government, Hoshino and Kaya, who joined her in suggesting that a top physician from the elite Imperial University should be called in, he would only consent to being treated by a doctor from the Tokyo Army Medical school. "If I were a field commander at the battlefront," he told them, "there would only be an army doctor to take my pulse. This is my battlefield and I'll have no special privileges. I still regard myself as being a combat soldier." He had, it appeared, rather more faith in traditional remedies than in modern treatments. It had been his habit in the past to use a Chinese medicine which he not only took himself but often pressed on others who complained of various complaints. The man who made this, on hearing of Tojo's sickness, visited him and prescribed that it should be applied to the general's stomach and the arch of his foot. Soon he was out of bed and, to his wife's distress, was bounding up and down the staircase of the house. When she protested that he should take things more carefully, he retorted, "There's a stairway in the Diet."[1]

When he addressed the Diet at the end of the month, he was in a defiant mood. Japan was no longer a have-not nation, he declared, and had secured ample resources to wage war "on whatever scale might be necessary." Yet there was in the latter phrase and in his mention of dispositions made for "both offensive and defensive" warfare an implied admission that things were no longer going all Japan's way.

Now, with the war going into its fifteenth month, it was clear enough that the possibility that a demoralized America would, after the shock of Pearl Harbor, shrink from counter-attacking in the Pacific had never been anything but a fantasy. The proud Japanese navy had been humbled and grievously weakened —indeed, it was never to recover fully from its Midway defeat. In Burma, the Japanese army had been halted at the borders of India. In New Guinea the remnants of a 15,000-strong Japanese force which, a few months before, had come within a few miles of capturing Port Moresby, had perished virtually to a man on the beach at Buna. Australia was now secure from the threat of invasion. From this great war base with lines of communication and supply back to the arsenals and manpower of the United States, General MacArthur had already launched the allied counter-offensive.

The depredations of Allied submarines (for which virtually no defensive preparations had been made by the Japanese supreme command) were on a scale completely unforeseen. Before the war ended, Japanese shipping losses were to exceed a staggering total of six million tons, and they were already severe enough to indicate the inherently precarious situation in which increasingly the resources of which Tojo had boasted were to get no nearer to Japan than the bottom of the Pacific.

In March 1943, as the Japanese people were being exhorted by press and radio to be publicly cheerful with the inauguration of National Smile Week, another great naval defeat was suffered in the Battle of the Bismarck Sea. A Japanese convoy on its way to reinforce the New Guinea base of Lae was virtually annihilated by American and Australian land-based planes. Of the

15,000 reinforcements only a handful survived to struggle ashore, where they were hunted down by Australian troops.

In the same week, Tojo sounded a new note. "If by chance," he said, through an army spokesman to members of the Japanese Patriotic Press Association, "Japan should lose the war, it would be at a time when public opinion is divided. Individual antagonisms and differences—which we cannot say were absolutely absent in the past—can never be permitted now." Tojo was speaking from the heart. Almost two years in office had confirmed the realization that his confident proclamation when he assumed the premiership that nothing could stop "one hundred million people merged into one in iron solidarity" had been visionary. He was bitterly aware now of the consequences, present and future, of the rivalries and suspicions that still divided important sections of the nation, the army and the navy, the government, of which he was now the representative, and the supreme command of the armed services which still regarded the conduct of the war as its own closely guarded prerogative. Unable to do much about this frustrating and abiding problem of assuming the real control over the conduct of the war, he turned for support to another and hitherto unlikely quarter.

Mamoru Shigemitsu, the former ambassador to London, had just returned from Nanking where he had been serving as envoy to the Japanese-sponsored government of Wang Ching-wei. Shigemitsu, a veteran diplomat and, if anything, pro-western, was now sought out by Tojo and asked to take over the foreign ministry.

The former ambassador, who had always opposed the idea of going to war if only on the practical grounds that his knowledge of international affairs told him that Japan could never win, was on the other hand a devout believer in the right of Asiatics to be free of western colonial domination. He just as sincerely believed that Japan, as the strongest and most advanced of Asiatic nations, would inevitably benefit from genuine co-operation with sovereign Asiatic states. He now took the opportunity and, he later held, made it a condition of his taking the office of foreign minister that Tojo should take a new look at the situation of the "one billion diligent people of Asia who," as Tojo had proclaimed, "are with us."

While not openly contemptuous of Asian nationalist leaders as some other senior army officers were, Tojo had paid little more than lip service to the slogan of Asian independence so far. After the early victorious onrush when the war was represented as one of liberation for the enslaved oriental masses, there had been little difficulty in finding collaborators like Laurel in the Philippines and Sukarno in the East Indies. From India, too, the Japanese had the anti-British Subhas Chandra Bose, who had fled his country and espoused the Axis cause even before the Japanese went to war.

The Indian army was growing into the greatest force of volunteers ever assembled, and its splendid soldiery was to play a significant part in defeating Japan. Even India's nationalist leaders, determined to be free of British rule and to take no part in the war, were impervious to the bait of Japanese assistance to achieve self-rule. To Tojo's suggestion that Japan would not "grudge her support" in this golden opportunity for Indians to rid themselves "of the ruthless despotism of Britain and participate in the construction of a sphere of co-prosperity in Asia," the revered Mahatma Gandhi, wise in the nature of conquerors, had replied in an open letter to Tojo in August 1942.

The Japanese premier's reported profession, the Mahatma wrote, "sorts ill with your ruthless aggression against China. You will be sadly disillusioned if you believe you will receive a willing welcome from India. . . . We need no aid from foreign powers." Nevertheless, despite this and the Mahatma's further warning that it would be a tragedy for the world if Germany or Japan won the war, Bose was now heading a Japanese-sponsored "Indian National Government" and endeavoring, with remarkably small success, to recruit an army from the thousands of Indian prisoners in Japanese hands.

While India was spared from Japanese invasion, the occupied countries, supposedly liberated, had soon found themselves—like millions of unhappy Chinese—under oppressive and often brutal military rule. The nationalists collaborating with the Japanese, although given an outward show of respect when they visited Japan, were treated as no more and often less than puppets by the arrogant *neo-samurai* who governed back in their own countries. "To be feted in Tokyo," as historian Richard Storry put it, "did not quite make up for having one's face slapped in Rangoon or Manila."[2]

The Chinese had been the first to discover the mockery of the high-sounding "East Asia Co-Prosperity Sphere." From China, Shigemitsu now confirmed rumors, long current, of corruption and tyranny there, involving Japanese army officers and businessmen working with Chinese entrepreneurs.

Tojo's tour of the occupied territories in the early summer of 1943 was probably too late to repair the situation even if it had been in his power to effect any real change. It was one thing for him to declare in his speeches on the tour that "activities detrimental to the occupied peoples must be liquidated" but another entirely to enforce his fiat. The soldiers were the real government in the occupied territories, as he had once been in Manchuria. Nor could his assurance that the "baneful tentacles" of Britain and America would never again be extended into Asia change the course of the war. It was the Japanese octopus whose tentacles were in the first painful processes of being lopped off one by one.

In May, an emotion-choked radio announcer reported to the Japanese people that they had lost Yamamoto, their greatest naval commander, "on the very front line while directing operations from a military airplane." The Admiral's plane had fallen into a successful and elaborate ambush by a special killer team of American fighter planes and had been shot down over Bougainville in the Solomons. A week later came the report that the garrison on Attu island in the Aleutians had all perished after U.S. troops attacked under cover of thick fog and following intensive air and naval bombardment. "Japanese troops," the official Tokyo announcement read, "launched their final attack after shouting *banzai* for the Emperor and bowing towards the Imperial Palace in Tokyo. Wounded, unable to take part, had committed *hara-kiri.*"

Mrs. Tojo especially remembered the fall of Attu. "When the island fell, a lieutenant-colonel, who was my husband's secretary, telephoned from his quarters and said he was coming immediately to make a report, so I went to my husband's room to awaken him. He slept in the next room to his study and always had his military uniform next to his pillow. When the secretary arrived, I showed him into the study and my husband was uniformed and waiting to see him. As he listened to the last message from Colonel Yamasaki, the commander of Attu, my husband was shaken with emotion and the secretary had to wait silently until he had composed himself and then finished reading. My husband suggested afterward that I should go and comfort the widow of Colonel Yamasaki. So as the signs of Japan's impending defeat became clearer, my husband became depressed and sick at heart."[3]

While the allies were piercing the Japanese outer ring of defense in the Pacific, news from Europe was demolishing finally the belief that had so greatly influenced Japanese leaders to go to war—that the Axis would be victorious there. A great German army had surrendered at Stalingrad; Rommel had been chased from North Africa; and in September, shortly after the Allies landed in Sicily and Mussolini fell, the Italians surrendered unconditionally. This "shameful act of betrayal," as it was characterized in a statement issued after Tojo had been received in special audience by the Emperor, shook the Japanese far more than was conceded by the brave assertion that "it was not unexpected."

The fact that Badoglio, the man who had taken over from Mussolini and capitulated, had been one of his generals, touched off a surge of panic among the younger Japanese officers. The cry went up that there must be no Badoglios in Japan. And among the generals there was a corresponding anxiety to avoid any suspicion that they might be casting themselves in the role of a future Badoglio.

Two weeks later Tojo announced over the radio drastic measures to concentrate the nation's energy and resources. "No slackening of effort can be tolerated," he warned. "The British and Americans are attempting, without regard to their own high losses, to force the Japanese empire to its knees by fresh offensives. Heavy battles are in progress and others must be expected. The time has come for the Japanese people to adapt themselves to the present war situation and a determined battle front will be established at home and measures taken to ensure an epoch-making increase in war output."

The measures subsequently enforced to effect a complete mobilization of the Japanese people provided for working right through the week. The age limit for war work was removed. Women were to be employed on a greater scale. Later, *geisha* and tea houses, which had kept in flourishing business despite the war, were closed. An Imperial Rescript issued on the occasion of the new emergency measures described the situation as "truly grave," and this was less an exhortation than a grim statement of fact.

In June, a supreme command headquarters communiqué announcing that there were "increasing signs of an Anglo–American offensive on a large scale" had rapidly been borne out by events in the Pacific. In July the Americans invaded New Georgia. In naval and aerial action the Allies inflicted heavy losses on Japanese naval units trying to reinforce island garrisons by night—as they were now compelled to do by Allied mastery of the sea and air by day in the New Guinea and Solomons area. In September, the important New Guinea base of Lae fell.

November brought even more severe reverses. In the early part of the month, the biggest air and sea battle since Midway was fought when Japanese forces set out to engage an American fleet thought to be threatening the vital Japanese bastion of Truk. The American move proved to be a feint and was followed by the real one two weeks later, when a powerful amphibious task force attacked Tarawa and Makin islands in the Gilberts. These assaults, which were to set the pattern for the island-hopping offensives toward the Japanese home islands, employed self-contained armies each supplied by a complete mobile base at sea. Tarawa was given, in the words of the American official communiqué, "a pasting like nothing ever before in the history of warfare —more concentrated than the bombing of Berlin." The Japanese garrison fought, as always, with fanatic courage, but on the 25th of November the Americans announced that "few live Japanese remain in the Gilberts."

During the month, Churchill and Roosevelt had met in Cairo and, following their conference there, issued in early December a declaration that "Japan shall be stripped of all the islands in the Pacific mandated in the 1914 war and that all the territories that Japan has stolen from the Chinese . . . Manchuria, Formosa and the Pescadores, shall be restored to the Republic of China. Japan will also be expelled from all other territories which she has taken by violence and greed, and the enslaved people of Korea will become free and independent." The allies, the proclamation went on, would "continue to persevere in the serious and prolonged operations necessary to procure the unconditional surrender of Japan." Tojo, in a broadcast to the nation, categorized this as a "laughable" and "silly childish propaganda effort, born of necessity to cover up their present series of failures." The Japanese Imperial forces were still winning "brilliant victories" in the Gilberts and other fighting areas although, he added, "the officers and men of our Imperial forces do not, of course, entertain the idea of ever returning alive." The people of Japan, he said, "must renew the determination with which they rose two years ago. . . . Victory in war cannot be won with folded arms."

Less than a week later, Allied troops landed in New Britain. Within five more days a supreme command headquarters announcement from Tokyo admitted that the victory Tojo had claimed in the Gilberts was an utter defeat. The garrisons at Tarawa and Makin had "died heroically to the last man." "The real war," Tojo told a subdued Diet on the 27th of December, "is starting now."

Twenty-seven

The first four days of January, when the Japanese celebrate their New Year, is a great time for shucking off the old and preparing for the new. Practically, by clearing up unfinished business and paying off debts, and symbolically by personal cleansing and the taking of the first meal of the traditional *o-mochi* (specially prepared rice cakes), the coming year must start off exorcised, as far as possible, of all inauspicious influence from the old. Especially, it is a time for facing up to the mistakes and follies of the past and earnestly considering the prospects ahead. In Japan these thoughts are often committed to diaries, of which the Japanese are inveterate keepers. As revealed by his own journal, the thoughts of Marquis Kido, the Lord Privy Seal, in the early days of 1944, were turning increasingly to speculation on how Japan might be extricated from the war.

It was not the first time that the privy seal had thought of getting out of the war. In the previous year he had talked with Prince Konoye on the way the struggle was going. They had agreed then that the prospect of victory was bleak, and the prince, as ever, was preoccupied with the likelihood of a Communist seizure of power in the upheaval of defeat. With the return of Kido's old and trusted friend Mamoru Shigemitsu to the Foreign Office, Kido had found someone he could talk to frankly on the possibilities of ending the war. Their conversations were always in private. To have revealed that anything resembling a peace move was in being would have been to invite either imprisonment or assassination by extremists. The *Kempeitai* agents were increasingly active, and high rank would not necessarily have been any protection.

The fall of Benito Mussolini had set Kido to speculating on what would happen if Tojo also fell. This, he thought, might happen with the possible collapse of Germany at some time in 1944. Once more he and the *jushin,* the council of former prime ministers, would be faced with the problem of who would replace Tojo. When that time came, he resolved, they must see that the succeeding cabinet and prime minister consisted of men who would get Japan out of the war on the best possible terms. Like many Japanese in high places, he refused to take seriously the Allied call for "unconditional surrender." He hoped that Japan would still be able to arrange some negotiated peace through either China or Soviet Russia before, as he noted in his diary, Japan was "isolated and subjected to attack by all the powerful nations of the world." Events, however, were moving with a speed the pessimistic Kido had not foreseen.

Tojo was perhaps nearer to reality when he told the Diet at the end of January 1944 that "there is only a hairbreadth between victory and defeat" and warned that the nation must be prepared for difficulties that would become "more and more severe." In the previous October, with the Japanese outer perimeter of island defenses thoroughly breached, an Imperial Conference had been held. After debates, described as acrimonious, between the army and navy, it had been decided that the original defense ring, once thought to be impregnable, must be contracted to an inner line stretching from the Burma front, through the Andaman Islands, the Philippines, the Carolines, the Marianas, the Marshalls, the Ryukyu islands of Iwo Jima and Okinawa, and the Kuriles to the north of Japan.

On the 1st of February, a few days after Tojo's warning to the Diet, the first Allied thrust into the Japanese new defense line came with the start of a powerful amphibious operation against the Marshall Islands. "For the first time," Tojo admitted to the Diet, "the enemy has really attacked Japanese soil." On the twentieth of the month, as U.S. troops were disposing of the survivors of the garrison on Kwajalein island, the main fortress of the Marshalls group, Tojo at last assumed full control by taking over the post of chief of army general staff. He thus took the unprecedented step of combining all the functions of premier, war minister, education and munitions ministers, and head of the army. Referring to him as "Total Tojo," a western leader wrote sardonically that he now had under him "as many departments as Poohbah." At the same time, Admiral Shimada, his ever-obliging navy minister, took over the post of chief of the naval staff from Admiral Nagano.

High ranking civilians like Kido and Shigemitsu, with inside knowledge of the war situation, were not the only people becoming convinced that somehow Japan must get out of the war. In the navy, although they had prudently kept quiet, several senior officers on the naval staff had remained pessimistic about the chances of Japan's success. One of them, Admiral Tagaki, now found himself in an embarrassing position. Earlier in the war, Tagaki had been instructed by the navy minister, Admiral Shimada, to carry out a study of the war situation. His findings, when he completed them in February 1944, were so depressing and his conclusions so heretical that Tagaki decided it would not do to pass them on to Shimada.

Tagaki's fear was that when Shimada, widely considered to be Tojo's toady, brought his recommendations—which envisaged Japan's almost complete withdrawal from overseas territories—to the premier's notice, Tojo would undoubtedly ignore them. But worse, he might well be goaded into extreme measures, possibly including reprisals against those he suspected of supporting Tagaki's conclusions in the navy. He decided, therefore, to hand his report to the former premier, Admiral Yonai, who as a member of the *jushin* had access to the Throne.

How correct Tagaki's fears of Tojo's probable reaction had been was demonstrated when, having had the findings shown to him by Yonai, Admiral Okada, another member of the privy council, approached Tojo. He and the other *jushin,* the old admiral told him, were seriously concerned about the course the war was taking. Tojo, thoroughly angry, refused to hear him out and exclaimed that the ex-premiers were conspiring to overthrow him.

Even the army had its doubters now. At the Sanno Hotel in Tokyo, which in the 1936 uprising had been the headquarters of the army mutiny, a group of young officers had been regularly meeting under the chairmanship of Colonel Matsutani, a junior member of the army general staff. Matsutani had formerly served as a military attaché in Britain and had maintained his contacts with the Japanese foreign office. Through these, he and his colleagues were less ignorant of the real situation than the great majority of army officers.

So concerned did Matsutani become, in fact, that he produced his own report, recommending that Japan should get out of the war, and this he eventually contrived to present personally to Tojo. After an interview, described as stormy, Colonel Matsutani the next day received orders for his immediate transfer to the China front.

In the following weeks, the bastion of Truk was heavily attacked by hundreds of U.S. planes which inflicted severe losses on ships there. American troops landed in the Admiralty islands, and U.S. marines made the first land assault on New Britain. By April 24, with the capture of Hollandia, the Japanese army in the New Guinea area—less than half of the original quarter of a million men who had been destined for the invasion of Australia—was declared by General MacArthur to be "neutralized and strategically impotent."

Only from China and Burma was there news of Japanese successes. In China a large-scale offensive aimed at neutralizing American "bomb-Tokyo" air bases there had been ostensibly successful, but the Chinese still had immense areas of space to trade for time, and guerrilla units, particularly those of the Chinese Communists, were proving a far more serious menace to the invaders than the incompetent generals of the Kuomintang regular armies. In Burma, the Japanese army had started operations grandiloquently announced as the "march on Delhi." A large Japanese force, skilfully infiltrated through the jungle, had invested the British bases at Kohima, Ukhrul, and Imphal on the Assam front, opening what promised at first to be the long-threatened invasion of India.

But in Burma, too, the days of easy successes were over. The British–Indian Fourteenth Army under General Slim was not only holding but, by large-scale movement of troops by air, had thwarted early Japanese capture of bases vital to them if their advance was to be sustained. In the following months, while the bulk of the Japanese forces was thus being ineffectually expended in besieging Imphal and Kohima, a special American combat force under General Merrill captured Myitkyina, the railhead town for Mandalay. Japanese attempts to reinforce their troops for these important operations were blocked by the Chindits, British and Indian long-range penetration groups formed by General Wingate who landed by glider across the Japanese lines of communication.

In the Pacific, the allied attack pressed on with landings in Biak, described by the Japanese supreme command as "of paramount importance" and whose fall would greatly impede their defense of the Philippines. And, in June, dismay now began to turn to despair among Japanese in high places as one disaster to their own and the Axis arms in Europe followed another. Rome fell on the June 4 and, two days later, the greatest amphibious assault of all time, the British–American landings in Normandy, was mounted. "This was more than enough to dishearten us," Toshikazu Kase wrote, "as the defenses of our home islands were far more vulnerable than the European invasion coast."[1]

If there was any disposition to imagine that the huge Allied operations in Europe meant that effort was going to slacken against Japan, prompt notice was served to confound it. On June 15 Tojo hurriedly met with his cabinet to consider the bombing of Japan's largest steelworks a few hours before by a force of U.S. "Flying Fortress" planes from Allied bases in China. And on the same day and after five days of saturation bombardment by sea and air, American assault troops stormed ashore on the island of Saipan in the Marianas.

On the 9th of July, as news from Burma made it clear that the Japanese attempt to invade India had turned into utter disaster for their army there, it was announced that Saipan had fallen. The cost on both sides had been grievous. The twenty-five thousand Japanese defenders had perished almost to a man, and among the dead was Admiral Nagumo, who had commanded the Pearl Harbor attack force. The main Japanese fleet, moved in a desperate effort to relieve the garrison, had been decisively defeated again. The Americans had suffered over 15,000 casualties, but with the fall of the island, which Imperial headquarters in Tokyo had boasted was an "impregnable shield," the Allies had broken deep into the Japanese Pacific defenses. Even as the Japanese pinned down in the northeast tip launched their last hopeless counter-attack in the final hours of the Saipan fighting, American naval units were moving into the island's deep-water harbors. Within a few days, heavy bombers were roaring down onto Saipan's two airfields, and poised for attack on the Japanese home islands less than 1500 miles away.

With the shock of the reverses of May and June, culminating in the American landing on Saipan, the movement to end the war began to take on the proportions of a plot to get rid of Tojo. Great care still had to be taken. He was not the kind of man to yield easily, and he could still count on a lot of support from the armed services, where the clamor by the young officers to recapture Saipan was loud. One of the former premiers, Admiral Okada, cynically suggested that they should be allowed to try, even though the naval defeat had made it hopeless, since this would be the only way to bring home to them the reality of the situation.

There was, too, the increasing danger from the secret police. Toshikazu Kase, who was taking a very active part in forming a liaison with end-the-war figures like Shigemitsu, his superior at the foreign office, Prince Konoye, Kido, and the various *jushin,* wrote of the attentions to which they were subject. "I knew my telephone was tapped. I received frequent visits from police agents who, with artificial smiles invited my comments upon the futility of continuing the war or upon the 'brutality' and 'misgovernment' of General Tojo. Many walked into these traps and were summarily taken to jail."[2]

On the home front there was widespread hardship and apathy. The air raid on Kyushu had been followed up with another a week later, an omen of the devastation to be wreaked on Japanese cities and their dwellers as Allied land-based planes came increasingly within range of Japan. And the recent military disasters, national and international, had come too thick and fast to be glossed over any longer.

On the face of it Tojo could not evade responsibility now, particularly since he had virtually assumed full control in

February. But it was already clear that the general was as obstinately opposed as ever to conceding personal failure. As he had already intimated to Kido, he felt he should receive some formal endorsement from the Emperor absolving him from blame. It would be dangerous to change the government in the middle of the crisis, he held. What he proposed was to retain power himself by yet another reshuffle of his cabinet. To this end, he was canvassing support among the former premiers, inviting certain of the *jushin* to join his cabinet, even being prepared to sacrifice his navy minister, Shimada, to make a place for Admiral Yonai. Moreover, he told the *jushin,* he was now ready to consider their advice and work more closely with them in the future.

Their advice thus invited was prompt, and scarcely what he had been hoping for. On July 17, Admiral Okada presented to Kido for transmission to the Emperor a resolution passed at a meeting of the ex-premiers which recommended that Tojo should not continue as premier. If the nation was to survive, it said, "a partial reorganization of the cabinet will serve no purpose."

Despite the open declaration of no-confidence by the *jushin,* Tojo still aimed to reform his government. At hurriedly called meetings with his ministers, he found that the attack on him was two-pronged, from within his cabinet as well as from without. The navy minister, Shimada, as obliging as ever, had resigned, and although ex-premier Yonai had refused to take his place, the post was now occupied by another admiral. He did not envisage dropping Shigemitsu from the foreign office, but the foreign minister—alerted by Kido that the time had now come to oust Tojo—insisted that the only step left was for the entire cabinet to resign and the premier with it. Uchida, the minister of agriculture and a career politician, came out on the side of Shigemitsu. The unkindest cut came with the knowledge that Kishi, Tojo's young protegé from his Manchurian days, had deserted. Kishi, with his weather-vane sensitivity to the winds of change, also refused to step down and be replaced by someone else. Taking his cue from Shigemitsu, he told the premier that he would resign only if the rest of the cabinet went with him. He refused to change his mind despite a personal appeal to him from Tojo, who was reported to be in tears.

On the following morning, the 18th of July, as he was

preparing to leave his official residence, Tojo said to his wife, "It has been decided that I will not carry on. Please make arrangements to go home." Mrs. Tojo was taken by surprise. She had seen her husband, as she said, very tired and giving unsparingly of himself, but had never considered that anything short of death would make him give up. She said, "You are going to quit but will that end your responsibility?" He told her, "I am not evading my responsibilities. I have done everything I can but even if I wanted to carry on, conditions have made it impossible. There is no help for it."[3]

From his residence, he went to Tokyo Radio to make his last address to the nation confirming that Saipan was lost. "I am profoundly pained," he said, "by the thought of the grave disquiet this loss has caused our Emperor . . . but our enemies have increased the intensity of their counter-offensive. Opportunities will now occur to crack them." This done, he proceeded just before midday direct to the Imperial Palace to present his own resignation and that of his cabinet. To Kido, the privy seal, to whom he reported before he was received in audience by Emperor Hirohito, he made a bitter attack on the *jushin* whom he accused of bringing about his fall.

He left the palace for his official residence for the last time. There Mrs. Tojo had preparations for return to their home in the Tokyo suburbs well in hand. He spent some time in saying good-bye to members of the staff and meticulously thanked them all. Years later, one of the regular residence police guards recalled Tojo as being the one he had liked best and found most considerate of all the prime ministers he had served under in over thirty years in the job. That afternoon, as Tojo was collecting his papers together, Tokyo Radio went on the air. "Using all means available," the announcer read, "the present cabinet was not able to achieve its objective. The government has finally decided on a complete reconstitution in order to prosecute the total war."

Part **F**our

THE SUMMER GRASS

> *"A wilderness of*
> *Summer Grass*
> *Ah, the reminder*
> *Of a Warrior's Dream"*

BASHO
(1644-94)

TOJO:

THE LAST BANZAI

Commodore Matthew Perry, whose warships peacefully opened Japan for American interests in July, 1853. His coming ended over two centuries of Japanese feudal hermitage.

Admiral Togo, a key figure in the Russo-Japanese War of 1904-05, with his two sons around the time of the conflict.

H. C. White, New York

Brown Brothers

apanese infantry approaching
iko Yang in what was to
ecome a nobly embarrassing
usso-Japanese War.

A contemporary lithograph of
Japanese troops during the
capture of Taishu in the
Russo-Japanese War.

RUSSIA'S MOVE

At a celebration in Hankow, November 3, 1938, a column of Japanese marines march before the high command of the Japanese army and navy.

Outnumbered, they were victorious. Jubilant Japanese troops after the capture of the 29th Chinese Army headquarters, Tungchow, China, August 17, 1937.

Japanese troops barricade themselves from enemy guns during bitter fighting on the Paoshan Road in Chapei, February 25, 1932. The Chinese later demolished the area.

Brown Brothers

Brown Brothe

A Japanese naval landing
party, armed with the most
modern weapons, advances
toward a bridge leading to the
Kiangwan sector of Shanghai.

The sinking of U.S. gunboat
Panay on patrol in Yangtze
River (1937) brought
Japanese apologies, but led to
pointed warnings for U.S. to
get out of Asia.

The young Hideki Tojo (about
1919) as a family man. L to R:
Mrs. Katsuko Tojo; daughter,
Mitsu; eldest son, Hidetaka;
second son, Teruo.

Japanese troops shouting
Banzai at Mt. Limay, Bataan,
Philippine Islands in 1942.
This was a captured photograph.

An emergent Captain Hideki
Tojo (about 1920).

General Hideki Tojo, prime minister of the "land of the rising sun."

"Further and Deeper." A cartoon by Low that appeared in the London *Evening Standard* of January 19, 1938.

Former Premier Hideki Tojo
as he is sentenced to death at
the Japanese War Criminals
trial in the Far East Tribunal,
June 12, 1948.

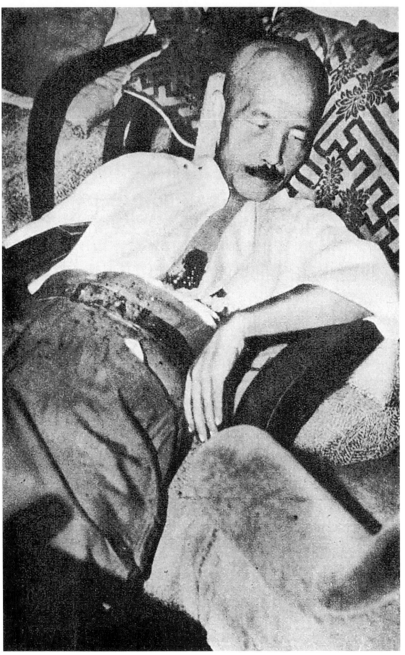

Not quite close to death.
Hideki Tojo after his
attempted suicide when facing
arrest by American
Occupation forces,
September 11, 1945.

Wide World Photos

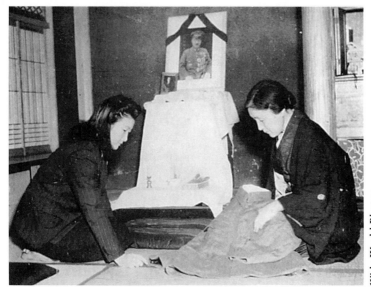

Tojo's wife and daughter burn incense at the family altar soon after he was hanged in Tokyo early December 23, 1948.

Mrs. Katsuko Tojo (1966).

Twenty-eight

In the last hours of his attempt to stay in power, as Tojo was arguing and pleading with the members of his cabinet, an urgent paper was delivered to the cabinet offices from the war office. In the form of a draft communiqué which the army proposed to issue and sent ostensibly for prior approval, it violently denounced the *jushin* for conspiring to overthrow the Tojo government. Whether Tojo had a hand in this or not, there is no doubt of his personal conviction that his fall had been plotted by the ex-premiers and Kido. He had revealed this in his angry outburst to the privy seal just before he handed in his resignation. The real purpose in sending the communiqué to the cabinet for "approval" had rather obviously been to intimidate those members suspected of involvement in the move to get rid of Tojo. Despite tacit disapproval by the cabinet which, urged by Mamoru Shigemitsu, tried to suppress the attack by taking no action on it, the war information office published it anyway a few days later. By the time it appeared in the newspapers, it was something of a damp squib. Tojo had gone, and his successor, already nominated and on the point of taking over, was another ex-Kwangtung man, known to be pro-Axis and expansionist.

For the end-the-war faction, the ousting of Tojo—like Pearl Harbor—had been only half-victory. Much as Kido and the *jushin* would have liked to install the moderate Admiral Yonai as Tojo's successor, they were still bedeviled by the fear that the army would heed no one but a general. In the frantic consultations during the hours after Tojo's resignation, it was decided as a last-minute compromise to bring in the retired General Koiso, a one-time Kwangtung Army commander, from his post of governor general of Korea, the intention apparently being that he should head the cabinet while actually sharing the power with Yonai. No one, unfortunately, thought to mention this to Koiso who proceeded on the assumption, which his colleagues were too embarrassed to correct, that he had been appointed to prosecute the war to a successful conclusion with Yonai as his navy minister. In his inaugural broadcast to the nation on July 22, 1944, he stressed that the change of government denoted "no basic change. Victory will be ours," he told his listeners, "if we have full confidence in our moral right." Ties with Germany would be strengthened "in positive pursuit of the common war objective."

Tojo, whatever he might have been hoping up to the time that Koiso was appointed and however much he might have been privately mortified, accepted his removal from power as final. This was made complete, militarily as well as politically, when on the 20th of July, 1944, he was put on the retired list. With no excuse for other than personal activity the General, now coming up to his sixtieth year, occupied himself as best he could at the family house in the Setagaya suburb of Tokyo.

The man who had so often told his wife that a military man spends twenty-four hours in the service of his country now had leisure to regret that he had never spared himself time for *shumi* or *doraku* (hobbies, pleasures). The day had come when, as Mrs. Tojo sadly observed, "he had too much time and he didn't know what to do with it." For him there was not even the relaxation of the traditional chess games, *shogi* and *go,* to fall back on. He was also denied the solace that most educated Japanese find in committing their thoughts to paper in the form of *waka* or *haiku* verses. He complained to Mrs. Tojo, "If only I could write a poem or something. I ought to have taken more of an interest in those things."[1]

In the house, he was the only male. Hidetake, the eldest son, had failed to get into the army on medical grounds and was working in Manchuria; the second eldest, Teruo, worked at one of the factories of the Mitsubishi *zaibatsu;* the youngest son Toshio was at military academy. Mitsue, the eldest daughter, so devoted to her father that she had remained single, helped at home with two other daughters, Sachie and Kimie, who were still children. The second daughter, Makie, married to Major Hidemasa Koga, who was stationed with the First Guards Division in Tokyo, was also staying at the Tojo home with her child.

Donning old clothes and a straw hat, Tojo worked a lot in the garden, still dominated by two large pine trees, but most of it turned over to the wartime cultivation of vegetables and chicken-keeping. He spent some time writing in a cottage, which he used as a study until their neighborhood was showered by fire-bombs on May 25 and the cottage and pine trees were destroyed. After the raid, in which many of his papers and personal records were lost, he converted the western-style room in their house into a study. Listening to the latest news on the radio was a ritual, and he supplemented his knowledge of the way things were going by avid newspaper reading and from talking with former army colleagues who occasionally visited him. He could have derived little comfort from what he learned.

In late September, Prime Minister Churchill was able to announce to the British House of Commons that in Burma "the largest and most important ground fighting that had taken place against the armies of Japan has resulted in the slaughter of between 50,000 and 60,000 Japanese." The British–Indian Fourteenth Army advancing on Mandalay often found "corpses in the jungle where each one had committed suicide in succession, with the officer who had supervised the proceedings blowing out his own brains last of all." Most of the force, Toshikazu Kase pointed out, had perished in battle or later of starvation. The disaster of Imphal, he wrote, "was perhaps one of the worst of its kind chronicled in the annals of war. . . . One of the regimental commanders who survived the retreat called upon me in Tokyo in his tattered uniform. I could hardly recognize him. He told me how the ranks had thinned daily as thirst and hunger overtook the retreating column, and how the sick and wounded had to be abandoned by hundreds . . . Only 70,000 of the original force survived."[2]

On the 9th of October Premier Koiso warned the

nation that although Japan was waiting for an opportunity "to crush the enemy with a single stroke . . . production on the home front, particularly of aircraft, has just barely reached a point where we can harbor hopes." Less than two weeks after he had spoken, the Allies brought off in the Pacific the greatest amphibious operation since Normandy with the invasion of the Philippines at Leyte. Wading ashore, General MacArthur, who was in personal command of the assault, delivered himself of a typically momentous declaration. "I have returned! By the grace of Almighty God our forces stand on Philippine soil. . . . Rally to me. . . . For your homes and hearths, strike!" Later, he added in less heroic vein, "I am particularly anxious to get at the Japanese 16th Division. . . . It did the dirty work at Bataan."

From Tokyo, an order was issued to the Japanese navy. "We are throwing our entire strength into the impending battle. You are expected to render your life to the beloved fatherland." By October 24, U.S. Secretary of the Navy James Forrestal was able to announce that in trying to save the Philippines, two-thirds of the Japanese navy was estimated to have been sunk or damaged. The result was, as Mamoru Shigemitsu noted, that "for all practical purposes our navy was destroyed at Leyte."[3]

On the same day, the 24th of October, U.S. Super Fortresses from Saipan made their first sortie over Tokyo in a heavy, concentrated attack, the first in a sustained aerial assault that was, almost unopposed, to scourge the Japanese homeland from now on.

The defeat of General Yamashita's army on Leyte was announced by MacArthur's headquarters on the 26th of December 1944, much to the mortification of Premier Koiso who had unwisely proclaimed that the Leyte battle was to be another *"Tennozan,"* a historic Japanese victory. Two weeks later, on January 9, 1945, MacArthur's forces descended on Luzon, the main Philippine island, and began their drive toward Manila. By February 16, only a few Japanese marines, trapped in a few hundred square yards of the capital's old town, were still holding out.

That morning, beginning at 7 A.M., a new element was added to the air raids, so far carried out by land-based U.S. Super Fortresses from China and Saipan. A powerful force of the American Fifth Fleet sailed to within 300 miles of the coast of western

Japan and mounted an assault by 1500 carrier aircraft. In wave after wave the naval fliers systematically devastated the Tokyo and Yokohama regions, leaving smoke rising to seven thousand feet when the last attackers flew off after nine hours of continuous bombing.

On the same day, as if to give mocking confirmation of the futile sacrifice of the Japanese navy at Leyte, an American task force moved in on the volcanic island of Iwo Jima, unimpeded by surface opposition though sorely tried by the suicidal sorties of Japanese *kamikaze* pilots on whom the Japanese high command was now placing desperate reliance. American marines who landed across the island's sands began that day one of the most epic and costly battles of their entire history, as they struggled up the lava-strewn slopes of Mount Suribachi. There the main garrison of 15,000 Japanese was concentrated, dug deep in caves and crevices, sheltered from the effects of saturation aerial, artillery, and rocket bombardment, and determined to carry out their commander's order of the day: "No Japanese must die before he has killed ten enemy soldiers."

Twenty-nine

That a high price in American and Allied lives would be exacted by the Japanese for every square yard of earth wrested from them had never been in doubt; that it was going to be higher still as the enemy struck nearer to their homeland was evident in the savage contest for Iwo Jima, 700 miles from Japan. But also increasingly apparent to the Emperor, kept well informed of events through Kido and the *jushin,* was the spuriousness of the assertion by those who had plotted Japan's road to power that the Allies would not be prepared to pay that price.

Among the Japanese, save the most blindly committed, confidence in the mystic equation that the fanatic spirit of the Japanese warriors more than compensated for the enemy's material superiority had wilted rapidly. The Allied fighting men had proved to have their own kind of courage of the highest order, stubborn and intelligently applied and—even if lacking what General Wingate had described as the Japanese "humorless capacity for self-immolation"—sacrificial where called for. In Burma and the Pacific, the Japanese generals and admirals were now being consistently outfought and outguessed. And the inequality in resources was seen to be more massive than ever envisaged, as much from Japan's inability to achieve declared targets as from the extraordinary production of the Allies and, more especially, of the vast American arsenal.

In January, Emperor Hirohito had taken the unusual step of summoning, of his own accord, all the senior statesmen to get their views on the war situation. With the double aim of avoiding suspicion among the army and extremists, which a large gathering of statesmen would inevitably arouse, and of enabling each of the *jushin* to speak his mind frankly, uninhibited by the presence of others, it was arranged that he would receive them separately on various days under the official cover that they were going to the Imperial Palace to pay their New Year respects. As a former premier, and therefore a member of the *jushin,* Tojo had his turn. He was among the last to be received and the very circumstances in which he was ushered into the Imperial presence on the 26th of February were inauspicious.

Carrier planes from the American Fifth Fleet cruising off the shores of Japan had that morning resumed their attack on Tokyo and Yokohama. On the day before, the navy planes had joined with Super Fortresses from Saipan in a heavy assault, razing hundreds of acres in the center of the capital. Several bombs had even falling sacrilegiously near the Imperial residence, sending Premier Koiso hurrying to the Palace—as Radio Tokyo announced it—"in anger at the enemy's arrogance and lawlessness" to apologize to the Emperor for "unforgivable negligence." Manila had just fallen and, on Iwo Jima, the Stars and Stripes had been hoisted by American marines at the summit of Mount Suribachi. Yet Tojo's summing up of the situation revealed none of the anxiety and doubt which those *jushin* received before him had expressed. His attitude was one of—according to one's point of view —either indomitable resolution or complete inability to comprehend the true position.

It was plain, he told Emperor Hirohito, that the enemy was going all out for an early victory over Germany. Once Germany was defeated, they counted on Japan to concede the hopelessness of trying to stand up to the mighty coalition of power that would then be ranged against her. But, as he saw it, the position might not be as simple as that. When this happened, Stalin would probably be tempted to take advantage of Japan's situation, but the essential antipathy and mistrust between the Anglo–Americans and the Russians would cause them to retain large forces in Europe. There was acute war weariness among the Russian people, and this could well dissuade the Soviet leader from embarking on a new war in the Far East.

Japan had large and powerful armies in Manchuria, Korea, and Japanese-controlled north China. Whatever else had been yielded, these possessions on the Asian mainland were formidable assets. The navy was strong enough to secure the relatively narrow waters between them and the home islands and the army would effectively deal with any attempt to invade Japan itself. The spirit of the armed forces was as high as ever, as evinced by the young *kamikaze* fliers who were now undertaking one-way missions to certain death in defense of their country. As for the civilian population, food was short admittedly, but no one was starving. And the air raids on Japan he dismissed as puny compared with those mounted on Germany. Things would get worse, but if the army and the navy and the people could be united under the Emperor as never before, Japan could hold out. Even, as he now apparently accepted, if outright victory was no longer possible, opportunities could be awaited to negotiate an advantageous peace.

If Hideki Tojo's prediction that the marriage of convenience imposed by the war in Europe upon the nations fighting Germany would not long survive the destruction of their mutual enemy was correct in the long run, his reading of the implications in it for Japan were, even as he spoke, proving disastrously wrong. The stand-and-die command to Japanese fighting men had been all too faithfully carried out, as exemplified by the battle for Iwo Jima where the Americans had taken a total of nine prisoners. To the tens of thousands who had perished in the Pacific could be added another 136,000 cut off in various areas by the Allied island-hopping strategy, impotent to take any further part in the defense of their threatened homeland. To meet the invasion which, it appeared, was only a matter of time, it had been necessary to move much of the Kwangtung Army from Manchuria to Japan. Soviet forces already outnumbered Japanese garrisons on the mainland and, with the rapid disintegration of the German armies, were being reinforced with men and arms from the European front.

On the 9th of March, as it was reported that Slim's British–Indian Fourteenth Army had broken into Mandalay, Flying Fortresses carried out their heaviest raid yet on Tokyo, and there commenced in Japan a "frantic and disorderly exodus from major cities."[1] The Sumida River in the capital was, in the words of Mamoru Shigemitsu, at one time "covered with burnt corpses. Not even the Great Earthquake could equal the inferno."[2]

How near the battle was drawing to the homeland was demonstrated three days later. Flying Fortresses which devastated the industrial city of Osaka were able to use airstrips established at Iwo Jima, where U.S. marines were methodically burning and blasting out last-ditch Japanese defenders with flame throwers, phosphorus grenades, and high explosives.

By this time, Marquis Kido, Konoye and Shigemitsu and the others anxious to conclude the war had made some progress, inasmuch as they had achieved an almost equal balance of power with those determined to fight to the finish. In the Cabinet, where the possibility of peace overtures was openly discussed, the only war minister and the premier, the bumbling Koiso, persisted in the illusion that the war could be won.

At the beginning of the month Koiso had agreed to the formation of a new totalitarian party aimed at "discarding past encumbrances and co-operating in overcoming the national crisis through complete unity to replace the Imperial Rule Assistance Association." In the Diet, the premier continued to voice defiance. The enemy, he told the representatives, "is now moving for a direct advance on our mainland. If he attempts to invade, we will crush him back into the sea. If he should finally succeed in landing, we will annihilate him with sledgehammer blows . . . on our home ground we will carry out ingenious operations, thereby taking full advantage of a God-sent opportunity for decisive battle."

As if to underline Koiso's consistent failure in prophesy, the U.S. Tenth Army, supported by Admiral Nimitz's Sixth Fleet and a powerful carrier force of the British fleet, commenced their invasion of the island of Okinawa in the early hours of April 1. The landing, which came a month earlier than expected by the Japanese high command, was practically unopposed in the early stages. Except for *kamikaze* attacks, which were a severe enough hazard, the only initial defense was put up by a few lightly armed civilians including women, some of whom committed suicide rather than fall into the hands of the "American barbarians." Later the advancing U.S. troops came across the bodies of a further two hundred suicides, men, women, and children. The curious inaction on the part of the 128,000-strong Japanese garrison was maintained as the Americans expanded their bridgehead and fanned out inland halfway across the island, and on the second day they reported that U.S. casualties could be "counted on the fingers of two hands."

As news of the Okinawa landings reached Japan, Premier Koiso made a characteristically unsubtle move in his struggle to get some hand in the direction of the war. Since the admirals and generals of the supreme command maintained that a retired general could not sit in on their councils, he proposed that he should be restored to the active list. The supreme command, equally lacking in subtlety, declined to accept his restoration. This and the blow of the Okinawa invasion was more than enough for even the dogged Koiso. On the next day, the 4th of April, he resigned with his cabinet.

Hideki Tojo was one of those who attended a conference of senior statesmen on the day of Koiso's resignation to deliberate on the choice of a successor to him. Almost at once he was at issue with his old adversary, Prince Konoye. Before they talked of selecting a man, Tojo said, in effect, they must decide whether the new cabinet was going to prosecute the war or surrender. Konoye argued that since the direction of the war was in the hands of the supreme command, the cabinet could hardly decide on this basis. When Kido implied that the nation was fast losing confidence in the army and that the appointment of a militarily dominated cabinet would increase an already dangerous situation. Tojo disagreed. The threat of invasion, he maintained, made the role of the army more vital than ever and its direction of the government imperative. He proposed General Hata, the man who had in 1940 nominated him to be war minister in the Konoye cabinet.

Admiral Suzuki, a veteran of the Russo–Japanese war, who had been left for dead by the young army assassins in the 1936 mutiny, thought that the post should go to Prince Konoye and, when the latter declined, was himself proposed for the job. Once again, Tojo intervened, insisting that Hata should be nominated. If not, he warned the *jushin,* the army would bring down any new cabinet. They would, as he put it, "turn the other way." The privy seal, Kido, responding to this threat, reminded Tojo that with the people in their present mood they might very well turn from the army. Admiral Okada, who had also narrowly escaped an attempt on his life by an army murder squad in the uprising of 1936, asked Tojo if he seriously meant to say that the army would refuse to carry out its duties in defense of the nation under a prime minister approved by the Emperor. To this Tojo had apparently no reply. The conference went on into the night and was chiefly taken up with persuading Suzuki to assume the premiership. On the following day, still protesting his lack of experience, his great age and deafness, the old Admiral was officially commanded by Emperor Hirohito to form a cabinet.

At the conference of *jushin* which had elected him, no one had dared to say openly to Suzuki in front of Tojo that his task was to end the war. Nor in his interivew with Kido and the Emperor, had he been given a direct brief as to his role. Rather it was conveyed to him in terms of the ruler's concern for the suffering of his people that peace was a consummation devoutedly to be wished for. But Japan's rapidly deteriorating position could hardly have been more explicit, even to a confused old man like the reluctant new premier.

On the day that he took office, the Soviet government gave notice that its treaty of neutrality with Japan would not be renewed in the following year. Training of aviation recruits had ceased because of lack of oil; in fact, the supreme command planning staff had advised that their oil stocks would run out in three months. With overseas supplies cut off, all they had to fall back on was a project, barely started, for producing oil from pine roots. Food was falling below subsistence level, and as dissatisfaction was more openly voiced, the *Kempeitai* stepped up their oppression. During the month of April over four hundred people were arrested, among them the former ambassador to Britain, Shigeru Yoshida, and several other elder statesmen.

On the 5th of April, the eighty-year-old Suzuki told the nation over the radio that although he considered himself "utterly unfit" for his post, he had bowed to the Emperor's will because of the nation's grave situation. As he spoke, the Japanese garrison on Okinawa at last came to grips with the American invaders in a battle that was to be the most savagely fought in the Pacific war and—as it happened—was the last battle of World

War II. What was left of the Imperial navy set out, and again met with disaster. Sixteen warships, including the mighty 72,000-ton "Yamato," the world's largest battleship, were sunk before they could reach Okinawa.

In the meantime, there had occurred a remarkable interlude. On the 12th of April, Tokyo Radio interrupted its regular broadcasts to announce the sudden death of President Roosevelt. The announcer described the late President as "a great man" and the transmission closed with the playing of solemn music. Domei, the official Japanese news agency, followed this with a statement. "No one," read the report, "can deny that Roosevelt, as an individual, was one of the greatest statesmen." Premier Suzuki himself made an official expression of "profound sympathy" for the Americans in the loss of their leader who, he said, had "been responsible for America's advantageous position today." This generous tribute to an enemy was, it is true, followed by a declaration that Japan's fight for the "co-prosperity and coexistence of all nations against Anglo–American power politics and world domination" would go on. But the hollow ring of this by now virtually automatic defiance was almost deafening.

In Okinawa, the American Tenth Army had broken into the fiercely defended capital of Naha, where among the Japanese who charged to their deaths in the face of American fire were reported to be civilians carrying spears. When the fighting ended twelve weeks later, 12,250 Americans had died. Of the Japanese garrison, over 120,000 died, many by their own hand rather than become one of the 7000 prisoners counted by the victors.

Tokyo Radio announced that in Japan there were now over three million "disaster victims," homeless, wounded or dead from American round-the-clock bombing. In burning Tokyo, the Emperor's palace stood "a lonely moat-surrounded island in a sea of destruction."

Then, from Europe, the knell of Japan's imminent doom sounded. As Russian troops advanced over the rubble of Berlin's eastern limits, Adolf Hitler took his life in his command bunker, and on the 7th of May, 1945, a few days later, through monitored reports of BBC broadcasts, the first news came to Tokyo of Germany's surrender. In London, Winston Churchill reminded the British people that in the rejoicing over the defeat of the Nazi tyranny they should not forget that "Japan with all her treachery and greed remains unsubdued. The injuries she has inflicted . . . her detestable cruelties, call for justice and retribution." Announcing the victory over Germany to his American compatriots, President Truman, who had succeeded Roosevelt, included a grim reminder to the people and rulers of Japan. "The longer the war lasts, the greater will be the suffering and hardship. . . . Our blows will not cease until the Japanese military and naval forces lay down their arms in unconditional surrender." Japan was alone.

Thirty

General Koiso's most predictable, if not his most obvious, area of failure as premier had been that which had balked all of his predecessors in office, including Hideki Tojo: the problem of doing away with the autonomy exercised by the Japanese supreme command. Yet out of his failure in this, the heavy-footed soldier, most improbably and in a way that he could never have imagined, rendered his greatest service to the nation. Frustrated in his attempts to get himself included in the deliberations of the supreme command, Koiso had initiated a Supreme Council for the Direction of War. The council's six regular members comprised the premier himself, his foreign and services ministers and the army and navy chiefs of staff. Although its aim was modestly set as liaison between the supreme command and the government, the chiefs of the armed forces were compelled for the first time to keep the premier and his ministers, through this body, informed of the progress of the war and their plans to prosecute it. And through the navy minister, Yonai, and Shigemitsu—who had stayed on in the foreign ministry after Tojo's fall—this inner cabinet contained at least two members who were dedicated, if covertly for the moment, to ending the war. More important, the Emperor was now brought directly back as a factor in the balance of power. Special sessions could be convened by him and, if considered necessary, the Imperial presence could be requested at the council's meetings.

On the 6th of June, 1945, the Supreme Council met to consider the army's proposals, set out in two documents, for continuing the war. The mass of statistics they contained confirmed Japan's desperate if not impossible position but was coupled with the usual expressions of determination to fight on for the preservation of the sacred national structure. There was to be no surrender or talk of surrender. Still obsessed with saving face, the army leaders obstinately held onto the idea that even now one victory could turn the tide, and since Okinawa was virtually lost, this could be achieved in the homeland. When the invasion came, the whole nation must rise and fight, if necessary to the death. Every Japanese could, like the heroes of the Russo–Japanese war, become a "human bullet." Civilians, men and women, would fight along with soldiers armed with guns, explosives or, where necessary, bamboo spears, even grappling with their bare hands. They would take such a toll of the invader as to make him recoil.

The still persistent fear of the army and of each other on the part of those who attended the conference—transcending all the consequences for the nation—was summed up later by Admiral Toyoda, chief of naval staff. "No one expressed the view that we should ask for peace," he stated. "When a large number of people are present it is difficult for any one member to say that we should so entreat."

As the decision to carry on the war was communicated to the Emperor at an Imperial Conference on the following day, newspapers and radio told the Japanese people that every able-bodied man, woman, and child would be brought into a "People's Volunteer Corps" to defend their soil. Prepared for nationwide distribution was a "People's Manual of Resistance Combat," with instructions for attacking tanks, dealing with paratroops, hand-to-hand fighting, and coping with flamethrowers.

The official news agency anounced: "The enemy has achieved his first target in the invasion of Japan. Tokyo, Yokohama, Nagoya, Kobe, and Osaka have ceased to exist. The nation must prepare for imminent battle on its own soil." Later in the month, assailed by 2000 plane raids from American carriers that had come to only fifteen-minutes flying distance from the coast, the Japanese were called upon over the radio to "laugh and treat the present attacks as a joke." The enemy was feeling out Japanese defenses and endeavoring to destroy them in detail. But the Japanese air force was "silently accumulating its might to crush the enemy decisively," hence the apparent lack of resistance.

As the nation waited, the terror from the air continued unabated and unopposed. "There was no safe place in the whole archipelago. The enemy even began to announce beforehand a list of towns to be attacked."[1] Day after day in the summer of 1945, B-29s dropped leaflets about six by eight inches in size, printed in blue, and showing on the front a picture of B-29s dropping a shower of incendiaries. "They contained usually the names of some dozen cities which were listed as probable victims of the impending raid. On the back of the leaflets appeared warnings in Japanese captioned "Appeal to the People" which advised the noncombatant population to evacuate for safety. This was a very clever piece of psychological warfare, as people in the affected regions got extremely nervous and lost what faith they still had in the army's ability to defend the mainland. Although the attacks were thus widely advertised, not a single plane engaged the enemy air units."[2]

When the Supreme Council for the Direction of War met in the Imperial presence next day, the 7th of June, Shigenori Togo, who had taken over the foreign ministry from Shigemitsu in the Suzuki government, ventured to point out that Japan's chances of negotiating peace with advantage diminished as her military situation grew more desperate. From the other members there was continued embarrassed reluctance to speak out against the army's plans for the country's future—if, indeed, it could be called a future. Nevertheless, when the formal decision of the Imperial Conference of June 8 was drafted, there was tagged on to the end what represented their own qualifying clause in what otherwise read like a declaration for war to the finish. "It behooves us," it read, "to seize any opportunity that may occur of conducting the war under more favorable circumstances. Suitable measures should be devised that can be actually pursued, for instance in China or in Russia."

The Emperor, who had been compelled to maintain his traditional silence at the Imperial Conference in the absence of any appeal directly to him, now began to make it clear through Kido that he required his ministers to do something positive about bringing the war to an end. The almost unbelievable confusion and irresolution prevailing among them was plumbed by the privy seal as he bustled around a few days after the conference sounding out the prime minister and members of his cabinet. As reported by Mamoru Shigemitsu, Suzuki told Kido, "What can I do? Yonai is very stubborn." Yonai, the navy minister, complained that he could do nothing because "Suzuki is very set in his views."[3] And Togo, the foreign minister, asked querulously what he could be expected to do in view of the Imperial Conference decision not to end the war. All they had to offer was the hope—stillborn, as it happened—that the Soviet government could be persuaded to use its good offices in opening negotiations. At the Yalta Conference Russia had agreed with Britain and the United States to enter the war against Japan within weeks of the end of the European fighting. Unaware of this, foreign minister Togo had made moves through the Soviet ambassador in Toyko and the Japanese ambassador in Moscow. As weeks went by and the Russians were obviously equivocating, it was decided to send Prince Konoye, heading a high level mission, to make a direct appeal to the Soviet leader, Stalin.

The Prince, however, was not to have the opportunity of "laying down his life" as he tearfully assured the Emperor on the eve of his intended departure that he was prepared to do. From Moscow came word that the Russians would do nothing until after a conference of the Allied leaders, Truman, Churchill, Chiang Kai-shek, and Stalin, in Potsdam on July 17. When the conference ended on the 26th of the month, even the chance of China's mediation had gone. The published terms were uncompromising and precluded all notions of a negotiated peace. They called for the "unconditional surrender of all the Japanese armed forces." The alternative for Japan, they stated starkly, "is prompt and utter destruction."

With Premier Suzuki's dismissal of the Allied ultimatum the next day as a rehash of the Cairo declaration that would be ignored, the generals grimly proceeded with preparations for their "decisive battle" to hurl the invaders back into the sea when they landed, as was expected, in the area of the Kwanto plain lying before Tokyo. The nation waited apprehensively, watching the skies but still, like the generals, thinking of the ordeal ahead in terms, appalling enough, of warfare as they had known it. Eleven days later, on the 6th of August, they learned that the threatened destruction would surpass any terror yet heaped on them from the air.

From the early morning, reports began to arrive in the capital that the town of Hiroshima, a few miles from the Inland Sea naval base of Kure, had been obliterated by a single bomb of an "entirely new type." The immediate security clamp down in the early hours after the attack could not long conceal the fact that the people of Hiroshima had been subjected to a holocaust hitherto unimagined. And, in Washington, President Truman revealed that the new weapon had been the first atomic bomb. Japan, he said, now that its leaders had rejected the Potsdam call for unconditional surrender, might expect "a rain of ruin from the air, the like of which has never been seen on this earth."

The historic destruction of Hiroshima almost overshadowed another disaster on the 8th of August when, at long last, Russia gave her reply to the Japanese request that Konoye go to Moscow on his peace mission. Since Japan had turned down the Potsdam terms, Russia had declared war. The next day Nagasaki, in the southern island of Kyushu, was blasted by a second American atom bomb.

For some time, as the bombing mounted, Hideki Tojo had been urging his wife to leave the city with the family. "I have to remain here," he insisted, "since the Emperor may call on me." Mrs. Tojo had always refused to leave. There was strong rumor, allegedly from a statement made by a pilot of one of the raiding U.S. planes which had been shot down, that Tokyo was to be next on the list for atomic attack and Tojo was inclined to believe it. The new bomb, he said, was apparently most effective on flat land bordering the sea and Tokyo was the likeliest target in the future. The thought of giving in was as far from his mind as ever. It was now, he told his wife, a matter of survival. "Our ancestors must have lived in caves at one time," he said. "So can we. The best thing to do is to dig a horizontal hole in a rugged area and come out during the daytime to dig potatoes and get food. If we don't take baths for seven months we aren't going to die and if we can stand it that long, we will win." There was a suitable place at Oume and a man there who would take them in. On the 11th of

August, he had certain of the family belongings moved there in advance.[4]

The Tojo family were not to test out this theory of atomic survival or know the rigors of ancestral cave life. As soon as news had reached Tokyo of the second atomic bombing of Nagasaki, the Supreme Council had been called into emergency session. That night, in a bombproof shelter thirty feet underground in the Imperial Palace, Emperor Hirohito emerged from behind a golden screen in the conference room to receive the reports of his chiefs of staff and ministers. It was soon clear that the conference was deadlocked between the civilian ministers who advocated immediate acceptance of the Potsdam terms on condition that the Emperor's status was assured, and the services ministers and chiefs who protested that they could still repel any attempt actually to invade Japan. Eventually Premier Suzuki rose. Enough time had been taken, he declared, and, for the first time since the war began, the Emperor was asked to decide.

The Emperor spoke at length. To continue the war, he said, would bring utter ruin to the nation. The army said that the war could go on, but there had always been a great discrepancy between what the army had said and what they had performed. Even now, measures which they claimed to have taken for defense of the homeland were, he learned, far short of achievement. The Potsdam declaration should be accepted.

As the Emperor finished speaking, the war minister, General Anami, approached him and knelt on the carpet. In tears, he begged the Emperor to reconsider. "Everyone in the room, with the exception of the Emperor, was weeping. Some were sobbing like children under the impulse of hysterical emotion."[5] The ruler told the prostrate war minister that he understood his feelings but that the Imperial decision could not be changed.

Tojo learned of the acceptance of the Potsdam Declaration at a meeting of the *jushin* called on the 10th of August. At first, as might have been expected, he showed some disposition to argue. Cut short by being reminded that he had been called merely to be advised of the Imperial decision about which there could be no argument, he said that, in that case, there was no help for it. Having no longer any official responsibility, he was more fortunate than the war minister, General Anami. To the war minister, torn between deference to the Imperial will and his own deeply held belief that a Japanese soldier could not surrender, fell the task of explaining to his subordinates that they must now be prepared "to eat stones."

There was among the younger officers, as in the uprising of 1936, a fanatic group ready to raise the cry that the Emperor had been misled by insincere advisers. Parties of these frantically endeavored to get backing for a military takeover, first from General Umezu, the army chief of general staff, and then from Anami himself, to prevent the negotiations now proceeding between the Japanese and American government from being consummated. Both of the generals to whom they excitedly confided their plot for a coup declined to go along with them. Yet even at this critical stage, they felt too much sympathy with the conspirators to denounce them.

There is no evidence that any effort was made to involve Hideki Tojo in the plot or that he was consulted about it, even though his family was to have a tragic link in the affair as it unfolded. On August 13, Major Koga, the husband of Makie, the Tojos' second daughter, made an abrupt and unexpected visit to the house. Grim-faced, he said he wished to speak to his wife privately and went with her and their child into the cellar. Shortly afterward, they returned and he left as suddenly as he had arrived without even pausing to embrace his child, as he had always done before. If he had revealed to his wife, which was unlikely, the venture he was about to engage in, she did not tell her parents. But of its desperate nature and probable outcome he left no doubt. In this last meeting with his wife, Koga confirmed from her that she had clippings of his nails and hair, relics traditionally preserved by Buddhists of close relatives after their deaths.[6]

On the next day, the 14th of August, two young officers, one of them Koga, were admitted to the office of General Mori, the commander of the Imperial Guards Division in his Tokyo headquarters. For some time they argued and pleaded with the general to join them with his troops in a bid to take over the government by force. When Mori refused, the young fanatics shot him and one of his aides down. Using the murdered commander's seal, the mutineers forged an order and with parties of his troops set out for the Imperial Palace.

Somehow the plotters had learned that a formal announcement of surrender had been recorded that night by the Emperor for transmission on the radio the next day, the 15th of August. Detachments of the rebels entered the radio station and the Imperial Palace grounds in search of the recording. Back in his house that night, war minister Anami, as he heard the sound of shooting signaling the start of the coup, penned a last message of apology to the Emperor and, in *samurai* fashion, plunged a short *seppuku* sword into his abdomen. During the long hours of the night as he lay dying, a loyal guards detachment headed by General Tanaka, commander of the Eastern District Army, moved against the insurgents. By eight o'clock in the morning of August 15 the rebels had been persuaded to give up. The recording, hidden in the Empress's quarters in the palace, had not been found and, early that morning, as planes from Admiral Nimitz's force returned to their carriers from a dawn raid on Tokyo, radio listeners were told to tune in for a very special broadcast at midday.

Long before noon, all over the land, people gathered around radio sets at home or loudspeakers set up in factories and schools. And, as the time approached, trains pulled up in stations, traffic came to a halt. In the Tojo household, the general and his wife knelt on the *tatami* matting before the radio set placed in the *tokonoma* recess usually reserved for a display of flower arrangements and the hanging of a *kakemono* scroll. At twelve o'clock, as the strains of the national anthem "*Kimigayo*" solemnly ended, they heard with an awed nation the voice, tremulous and high-pitched, of the Emperor himself. He spoke in the archaic court Japanese which many of his subjects found difficulty in comprehending. Mrs. Tojo recalled that there were some details she did not understand. Her husband, she thought, knew what was coming but had said nothing in advance. The declaration, even in translation, reads enigmatically, but the burden of it was clear enough to her and the millions who listened:

To our good and loyal subjects. After pondering deeply the general trend of the world and the actual conditions obtaining in our Empire today, we have decided to effect a settlement of the present situation by resorting to an extraordinary measure.

We have ordered our Government to communicate to the

Governments of the United States, Britain, China and the Soviet Union that our Empire accepts the provisions of their joint declaration.

To strive for the common prosperity and happiness of all nations as well as the security and well-being of our subjects is the solemn obligation which has been handed down by our Imperial ancestors, and which we lay close to heart. Indeed, we declared war on America and Britain out of our sincere desire to insure Japan's self preservation and the stabilization of East Asia, it being far from our thought either to infringe upon the sovereignty of other nations or to embark upon territorial aggrandizement. But now the war has lasted for nearly four years. In spite of the best that has been done by everyone . . . the war situation has developed not necessarily to Japan's advantage, while the general trends of the world have all turned against her interests. The enemy, moreover, has begun to employ a new and most cruel bomb, the power of which to do damage is indeed incalculable, taking toll of many innocent lives. Should we continue to fight, it would not only result in the ultimate collapse and obliteration of the Japanese nation but would lead also to the total extinction of human civilization. Such being the case, how are we to save the millions of our subjects, or ourselves to atone before the hallowed spirits of our Imperial ancestors? . . .

The hardships and sufferings to which our nation is to be subjected hereafter will certainly be great. We are keenly aware of the inmost feelings of all our subjects. However, it is according to the dictate of time and fate that we have resolved to pave the way for a peace for all the generations to come by enduring the unendurable and suffering what is insufferable.

Having been able to maintain the structure of the Imperial State, we are always with you, our good and loyal subjects, relying upon your sincerity and integrity. Beware most strictly lest any outbursts of emotion which may engender needless complications, or any fraternal contention and strife which may create confusion, lead you astray and cause you to lose the confidence of the world. Let the whole nation continue as one family from generation to generation, ever firm in its faith in the imperishableness of its divine land. . . .

When the broadcast ended, once more to the strains of the national anthem, Tojo said to his wife, "Well, until now, it has been our life for our country. Now the direction has changed. Reconstruction may be more difficult than giving our lives. But if this is the Emperor's will, we must all do everything to achieve it as long as there is a breath of life in us."

"To me," Mrs. Tojo said, "the 15th of August meant blank hours, so empty that I felt I was losing consciousness." About an hour after they had heard the Imperial Rescript, the telephone rang. The call was for Tojo from the war ministry and Tojo, when he had spoken and hung up the telephone, called his daughter Makie. Her husband had killed himself. "His body is being brought here in one hour," he told her. "Prepare yourself."[7]

In the following days, many of the young officers who came to pay their respects to Major Koga at the house spoke to Tojo, arguing that they should not give up without further struggle and asking whether they could not still make a final stand. He listened to them patiently but told them that the Imperial will had been expressed and that, like him, they should accept it. When there were no visitors, he spent much of his time writing. He now began burning what was left of his papers, even address books. "I knew without any word from him," his wife said, "that he was already prepared for death."

The great majority of Japanese who had heard the "voice of the Sacred Crane"[8] returned to their homes or work more or less apathetically. For most the business of daily survival among the devastation would be as grim tomorrow and for many more days to come even, if only in terms of eking out scanty food and clothing rations and having a roof over their heads. For some the release from tension was too great. Hundreds felt impelled to go to their shrines or gather in the streets to lament and pray. In Tokyo, crowds made their way to the plaza in front of the Imperial Palace to bow, some to end their lives there.

Despite the opinion expressed by one officer just before the surrender that "all the army leaders should commit suicide," the number who actually took their lives—although on a scale unthinkable to the western mind—was relatively small. General Anami's suicide was followed by those of other senior officers. General Sugiyama, who had been chief of army general staff under Tojo's premiership and latterly commander of the Eastern Defense Area, shot his wife and then himself; General Tanaka, whose loyal action had prevented the attempted military coup on the eve of the surrender, committed suicide. A few others also killed themselves, among them the commander in chief of the notorious *Kempeitai,* General Shirokura, who thus avoided certain arrest and probably execution at the hands of the Allied victors later.

Reaction among the younger officers was predictably more violent. Scores took their lives. The ringleaders of the attempted mutiny, like Major Koga, had shot themselves after its failure; about a dozen others later gathered on the Yoyogi parade ground and committed mass *hara-kiri*. Another group of armed fanatics assembled on a hill, not far from the Imperial Palace, and, after holding off besieging police and troops for some time, destroyed themselves with grenades.

In the limbo of days and nights which dragged on between the surrender announcement and the setting of the first invaders' feet on their soil, the Japanese, as before in their history, seemed to be reaching back into their past for reassurance and direction. Three quarters of a century earlier, when the Tokugawa military usurpers had been helpless to prevent the coming of the foreigners, the restoration to power of the Emperor Meiji had saved Japan. Now, the divine intervention of Emperor Hirohito had halted the military just as they had brought the nation to the very brink of annihilation. In the press and on the radio, the nation was exhorted to pin all its hopes on the sacred Imperial descendant of a line unbroken for over two thousand years.

"The entire people should know that the only way to set the mind of his August Majesty at rest at this critical moment," the *Asahi* leader writer told them, "is to solidify their unity." In the *Mainichi* they were called upon to "bow their heads low before the Imperial Palace embodying their perennial history." From the palace, "quiet beneath the dark clouds," a radio reporter described the crowd assembled there. "Honored with the Imperial edict, the loyal people are bowed to the ground in front of the Nijubashi. With the words, 'Forgive us, Emperor, our efforts were not enough,' heads bow low and tears run unchecked. Alas, in their shame, how can the people raise their heads? Ever since the 8th of December when we received the Imperial Rescript causing His Majesty deep anxiety . . . ." Here the broadcast suddenly broke off, possibly because the reporter was himself too overcome with emotion to continue.

As a vast armada of American, British, Australian, New Zealand, and Dutch warships anchored in Sagami Bay within sight of Mount Fuji, there was even speculation—with the approach of the typhoon season—that they might yet be scattered by the divine wind, the *kamikaze,* as the fleets of the invading Mongols had been six centuries before. In an edict reminiscent of the Tokugawa's attempt at the time of the coming of Perry's black ships to keep the Japanese insulated from the importunate foreigners, a no-fraternization rule was promulgated in Tokyo. There was to be no direct contact, the Domei news agency announced, between the general public and Allied occupation forces.

There was understandable fear of the advent of vengeance-seeking Allied soldiery and of reprisals for the acts of their own occupying soldiery that could now be visited upon them. Unrest and, in some cases, panic was touched off as rumors swept the country that the Americans and Chinese had already landed. "The Yanks were coming. Their atrocities, people were told, knew no bounds. Seized by a wave of terror, men fled from the cities into the country in order to hide their wives, daughters and family possessions."[9] Uncertain itself what the consequences and character of the Occupation were likely to be, the government tried to reassure the nation. The Allied forces were coming "to see that the terms of the Potsdam declaration were faithfully observed. The sooner the Japanese people convince the Allied powers that these have been carried into effect, the shorter will be the period of occupation. Allied forces will not enforce military administration. The administration of the Japanese people will be carried out by their own government."

Another echo of the past, harking back to the words of the Meiji era statesman Count Hayashi, after the humiliation of the Triple Intervention in 1895, was strongly discernible in other radio and press comment that sought to explain the defeat. "We have lost. But this is only temporary. . . . We have bowed to the enemy's material and scientific power. In spiritual power we have not lost yet." Domei took up the same theme. What had finally brought about the defeat, it reported, "was the enemy's scientific offensive. . . . After the preservation of the glory of our national structure the most important thing is scientific progress."

The nagging worry that more primitive and irrational emotions might still bring irrecoverable disaster was voiced by the Japan *Times,* which warned that the disembarkation of alien armies of occupation on the soil of Japan "may be too much for some of the military officers to bear." In Singapore, General

Itagaki, the veteran conspirator from the Kwangtung Army, now commander of Japanese forces in Malaya, sullenly declared in a radio address that the Imperial army still had "an unchallenged dignity" and was ready to "crush its foe." On the afternoon following the Emperor's surrender broadcast, naval *kamikaze* fliers from the Special Air Attack Corps stationed at Atsugi airfield had swept ominously low over Tokyo scattering leaflets demanding that the Imperial Rescript be ignored. Placards appeared in the capital calling for the deaths of the "Badoglios" who had betrayed the nation.

On the night of the 15th of August, Tokyo radio announced the resignation of Prime Minister Suzuki, whose government had been succeeded by a caretaker cabinet under the premiership of Prince Higashikuni. Other princes of the royal house were dispatched to forces overseas to convey directly the Emperor's order to lay down their arms. At Atsugi airfield, Prince Takamatsu, the Emperor's brother, was engaged in a touch-and-go effort to get the area cleared of fanatic young *kamikaze* pilots. These were still declaring that they would carry out suicide missions against the Allied forward elements whose airborne arrival was expected at the airfield within seventy-two hours. It was not until the 25th that the Prince was able to report that Atsugi was clear.

On the evening of the 29th of August the first planes bearing soldiers of the U.S. 11th Airborne Division touched down at Atsugi. Many of the Americans who emerged watchfully in full combat order from their aircraft confessed later to very natural feelings of apprehension. They were entering the heartland of a people who they had always been told were likely to be desperate and treacherous and who, from their own experience against its fighting men certainly had been. Their fears were unnecessary. Japanese troops guarding the airfield and civilians working there greeted them with smiles and bows and Allied correspondents described their welcome as "obsequious." On the following day 42,000 troops, mostly airborne, occupied Yokohama and Tokyo. General MacArthur's plane arrived at Atsugi on the same day. The General, in rumpled drill uniform and smoking his corncob pipe, paused at the head of the gangway for a brief conquering glance around him and for the benefit of newsreel and still photographers assembled to record the historic moment, before he descended and drove off to his temporary headquarters at Yokohama.

On the 2nd of September, Stalin announced the end of his six-weeks war with Japan. Soviet troops had swiftly overcome the depleted Kwangtung Army and occupied Manchuria and north Korea. "We have a special score to settle with Japan," Stalin declared. "The defeat of 1904 left painful memories in the minds of our people who trusted for the day to come when Japan would be routed and the stain wiped out. For forty years we have waited for this day." Many years later it was to be claimed in Moscow that the United States "had been unable to achieve decisive successes in the war against Japan" but that the Russian intervention "had made it possible for the American troops to land in Japan without firing a single shot."

The Japanese were at least to be spared the division of their land among the victors as had occurred in Germany. The Russians took over southern Sakhalin and the Kurile Islands, but they and the Chinese—whose coming the Japanese dreaded most of all—were excluded from the occupation of the home islands, which was to be, for all purposes, an American one under Mac-Arthur. The British, intent on securing not only their own colonies but those of the French and Dutch as well, had no forces to spare for Japan. Some months later, largely on Australian insistence, a mixed Commonwealth force of British, Indian, Australian, and New Zealand troops arrived in Japan to share in occupation duties.

At dawn on the 2nd of September, Mamoru Shige-mitsu, who had been chosen to head the Japanese delegation to sign the instrument of capitulation, assembled with other members of the party. For all of them it was a painful duty. General Umezu, designated to sign on behalf of the army, had angrily refused when first approached, agreeing to go only on the understanding that he was directly commanded by the Emperor to do so. Bowing in the direction of the Imperial Palace, they set out by car through the desolation of bomb damage which stretched right to Yokohama. There an American destroyer took them out to the American flag-ship, "Missouri," where the ceremony of surrender was enacted in the presence of General MacArthur, the supreme commander of all the allied forces, and attended by naval and military representatives of all the Allied nations.

A few days later, on the 8th of September, General MacArthur, at the head of American troops, led by the 1st U.S. Cavalry Division, formally entered Tokyo and took the salute at a ceremonial raising of the American flag at the U.S. Embassy, where he established his residence. From there, his daily emergence for the short journey to SCAP headquarters set up at the Dai Ichi Building facing the Imperial Palace Plaza and the return trip in the evening, in limousine and attended by a flying column of siren-sounding jeeps and motorcycle outriders, was to take on the appearance and significance almost of a state occasion. Dubbed irreverently "Our Father Which Art in Tokyo" by some of the occupationaires under him and facetiously alleged by others to have been observed at dawn walking on the waters of the palace moat, Douglas MacArthur was referred to rather more aptly by the awed Japanese he had been sent to disarm and democratize. To them he was the "blue-eyed *shogun,*" remote as any Tokugawa. He brought to the Japanese almost exactly the measure of authority and grandeur they required at the time. And, it should not be forgotten, he also brought to his task both competence and compassion. Under his control began one of the smoothest and, on the whole, most beneficial military occupations in history.

Thirty-one

In the days following the arrival of the first occupation forces, Hideki Tojo warned his wife that what he described as "some major development in connection with his person" could be expected. As to the nature of this he only hinted. In the meantime, although he insisted that he must remain in the capital himself, he urged her to join the younger children in Kyushu, where they had been sent. Mrs. Tojo kept a few things packed and ready to go at short notice, but she could not bring herself to leave him.

There can be no doubt that Tojo's instinct, after learning of the decision to surrender, had been to take his life. The Allied leaders had let it be known in their utterances at various times and in unmistakable terms that they proposed to exact retribution from those who had led Japan into the war. Their action after Germany's surrender in hunting down the Nazi leaders who had not destroyed themselves had shown that they were in earnest. As the first minister in the land when Japan went to war, Tojo was in no doubt that he would be high on the Allied wanted list.

One of his first acts had been to ask Dr. Suzuki, a neighbor whose house faced the Tojo residence, to show him exactly where his heart was. So that there could be no error, he went to the extraordinary length of getting the doctor to mark the spot on his chest with *sumi* ink used for brushwork writing "My life doesn't matter," he told his wife. "A military man has always to be ready to die." But was he justified in taking the warrior's way out? If he was not there to take the responsibility, who would the Allied victors call to account? Was it possible that the emperor himself would be held culpable? Almost unthinkable though it might be, the possibility had to be considered. The fact was that there was no assurance that the conquerors would respect the Ruler's divine status. In America and in the Allied countries Emperor Hirohito had been depicted by word and in cartoon as a war criminal. The agonized indecision among Japan's leaders before the Surrender had turned ultimately on the single issue of whether —though all else was lost—the terms of the Potsdam declaration would permit the Imperial house to remain in being. But the Japanese government's submission had been made on the wishful assumption that though there had been no clear assurance it would so remain, the Allies had not specifically stated that it would not.

Tojo seems not to have been the only one apprehensive of the consequences that might follow if he were, by self-elimination, to be unavailable to the Allies for whatever fate they had in mind for him. In early September, Tojo received a message asking him to go to see General Shimomura, who had been recalled from his command in China to replace the former minister of war, General Anami, after the latter's suicide. Shimomura, who had apparently heard rumors that Tojo might also take his life, asked him what his intentions were.

Tojo told him that he wanted to avoid trouble for the Emperor and that he proposed submitting a statement to the Occupation forces commander, General MacArthur, holding that the war had been forced on Japan. He was fully prepared to take the entire responsibility for war himself, but he did not want to be arraigned before a court where, as he said, "the victor judged the conquered." Shimomura told Tojo that, in his opinion, he would serve the Emperor best by saying publicly who had the responsibility for war. Tojo, Shimomura said, should think about this very carefully and, if he had thought of taking his life, to reconsider it.

Tojo could have been excused if he got the idea that Allied victors were themselves subject to some indecision, as almost two weeks passed with no move made against him. He and his wife had expected that they might get some forewarning if one was impending, perhaps through some army colleague still involved in the nation's affairs, "but there was no such warning," Mrs. Tojo recalled, "and so we continued our ordinary lives at home."[1]

There was, in spite of his previous refusal to leave, a possibility that Tojo could be persuaded to go away from the capital. The government was getting concerned about the wild rumors building up about the ex-premier and there was also the risk of an attempt on his life, possibly by an extremist among those who blamed him not so much for the war as for defeat. The ministry of the interior and the police department were, according to Toichiro Takamatsu, a journalist with *Mainichi* newspaper, planning to get Tojo quietly away from Tokyo.

It was realized that to do this officially would almost inevitably increase the kind of speculation they were anxious to avoid, attracting the attention of newsmen alert for any move concerning him. The scheme, therefore, was to arrange with officers of the Domei government news agency to have the general picked up by one of the agency's cars. In this he was to be taken to the Ueno railway station in the suburbs of Tokyo. There, with a ticket already provided for him, he would board the train incognito and travel to his wife's family home in Kyushu.

The plan was dropped when the first visitation from Allied personnel, indicating that the Occupation authorities were now ready to take action, made it clear that the time had passed when the Japanese government was to have any say in the disposal of Tojo's person. The initial call on him on the 10th of September was, in fact, made by a number of news correspondents who made their way with an interpreter to the Tojo residence by taxi.

The meeting for both the newsmen and Tojo himself was, if anything, anticlimatic. The general, inflated by repute and legend into someone approaching a latter-day Genghis Khan, appeared to the interviewers to be unimpressive and mild-mannered. Wearing shorts and, as Mrs. Tojo described him, "burned black" from working in their vegetable plot, Tojo sat down with the correspondents on some ceramic garden seats outside and offered them cigarettes. He smoked throughout the interview himself, using his customary holder, and the correspondents detected that he was nervous under his apparent self-possession.

"As one retired from government and as a defeated

general," he told them, "I cannot answer questions about politics or the war. I am just a farmer now. But I believe that Japan's war was a just one although I know your country would not accept that. History will decide who is right. As for me, I accept full responsibility for the war." He did not agree that he was, therefore, a war criminal, but being a war criminal, he implied, depended on whether you were on the winning side or not.

It is likely that Tojo realized that the newspapermen's visit was the prelude to the "major development" he had been expecting. He had already, a couple of days before, written his personal will. In it he asked that his funeral should be held not in Tokyo but in Kyushu. But if his body were to be required by the Japanese government "to be delivered to the enemy," this was to be accepted. Now, on the night of the 10th of September, he sat in his study and, taking up his writing brush, began to set down what he intended to be his last testament. He offered his deepest apologies to the Emperor for the inglorious conclusion of the war. His death, he explained, was to atone for his own part as a responsible person for the dishonor of defeat and for those who had died. "Looking towards the Imperial Palace from afar, I pray for the health and long life of His Imperial Majesty," he ended. "I am determined to devote the life of my spirit to the protection of the welfare and prosperity of the nation."[2]

The next day the Tojos had finished lunch and, as the general went to his study, Mrs. Shikata, wife of a former *Kempeitai* commander, called on them bringing some *ohagi* (Japanese sweetcakes). Mrs. Tojo placed them as an offering at their small shrine for the household deities, intending later to exercise the traditional and practical right to have them for tea. Then, in her own words, "it happened."

"A policeman came and said there was a disturbance outside. I went to the study where my husband was sitting writing something with a brush and he told me to leave right away." This time, Mrs. Tojo did not argue. Calling the maid to go with her and picking up her handbag and a broadbrimmed straw gardening hat, she looked in on Tojo before she left. "Take care of yourself," she told him, "and be calm. . . ."

"There was a person called Hatakeyama-san, a former policeman, whom Tojo knew personally and who used to come to our home almost every day. There was also a military policeman called Kakiuchi-san. They were in the house as I left my husband. I asked them to look after him. From what they told me later Tojo told them to leave, and he locked the door after them."

Mrs. Tojo went out by the rear entrance and detoured around, taking a side road past the house. As she did so, she saw there were four or five vehicles in front of it. This, she realized, "was no ordinary thing." As the commotion increased, she felt she could not leave without knowing what was happening. "I circled around to Suzuki-san's rear gate and asked if I could go into their front patch of ground for a time. They said, 'of course,' and I put on my gardening hat, took a weeding scythe and basket and went to the corner of Suzuki-san's field which was just in front of our gate. I wanted to see as much as possible to be able to tell our children in Kyushu about it. I wore *mompei* [peasant type trousers] and knelt in the field. While I pretended to be weeding, I kept an eye on our house from under the hat. Then several jeeps came and many soldiers—I believe they were military police—got off and I saw them surround that portion around the living room.

"My husband opened the south window and asked the people who had gathered whether any of them understood Japanese. One came forward. Tojo asked him who they were and what was their purpose and status. He told my husband they had arrived to take him away. Tojo inquired whether they had an arrest warrant and they told him they had a *renkojo* [warrant] to take him away. He was smiling but it seemed to me that he was inwardly strained. After talking for a while to the people outside, there was the sound of a window closing and then in about the time it takes to walk three meters, there was the sound of a pistol shot. I heard that sound as I knelt in the garden across the street. I said to myself, at this moment my husband must be suffering greatly. I clasped my hands in prayer. I learned later from Hatakeyama-san what had happened inside the house.

"As soon as the shot sounded, the MPs forced the door open, kicked in the door of the study room. Tojo was sprawled in his chair as if he was looking toward the palace. His coat was hanging so it would not be soiled. He was shot in the position of his heart.

"Hatakeyama-san went to him. Cold sweat was pouring from Tojo's forehead and blood flowed from his chest. The pistol had dropped. Hatakeyama-san called to him and Tojo asked for some water. Hatakeyama-san immediately went to the kitchen and brought a cup of water. Tojo drank it and asked for another. Hatakeyama-san hastened to bring another from the kitchen. This time one of the Americans pulled it away, motioning that this was no good. Then they hastened to call a doctor. I saw a jeep rush away. I learned later it brought back the director of the Ebara Hospital.

"After some time, Mrs. Suzuki came to me and said she thought that the police might come to search their place. I thought I should not cause an additional burden on her so I left immediately for our relatives' house at Tsurumaki."[3]

"We want this bastard alive," an officer of the arresting party was quoted as saying by a western correspondent who wrote later that he would not have believed it possible for a man to bleed as much as Tojo and still live.[4]

The Japanese doctor, instructed by the arresting officer through the interpreter—"Tell him he's under orders to save the guy's life"[5]—had dressed the wound but declared Tojo's condition was hopeless. The near pandemonium that reigned in the room with cameramen and newsmen jostling to get pictures of the supposedly dying man and get some last words from him was described by one of them, in what would appear to be an outstanding piece of understatement, as "lacking in dignity." To a Japanese journalist there who was acting as interpreter, Tojo was alleged to have gasped, "Tell MacArthur I do not want my body to be put on show. Tell him to treat me as a soldier."[6]

It was undoubtedly the supreme irony of Hideki Tojo's life that his attempt to end it was thwarted by the action of an American army doctor who arrived with an ambulance about an hour later and administered a transfusion of American blood. While he was being summoned, some of the newsmen and members of the arresting party moved the apparently dying general from the chair where they had found him. When Captain Johnson, the army doctor, got to the house, Tojo was stretched on a bed in the study and covered with a *futon* quilt.

Ignoring the Japanese doctor's opinion and ignoring

also the patient's plea that he should be allowed to die, Johnson made a routine examination. Conscientiously observing a doctor's professional responsibility to do everything possible to save a life no matter whose and however hopeless it might appear, Johnson administered a blood transfusion and a shot of morphine. In a relatively short space of time, as the transfusion began to take effect, it appeared that the general would probably be able to survive a journey to a hospital. With his wound re-dressed, he was taken by ambulance to the one set up by the American army in Yokohama. There, further transfusions and penicillin drugs were given him. Some anxious hours passed with almost as much thought given to preventing Tojo from trying again—he was still protesting that he should be allowed to die—as to saving him from succumbing to his injury. But soon it was obvious that Hideki Tojo was going to live—at least, for as long as his captors decided.

Criticism of Tojo had begun, muted though it was, after the fall of Saipan. Now it broke into full cry. "Japan needed a scapegoat," Hessell Tiltman, the veteran Far Eastern correspondent, observed, "and General Tojo was the obvious choice for that role." Tiltman recalled that after the surrender, it was common in some quarters to refer to the ex-premier as "Idiot Tojo." He was satirized in a play at a Tokyo theater in which, in one sequence, an aide reported to Tojo that seventeen Japanese warships had been lost. " 'Alter that to seventeen American warships sunk and issue a victory communiqué immediately,' ordered the stage Tojo."[7] Letters from all over Japan reached Mrs. Tojo, some condoling with her, but many vindictive, like one that offered to send coffins for the entire Tojo family and inviting her and her children "to crawl in them and die."[8]

A leading Japanese lawyer later declared that he had refused to defend the General at his trial because, he said, "Tojo was personally responsible for the war." Nor did the outcry stop at criticism of his wartime leadership. Accusations of corruption were raised, alleging that he and his family had received favors from industrialists, a calumny disproved by official inquiry after the war.

Later he was even to be accused of being far from the austere personality and dedicated family man he had always appeared to be. A writer, Shiro Ozaki, in his published memoirs, wrote that General Tojo in 1944, when the war had taken a desperate turn for the nation, had found consolation in dalliance with a well-known Japanese danseuse with whom he kept discreet assignations at the Sagano, a Tokyo restaurant. The story was indignantly denounced as a lie by the madame of the Sagano when Mrs. Tojo brought it to her attention, and the former probably spoke no more than the simple truth when she declared that Tojo was "just not that kind of man."[9]

There was, further, not unexpected scornful comment on Tojo's desperate last-minute attempt to escape arrest and trial. To many of his own countrymen, no less than the Allied newsmen whose own reporting on the suicide attempt often took a cynical line, he stood condemned as a double failure: as a war leader and now, as a man who could not even accomplish his own death without bungling it. The American wife of a Japanese foreign office man, who had lived in Japan throughout the war, wrote of him that "he was despised for having failed at suicide, thus permitting the Americans to nurse him tenderly back to health to stand public trial. There was a saying, expressive of the people's resentment at such awkwardness: 'Going to be another Tojo, not even able to kill yourself?' "[10]

Kimpei Sheba, the managing editor of the *Nippon Times,* confessed that he was one of those Japanese who had been strongly convinced that Tojo had faked it. Having suffered the attentions of the *Kempeitai* and been held for a period in solitary confinement on suspicion of being pro-American, Sheba was no admirer of the general and began to change his mind only when he interviewed Tojo after the suicide attempt. He learned afterwards, he wrote, "that the bullet lodged a hair's breadth from his heart, too close for anyone to have pretended he was trying to commit suicide."[11] Tokisaburo Shiobara, one of the Japanese lawyers who served as a defense counsel at the International Military Tribunal, held that the general had missed his heart because the mark placed there had been smeared by perspiration.

The fact is that the wound was a grave one and Tojo would indubitably have died but for the prompt and skillful treatment by Captain Johnson. That it was not instantly fatal was apparently due to the angle at which the bullet pierced him. For this, Mrs. Tojo had an explanation. Her husband was, she said, "if anything, left-handed. He would hold a hammer, tennis racket and other things with his left hand. I don't know which hand he held the pistol in but from his usual habit, I believe it was his left hand. Because he tried to hit his heart on the left side with his left hand, the bullet entered below and missed it."

Some of the criticism directed against Tojo was to the effect that his suicide attempt was the panic action of one who had been procrastinating and who, it was implied, had not really made up his mind to kill himself. The clue to the truth here lies, perhaps, in his own reported words later. "I wanted to kill myself with the sword," he said, "but the revolver prevailed."

His early talk with Dr. Suzuki, his neighbor, certainly indicated that he proposed to shoot himself, and in the cupboard of his room was what has been described as a small armory of pistols. The one he had fired, an American 38-caliber service revolver, probably originally taken from a captured American airman, had also been used by his son-in-law, Major Koga, to shoot himself after the failure of the last-minute coup before the surrender, and had been passed to the Tojo family after his death with other relics. But Tojo had also ready in the house, in the shape of two swords, the instruments of a death by *hara-kiri* which he would have considered more fitting for one proud of *samurai* descent and imbued as he was with the warrior tradition.

Mrs. Tojo assumed, without ever discussing it with him, that this would be his way. On her hurried departure from the house, almost the last thing she had noticed was the short sword in its plain wooden scabbard and the long *samurai* sword in the living room, and she recalled thinking that "for any time and any occasion his death equipment was ready." His wife certainly believed that his decision for death was made and irrevocable. But he would not, she said, have "chosen death immediately" if the Americans had notified the Japanese government that he should present himself and be delivered over to them "with all the formalities." He would have gone, she held, because he knew he had a duty to put the record straight as far as his own part, his country, and his Emperor were concerned.[12]

The truth appears to be—and it would have been typical of his methodical mind—that he had decided to take his life in any case to expiate his failure. He was prepared to defer this while there was a chance that he might have an opportunity to exonerate the Emperor from any blame in the war and to justify Japan's decision to fight. This done, he intended to die at a time of his own choosing and by *hara-kiri*. Another and almost quite separate intention to kill himself had been taken, as it were, on a different level. He was determined not to submit to humiliation and arrest as a war criminal and had even, reportedly, expressed fear of being "sent to Washington in a cage."

Death by revolver, planned even to the extent of having the position of his heart marked, was to be an emergency measure against a sudden seizure of him that precluded the ritual of disembowelment, probably the most agonizing and complicated method of self-destruction ever devised by man. Properly conducted, it requires the presence of another to ensure that the ritual is observed, to stand by to give the *coup de grâce* if called upon, and, at the end, formally to report its execution. The apprehension of violent seizure, looming large immediately after the surrender, seems to have lessened as time went on with no move made against him. Then the unceremonious descent of an arresting party on the 11th, complete, or so it appeared, with a noisy circus of cameramen, journalists, and spectators, had decided the manner of his attempted demise.

"I had occasion to talk to my husband about this later at Sugamo Prison," Mrs. Tojo said, "and it is my feeling that it was because the American MPs came without warning. I can understand from his nature that he could not agree to them trying to remove a Japanese general by force. He told me that it was the military code that one's life must be taken if one is about to become a prisoner. So, while feeling regret that he could not carry out his responsibility, he chose death."[13]

Through that night, at the home of relatives, she knelt in lonely and silent communion before the picture of her husband, mourning him as dead. It was not until the next morning that she learned from the radio that he had lived, and her first reaction was one of sadness. "At the time I thought—how tragic for him. He would have been better off if someone had given him poison or somehow allowed him to die."[14]

Thirty-two

In a remarkably short period of time, considering how near he had been to death, Tojo recovered sufficiently to leave the hospital and, after a brief incarceration in the former allied prisoner-of-war camp at Omori, he was transfered to Sugamo Prison on the 8th of December 1945. There he found himself in the company of familiar faces. His name had been one of several on a list of those ordered to be arrested as war criminals on the 11th of September, and since then the net had been cast wider. Among those with whom he queued for food and took his turn with the prison chores were Marquis Kido, the former privy seal; Araki, the ultranationalist general and "Imperial Way" advocate; Generals Doihara and Itagaki, the Kwangtung conspirators; General Matsui, whose troops had been responsible for the Nanking massacre; General Umezu and Mamoru Shigemitsu who, a few weeks before, had both signed the instrument of surrender on the "Missouri"; Matsuoka, the former foreign minister who had led his country out of the League of Nations and into the Axis Pact. Among them, too, was Dr. Shumei Okawa, the eccentric co-founder of the Cherry Society, resuming in prison his old acquaintance with Colonel Hashimoto, the propagandist and plotter and perpetrator of the attacks on the British and American gunboats on the Yangtze in 1938. Hoshino and other members of Tojo's wartime cabinet, including the faithful Admiral Shimada, had been taken in. Former premiers were well represented, among them Hiranuma and Hirota, who had headed governments just before the war, and General Koiso, who had taken over after Tojo was ousted in 1944.

Of those whose names had been on the list of war criminals but who had put themselves beyond the reach of the allied victors, Prince Konoye was the most notable. The prince, on the 16th of December, the day on which he had been ordered to report to Sugamo Prison, took poison and died, a copy of Oscar Wilde's "De Profundis" and a farewell note at his side. He could not, he wrote, "stand the humiliation of being apprehended and tried by an American court. . . . It is a matter of regret to be named as a war criminal by the United States, with which I have tried to work together for a peaceful solution of Pacific affairs. . . . World public opinion, which is at present full of overexcitement . . . will in time recover calmness and balance. Only then will a just verdict be given at the Court of God." Outside Japan, in the former occupied territories, hundreds more major and minor figures were being rounded up. In Manila General Yamashita, the "Tiger of Malaya" and conqueror of the Philippines, was in the same prison with General Homma, also awaiting trial.

Mrs. Tojo came back from Kyushu and made her first visit to her husband in February 1946, seeing him for the first time since she had hurriedly left the house in September. He appeared cheerful although, as she told it, the war-criminal prisoners suffered from "harsh treatment and poor food" and were handled "discourteously and with contempt" until the Tribunal proceedings opened.[1] It appears that there had been some attempt in the initial stages of their confinement at Omori to give the prisoners a taste of the same kind of treatment in terms of convenience, bedding, and food which had been the lot of the Allied prisoners there. Apparently, there was also, on occasion, brusqueness and over-conscientious attention by the American guards to ensure that their prisoners abided by prison rules, particularly those designed to prevent any attempts at suicide. These latter particularly irritated Tojo since he had now decided to endure the trial, not with any hope of saving his life but in order to expound publicly his own and his country's point of view and to take the entire blame himself. What is certain, however, is that the imprisoned men were not subject to anything like the "severe floggings, deprivation, and sadistic forms of torture,"[2] related by former Allied prisoners of war who had, not long before, been inmates of Omori and other camps in Japan.

When the war criminals were moved to Sugamo Prison, their lot in material terms might well have been envied by tens of thousands of their countrymen who were living through a distressing lack of almost everything—housing, food, and clothing—in the aftermath of defeat. And when the indictments against the defendants were finally ready and the International Military Tribunal for the Far East opened its proceedings on the 3rd of May in the hall of the former Tokyo military academy, the appointment of Lieutenant Colonel Kenworthy as commander of the detachment of military police at the court (and described by Mrs. Tojo as "a splendid gentleman"), led to further alleviation.

"As soon as they started going to the tribunal," Mrs. Tojo said, "they had the same lunch as the lawyers and others. And since the tribunal did not open until one o'clock and they had free time until then, Kenworthy-*san* said he would permit members of their families to visit the twenty-eight men during that time if they wanted and he would take the responsibility for any trouble. But the Japanese got together and said it would impose a heavy burden on the guards if the families visited the men without restrictions. They voluntarily agreed to limit the visits to two a week with not more than three members of the family visiting at any one time. This made us happier than anything and I felt a big debt of gratitude to him. My husband said I should come every time and have the children alternate and so I went to see him twice a week."[3]

On one of these visits she asked Tojo whether she should accept a gift of 10,000 yen (about $100 at the current official rate of exchange) from the president of a newspaper company, a Mr. Konosuke Oishi, who had previously assisted the family to get down to Kyushu. "The General has taken responsibility for all of us," Oishi had told her, "but this puts a great burden on you." He proposed to make this sum available to the family every month. Tojo told her to accept it. He had personally seen the privation caused by runaway inflation in Germany after World War I and was grateful and relieved that his family was not being left entirely unaided now that Japan was similarly afflicted.[4]

Kenworthy, who had come to Tokyo from Manila, where he had been profoundly impressed by the courage and general demeanor of General Yamashita who had been in his charge there, appears to have become genuinely attached to Hideki Tojo, and in an article contributed by him to the Japanese periodical *Bungei Shunji,* as re-translated from Japanese back into English, he appears also to have come to admire him greatly. "From the moment I caught the first glimpse of the famous General Tojo through the barred window of Sugamo Prison," ran the article, "I never once had the feeling that I was his guardian and he my prisoner. It was rather a relation between teacher and pupil. Needless to say, he was the teacher and I the pupil. . . . I learned from General Tojo forbearance. . . . the virtue of tolerance. . . . General Tojo had become the leader of Sugamo Prison, who gave inspiration not only to his fellow prisoners but also to us whom the irony of worldly fate had placed into the position of his guardians."[5]

The tribunal set up to try Tojo as a war criminal was understandably more detached in its attitude, although it contained its dissenters, notably Justice Pal of India, who was against the whole concept of singling out individuals to stand trial for their country's lost war. In this he was at distinct variance with Joseph Keenan, the Chief of Prosecuting Counsel.

Keenan, whose career had started as a criminal lawyer and who had subsequently served as a government attorney, held from the start that the official positions held by the defendants in no way excused them from the crimes committed by their countrymen whether as individuals or as a group. Later in the trial, the chief prosecutor spelled it out more bluntly when he told the court, "These long proceedings were always intended to be more than a mere trial of individuals."

The first day of the tribunal's hearings, May 3, 1946, was well attended and was enlivened by the activities of Dr. Okawa. Unlike the remainder of the defendants who sat quietly and impassively in their collective dock, he fidgeted and muttered and had constantly to be restrained by the military police. Finally, the doctor capped his performance by leaning over and smacking the bald head of Tojo, who sat directly in front of and below him. As the General smiled mirthlessly at the unexpected assault,

Okawa was taken away. Prolonged psychiatric and medical examination afterward confirmed what might easily have been suspected of him for many years, that the doctor was mad. Declared unfit to stand trial, he was removed to a mental institution where he ended his days.

Thereafter, even the efforts of the chief prosecutor, Joseph Keenan, could inject little animation into the trial. His hectoring manner and delivery, strongly reminiscent of an American courtroom movie of the 1930s, was consistently anticlimaxed by the necessity for translation and by the flat, unemotional voices of the interpreters as they intoned their versions of the questions and replies. Forensic cut-and-thrust was confined almost entirely to bouts involving the chief prosecutor and Sir William Webb, the president of the tribunal, between whom a mutual antipathy was evident from the start. Evident, too, were the unfortunate occasions when Keenan's naturally florid complexion was flushed more than usual and when he might charitably have been described as being unfit to be in court.

In his interrogation of Tojo, he heavy-handedly made the point that he would not address him by his military rank of general because the Japanese army "no longer existed." Tojo most certainly gained in dignity in his various passages with the chief prosecutor, appearing at times, in comparison with his interrogator, to be a sympathetic and even impressive figure. On one occasion, at least, when Keenan was apparently endeavoring to elicit an admission from Tojo that Japanese institutions were much better under Allied Occupation rule, the General caused considerable amusement in the court at Keenan's expense by reminding him that since he, Tojo, had been imprisoned by the Allies for two years, he was in no position to comment.

Tojo's attitude appears to have been that the whole was a tedious charade. His underlying feeling, a weary wish that it should all be over with as soon as possible, was caught when, during a particularly tedious passage of cross-examination one day, a groan of frustration was picked up by the microphone in front of him and amplified all over the courtroom.

There is no record that Tojo ever complained that his trial had been unfair except on the general grounds that it was an entirely unprecedented one of loser by winner with no basis in international law. The Allied supreme commander, General Douglas MacArthur, later personally disclaimed that he had enough wisdom to weigh the principles involved in the tribunal's attempt to lay down standards of international morality required of a nation's leaders, the definition of which, he commented, might elude man until the end of time. No human decision was infallible but, he added of the trial, "I can conceive of no judicial process where greater safeguard was made to evolve justice."

Some years later, however, various of the Japanese defense attorneys claimed in interviews published in the magazine *Nippon Shuho* that the defense had been severely handicapped. About 80 per cent of the evidence they submitted favorable to the accused, they held, had been refused admission. More damaging was lack of money, and but for this none of the men on trial, they insisted, would have been hanged.

They had attempted, they revealed, to raise the sum of 10,000,000 yen (about $100,000) from the postwar government led by Premier Shidehara, and negotiations to get it had broken down when the government fell. Other attempts to get finance from publishing and industrial circles had met with no response. It was intended that some of this money should be spent on getting "better relations with the press, American counsel, the prosecution, and the judges." An idea of what was in mind was given in portions of the interviews republished in the *Nippon Times* of May 7, 1956.

The press had proved unfriendly to the accused initially, the lawyers recalled, "but after the Japanese counsel had drunk and eaten with the reporters as often as possible," things improved. And to get on better terms with the prosecutors and judges the attorneys made "an oblique approach—giving presents [Japanese fans] to their female secretaries." One of the attorneys commented that this had proved "quite effective."

The Japanese public, to whom the proceedings of the tribunal were open so that they might see and hear the misdeeds of their leaders unfolded and witness western democratic justice in action, soon ceased to attend in any large numbers. There was, at most, only a perfunctory interest in a trial the result of which was generally considered by them to be a foregone conclusion. As one month followed another few people, Japanese or western, bothered to come at all.

Interest revived on the day that the shrunken figure of the sixty-three-year-old Hideki Tojo took the stand at last—on the 28th of December, 1947. For many Japanese this was the man to blame, if not for leading them into war, then for losing it and for the purgatory of defeat now on them. Compared with the Nuremburg trials of the Nazi war criminals with its cast of well-known characters, the Japanese villains of the Tokyo trial were, for westerners, anonymous figures. The faces, foibles, and malevolence of Hitler, Goebbels, Ribbentrop, Goering, and Streicher had been familiar for years before the war. But it was not until 1940 that the emergence of the hitherto unknown "Razor" Tojo had given propagandists and cartoonists an identifiable figure to add to the Mikado image of Emperor Hirohito and the caricatured versions of the rapacious, buck-toothed, bespectacled Japanese soldier which had served until then to represent the Asian aggressor.

To many, including the president of the tribunal, the absence of the Emperor's name from the list of Japanese war criminals was a matter for comment and criticism. This course was alleged to have been opposed by General MacArthur who, it was reported, held that a million more occupation troops would have been required if there had been any attempt to bring Emperor Hirohito to trial. Keenan, the chief prosecutor, characterizing the ruler as a "weak character but always on the side of peace," had wanted to summon the Emperor as a witness at the trial. It was the British, he declared, who had maintained that "such a thing was intolerable as they had a king of their own."

"MacArthur needed the Emperor untried and un-reviled," wrote David Bergamin in *Life* magazine. "The American and the British public needed culprits to punish for the horrors of the Bataan death march and of the Burma–Thailand railway." And the fact that the full truth cannot be told twenty years later, he added, "testifies to the violence that was done to truth at that time."[6] Nevertheless, in the person of General Tojo, the Japanese soldier had been brought to book. And this, probably to the very great majority of western spectators and newsmen who crowded the wooden benches of the court and to most of their compatriots back home, was what the trial was really about.

Much of Tojo's time in Sugamo had been devoted, in consultation with his American and Japanese defense counsels, to preparation for this day. Now his statement, as read by them, took a marathon four days and, with the tribunal recessed for the Christmas holidays, was not concluded until the 31st of December.

He made it clear that he proposed to call no witnesses and that he assumed all responsibility for Japan's decision to go to war while he was prime minister. Before his appointment he had taken no part in politics and held, consequently, that he had nothing to defend prior to it. He denied that he ever been part of any "criminal, military clique" which his defense counsel, Mr. Kiyose, insisted—almost entirely truthfully as far as Tojo was concerned—had existed only in the imagination of the Allied powers.

Far from being the culmination of a long conspiracy by the Japanese, the decision for war had been provoked, Tojo said, by Britain and America. They had, he argued, waged cold war against Japan all through the 1930s. By economic sanctions and by aid to China they had brought Japan "to the point of annihilation." Their action in freezing Japanese assets in July 1941 had created a situation for Japan "fatally involving our national defense." And finally there had been an ultimatum, whether it had been called one or not, delivered for Japan to give up in China the results of ten years of struggle to save Asia from Communism. Japan's policy, in his opinion had been one of "neither aggression nor exploitation."

Japan had tried to fight the war honorably and though he regretted that the declaration of war had not been served on the Americans until after the assault on Pearl Harbor, it had not been intended to be a "sneak attack." He accepted that he had a certain, but not the entire, responsibility in his official capacity for the treatment of Allied prisoners of war. Here again there had been no intention of cruel behavior or inhumane acts. It was unfortunate that standards which a Japanese soldier would not find unbearable had apparently proved to be inadequate for western prisoners. Other hardships had been the result of shortages of food, materials, and transportation. Reports of sickness and deaths among prisoners had, when they reached him, been passed on to the Prisoner of War Bureau. But his personal power to prevent abuses or even to know of them had been limited because Japanese commanders in the field had complete discretion to carry out their operational tasks in wartime.

Unlike Marquis Kido who, in his defense, sought to put the responsibility on the military leaders, on Matsuoka, on Tojo, and according to the prosecution, on the Emperor himself, Tojo went to some lengths to claim that he alone should shoulder the blame. Much of his testimony was dedicated to absolving the Emperor who, he declared, "had no free choice in the governmental structure." Although the ruler might express his "hopes and wishes" through his privy seal, he was not able to reject the recommendations of his cabinet and the high command. "Accordingly, full responsibility for the decision of the 1st of December, 1941, to go to war" was theirs and not the Emperor's. Later, under cross-examination by Keenan, he said that he believed that the Emperor had been told of the "general outline" of the Pearl Harbor attack, but not by him. Emperor Hirohito's own benevolence, although not fully understood by Tojo himself and others serving him, Tojo held to be boundless and unquestionable. As an example of it, he cited the case of the Doolittle fliers captured in the 1942 raid on Tokyo. Although eight had received the death sentence because of "atrocities they committed in violation of international law" in bombing civilians including school children, the Emperor, on Tojo's recommendation, had intervened to reduce the number to be executed from eight to three.

Chief Prosecutor Joseph Keenan was almost immediately at issue again with the president of the tribunal, Sir William Webb, when the latter disallowed his opening question in the cross-examination of the prisoner, which began on December 31, 1947. Was Tojo, Keenan had proposed to demand, presenting his affidavit as a profession of innocence or was it intended "as a continuation of imperialistic militaristic propaganda addressed to the people of Japan?" To this, the general might, had the question been permitted, have retorted that the matter of his innocence appeared to him to be academic; but in the second part of his question the chief prosecutor had, in fact, a small part of a point in insinuating that Tojo's statement was addressed not so much to the court as to his own countrymen.

Foreign correspondents covering the trial in Tokyo

had noted that from the time that Tojo took the witness stand there had been a strongly discernible tide of feeling among the Japanese people in his favor and away from the condemnation and abuse to which he was subjected at the time of his suicide attempt. In his steadfast insistence that all the guilt should be put on him, they could now shed some of their own. "There can be little doubt," the correspondent of the London *Times* wrote, "that Tojo's defence of Japan's part in the Pacific war had created a deep impression here. Japanese newspapers have devoted all their available space to printing his testimony under headlines strongly reminiscent of Japan's war-time propaganda, such as 'War of De-fence Forced on Us,' and 'Japan's Tragedy,' and 'Emperor Not Responsible.' While many newspapers in their leading articles have expressed their disapproval of Tojo's assertions which, they say, show he is 'unmoved by remorse,' it is generally believed that he has been successful in freeing the Japanese people from any feeling of war-guilt and restoring to them much of their lost pride."[7]

Outside of the tribunal building after the hearings, a young Japanese widow who had lost her husband in New Guinea said, "He is *Boku-no-Tojo,* again," referring to the song, "Our Tojo," popular early in the war. A white-collar office worker of the type the Japanese call a "salary-man" observed, "Tojo made big mistakes in the war, I think, but he is an honest man. He isn't afraid to say what he thinks is true even now." Another member of the public said, "As a soldier, I suppose he couldn't do anything else but fight if he was forced to." A student, asked what he thought of Tojo's responsibility for the treatment and deaths of Allied prisoners of war, said, "After all, he's a soldier and he is your prisoner, but you are going to kill him."

This argument, although in this case casuistic, did voice the acceptance on the part of the Japanese that Tojo was doomed to die regardless of issues of guilt or innocence or even of the victors' desire to exact retribution from their enemy now that they had him at their mercy. It was, the general feeling seemed to be among them, not only inevitable but even appropriate that Gen-eral Tojo should die.

For himself, Tojo summed up what he considered to be the essential futility and injustice of it all. "Never at any time," he declared, "did I conceive that the waging of this war would or could be challenged by the victors as an international crime, or that regularly constituted officials of the vanquished nations would be charged individually as criminals under any recognized international law or under alleged violations of treaties between nations. . . . I feel," his testimony ended, "that I did no wrong. I feel I did what was right and true."

Thirty-three

Seven months were to elapse after the closing of the hearings and the final delivery of the tribunal's judgment, which took place between the 4th and the 11th of November, 1948. Other faces were missing besides that of Dr. Okawa when the defendants quietly filed into the dock again. While the trial had been in progress, the voluable and erratic Matsuoka had died; so had Admiral Nagano, whose preoccupation with the Imperial navy's need for oil had led him to decide for what he had described as the surgery of war. In the courtroom, crowded again for this final act of the long-drawn-out presentation, the findings were read by a team of thirty-five Japanese and Allied interpreters.

The Manchurian conquest and the war against China, the tribunal found, had been instigated by the Japanese militarists and deliberately provoked by the Japanese government. Through the mastery of the army over the government, Japan had embarked on a program of aggrandizement by military power. The people and the Emperor were, in effect, found not guilty. The army had assumed "such power that no individual or group was in a position to oppose its policies and actions" and the army leaders had deliberately lied to the Emperor.

Japan had negotiated with the United States "solely for the purpose of furthering her own aims in conjunction with those of Germany and Italy." A verdict of guilty was delivered posthumously on Prince Konoye for signature of the Tripartite Pact with the Axis powers and for being a chief protagonist of the plot to seize "all territory between Eastern India and Burma on the one hand and Australia and New Zealand on the other." He and Marquis Kido were judged among those primarily responsible for the setting up of a totalitarian state.

Generals Araki, Hata, Koiso, and Umezu, Marquis Kido, Admiral Shimada, and Colonel Hashimoto were among sixteen of the accused sentenced to life imprisonment. Shigenori Togo, foreign minister under Tojo, was given twenty years. Mamoru Shigemitsu was sentenced to seven years imprisonment for taking part in, though not conspiring to wage, aggressive war and for failing to have the ill-treatment of war prisoners investigated. The comparative mildness of the ex-diplomat's term was justified in that, with the military in full control, "great resolution" would have been required of any Japanese to oppose them.

Generals Doihara, Itagaki, Kimura, and Muto were sentenced to death for conspiracy to wage aggressive war, crimes against peace, and responsibility for atrocities against prisoners of war and civilians, thus sharing the same fate under the same indictment as Generals Yamashita and Homma who had already been tried and hanged in Manila. Death was decreed for General Matsui for failing to prevent the "wholesale massacres, individual murders, rape, looting and arson" carried out by his soldiers in Nanking. Koki Hirota, found more culpable than Hiranuma, his fellow ex-premier who received a life sentence, was the only civilian to have the death penalty pronounced on him. And Hideki Tojo, the last of the defendants in the courtroom to have sentence passed on him, was found guilty of conspiracy to wage aggressive war, crimes against peace, and responsibility for atrocities against prisoners forced to work on the Burma–Thailand railway.

On Tojo, the Tribunal's judgement read:

Tojo became Chief of Staff of the Kwangtung Army in June 1937, and thereafter was associated with the conspirators in principle in almost all their activities. He planned and prepared for an attack on the U.S.S.R.; he recommended a further onset in China in order to free the Japanese Army from anxiety about its rear in the projected attack on the U.S.S.R.; he helped organize Manchuria as a base for the attack. Never at any time thereafter did he abandon the intention to launch such an attack if a favorable chance should occur.

He became Minister of War in July 1940, and thereafter his history is largely the history of the successive steps by which the conspirators planned and waged wars of aggression against Japan's neighbors, for he was the principal in the making of plans and in the waging of wars. He advocated and furthered the aims of the conspiracy with ability, resolution and persistency.

He became Prime Minister in October 1941, and continued in the office until July 1944. As War Minister and Prime Minister he consistently supported the policy of conquering the National Government of China, of developing the resources of China on Japan's behalf, and of retaining Japanese troops in China to safeguard for Japan the results of December 7, 1941 [Pearl Harbor]. His attitude was that Japan must secure terms which would preserve for her the fruits of her aggression against China, and which would conduce to the establishment of Japan's domination of East Asia and the Southern areas.

All his influence was thrown into support of that policy. The importance of the leading part he played in securing the decision to go to war in support of that policy cannot be over-estimated. He bears the major responsibility for Japan's criminal attacks on her neighbors. In this trial he defended all these attacks with hardihood, alleging that they were legitimate measures of self-defense. We have dealt with that plea. It is wholly unfounded.

And the penalty was death.

Thirty-four

On the day that the verdict was to be delivered, Mrs. Tojo with her two daughters visited her husband at Sugamo Prison. She found him in good spirits. Yet, though it was their first meeting since the Tribunal had gone into recess to consider its findings seven months earlier, they found themselves at first at a loss for words. "We had said everything there was to be said and everything there was to be thought," she said, "and there was nothing more to say. When we looked at each other, all we could do was smile." Eventually he asked if she would take a message to Giichi Miura, the exponent of traditionalist philosophy whose teachings he admired greatly. "Tell him," he said, "that I am thankful that this trial is ending without too much trouble for the Emperor; that I have great confidence in the human race and so I am very optimistic about its future; and that he should please use his influence for the reconstruction of the nation."

Then, Tojo went on as if speaking to himself. "You know, about Japan's Imperial Family, this is the way I think. It is a miracle that one blood line has ruled a country for two thousand years and more. This miracle remains. Our forefathers fought for power among themselves but not one tried to overthrow the Imperial Family. There were rivals, but they put the royal line above all else. In the blood of the Yamato race there is a great tide." He broke off and told her to go home and not to wait for the verdict. Outside a Chinese newspaperman who knew Mrs. Tojo and the family warned her that reporters were at the house awaiting her return. Gratefully she accepted his offer to let her rest at his home and it was there that she heard over the radio that her husband was to die.[1]

At the Imperial Palace, the Emperor Hirohito was, according to members of the royal household, also sitting by the radio making notes with pencil and paper as the verdicts were announced. He was, reportedly, "rather shocked" at the sentences. And, that night, widespread speculation and rumors were abroad that the Emperor would abdicate following the blunt denunciation of him by the Australian Sir William Webb, president of the Tribunal, as "a leader in the crime" but who had been granted immunity from answering for it in the dock with the others.

"Judgment was given just after three o'clock," Tojo noted that day in his prison diary. "There is nothing strange about the sentence passed on me. I expected to be put to death by hanging. But the sentences on the others surprised me and I am indeed sorry for them. When judgment was passed I saw Teruo and Toshio [his two sons] in the gallery. I am grateful to them for having been present there in the final hours.

"Seven of us were taken back to Sugamo Prison after nightfall. Except for five blankets and my overcoat, I was allowed to keep practically nothing, not even my dentures and spectacles. . . . I thought it was ridiculous. Through the night, officers and many soldiers kept watch on me. They might as well have saved themselves the trouble." Nevertheless he slept well that night. The next morning he was angered again by the increased security measures. "They tried to make me have breakfast without my dentures," he complained, "but I refused. Eventually, they handed my dentures and glasses back to me. Incidently, I am fortunate to have a cell to myself; it is usually shared by two persons. I am grateful, too, that the reading of Buddhist *sutras* [chanted prayers] in the morning and evening refreshes me."

The next day he recorded that he again slept well, "in fact, I overslept this morning and they had to wake me up. It seems that it will be a nice day again and I feel fine. Yesterday they did not allow us to take a walk outside and no walk again today. To kill time I jotted down any poem I could recall." The security precautions continued to oppress him. "The only thing which disturbs me is the watch the guards nervously keep on me. I wonder how long this will go on? It is really annoying."[2]

The security precautions which, in any case, would normally have been stepped up after the prisoners were sentenced to death and were, presumably, more desperate, had been applied with increased meticulousness since the Nazi war criminal, Hermann Goering, had escaped the gallows by killing himself with a cunningly hidden poison capsule. Searches were thorough and they were not confined to clothing. They extended to an examination of a physical and humiliatingly personal nature. Tojo regarded all the precautions as "insulting." He understood that his captors were determined that he should not cheat them as Goering had done but, he said, "it only shows that they do not understand our Japanese mentality. We want to be executed with honor and, until then, we only wish to maintain our health."[3]

At his request, the prison authorities had provided him with a pencil and ten sheets of paper. Some of these he now devoted to setting out a formal petition to the Warden of Sugamo Prison.

"As a person who has already been sentenced to death," he wrote, "please allow me to state my last wish. I only desire to depart this life after discharging my duties as a Japanese by taking calmly and honorably the execution which is to be carried out at no distant date. Therefore, though there may be only a few days left, I would like you to consider the following points:

(1) I ask you, if I may, to tell the lower ranks to restrain themselves from insulting behavior.

(2) Please give us religious freedom. Needless to say, religious freedom is guaranteed by various treaties. Particularly those under sentence of death are entitled to receive every convenience in regard to religious matters.

(3) Though I may have only a few days' life, I should like to keep fit until the execution. Life demands sunshine. Though I think that solitary confinement at present has a reason in keeping us under observation, I wish to be in the sunshine at least once a day. This is only because of my heartfelt wish to accept my execution with dignity.

(4) Please create the circumstances in which I will be able to devote my last days to mental training.

(5) Please provide me with facility for handing my last messages to my family and others.[4]

During his imprisonment, as when he was ousted from government into enforced retirement in 1944, Tojo had found time to regret his lack of knowledge of things outside of work. He had tried his hand at writing *waka* and *haiku* poems, "crude," as Mrs. Tojo observed, "though they were." On the day he had been sentenced to death, he had written a *haiku* verse:

> Ah, look!
> See how the cherry blossoms
> Fall mutely.[5]

But more and more he had been spending time with the Reverend Hanayama, a Buddhist priest appointed as prison chaplain at Sugamo. On the evening of Wednesday, the 17th of November, he talked with Hanayama. He was, he told the priest, "relieved and consoled" now that the ordeal of the trial was over and that he had "more or less discharged" his duties. He repeated how painful it was to him that his colleagues were to suffer death with him and that he had not been able to take all the guilt on himself.

As for the trial, "I would rather not comment on it," he said, but he was "indeed sorry" for the treatment of prisoners of war and for the crimes against humanity. "I fully realize that the responsibility lies with me for not making His Majesty's benevolence generally known to the people." He asked that the Japanese government and the Allied powers be sympathetic to those bereaved in the war. Their sacrifice had been for the nation and, if anyone had to be punished, "we, the leaders should. To leave the victims of war as they are now," he warned, "is to drive the entire nation to Communism."

That night he recorded in his diary: "My health is good, and I feel refreshed. I am spending the days with Buddha, hoping that the execution will be carried out as soon as possible. I am calm."[6]

Tojo had refused his counsel's request for an appeal

to be made against his sentence. There was, nevertheless, a delay while Doihara and Hirota appealed unsuccessfully. The execution date was set finally for the 23rd of December, 1948. All of the doomed men were permitted to receive a last visit from not more than five people named by them. Tojo sent word to his wife that "he thought the males could forego it." He had therefore arranged that she and the four daughters should come to see him for the last time.

Again, words were difficult to find as they sat opposite each other at a table in the reception room at Sagamo Prison. Unlike previous family meetings, when the considerate Colonel Kenworthy had made a point of standing aside, all of the condemned men were now under constant guard against last-minute attempts to cheat the gallows. Tojo had a military policeman standing behind him and was manacled to an American army officer who sat at his side. Noticing that their youngest daughter was staring at the handcuffs, Tojo said to her, "Kimie, you seem to be bothered about my hands." Smiling he went on, "Don't be. They can bind my hands or feet, but no one has ever bound my heart." It was of religion that he mostly spoke to his daughters at this last talk with them.

"All his life, your father has done his best," he said to them, "but he was so busy that he drifted away from religion. Since I have been in these circumstances and have had a lot of free time I have come to realize how important it is. . . . You don't know what kind of difficulties you may find yourself in later. Take a grasp of some good religion—I don't mean just a religious cult. Your father finds Buddhism best for him. But it can be Christianity or some other religion that fits your heart. Then, no matter what, you won't be afraid."[7]

On the night of the 22nd of December, Tojo received the Reverend Hanayama in his condemned cell again. He handed the priest a *haiku* verse he had composed for his wife. Some time before he had made her promise that for the sake of their children she would not, as he put it to her, "join him" when he met his death. His realization and concern now for the solitary and difficult years ahead to which her promise bound her was evoked in the poem:

> A lonely goose
> In the sky
> My heart aches.[8]

In his last two weeks in prison, he had been working on a long document, his final testament. This he also entrusted to Hanayama. Realizing that it would probably be appropriated by the American authorities—as, in fact, it was—he spent a great part of the time they were together dictating portions to the priest so that his thoughts could be made public when "the bitter wake" of the Pacific war had subsided.

When ultimately they were published in 1961, they contained no significant message or, indeed, little that he had not said before. Written in captivity, they revealed perhaps more than anything how Hideki Tojo had been a prisoner for much longer than his relatively short physical confinement. To the end he remained the captive of convictions and attitudes formed early in his life and which had never basically changed. He apologized to the Emperor and to the Japanese nation for having led them into war; expressed his firm belief in the eternity of the Imperial line; and criticized the trial of Japanese war criminals. A third war between the United States and the Soviet Union, he predicted, "was inevitable" and would be fought in Asia. "I believe that to eliminate war one must eliminate greed, but it is impossible for nations to do this. Accordingly it is impossible to do away with war even though this may mean self-destruction.

"I would like to say a few words," he said, "to the Americans who are now in actual control of Japan. I would like to ask them not to alienate the feelings of the Japanese people. I would like to ask them not to allow Japan to become Communized. . . . The leaders of the United States made a big mistake in destroying bulwarks against Japan's Communization."

He spoke of the Asian mainland where Japan had spent vain years, effort, and dreams of glory; of China, where the Chiang Kai-shek government which had defied the might of Japan for fourteen years was in the last throes of overwhelming defeat by the communist armies of Mao Tse-tung; of Manchuria, the land so fateful for Japan, now already under Mao's control; and of Korea, divided by opposing ideologies and where the Moscow-installed

Kim Il Sung ruled in the north. Britain and the United States, he declared, were to blame for the triumphant march of communism in Asia. Of Japan, deprived of weapons by those who had vanquished her in a world still armed, he said that "unilateral disarmament is much like doing away with police while thieves still run wild." And for himself, he said, "my execution is some consolation, although it certainly cannot compensate for my responsibility to the nation. But internationally, I declare myself innocent. I only gave in to superior force. . . . I now walk to the gallows happy to shoulder my responsibility."

Less than three and a half hours after Hanayama took down the general's last words to the world and his people, they met again. This time the meeting was brief and solemn. Just before one o'clock in the morning, American military police guards entered the cell where Hideki Tojo was fully dressed and waiting composedly for them. Manacling him, they led him out along the corridors in the direction of the prison's Buddhist chapel. There he joined the other condemned men, Doihara, Muto, and Matsui, whose hour had also come. In the room, with the air scented and heavy from the joss-sticks each had put in the altar incense burner, they stood with bowed heads while the priest chanted Buddhist *sutras*. Then the quiet of the chapel was broken as, after subdued farewells to each other and thanks to the Reverend Hanayama and the guards who were attending them, Tojo joined with the others—all, like him, elderly men now—in cries of *"Banzai"* for the Emperor and *"Dai-Nippon."*

Outside in the prison courtyard, waiting official witnesses of the Allied nations saw him emerge, blinking in the sudden brilliance of the floodlit courtyard. He looked diminutive flanked by the grim-faced American escorts who towered over him, even smaller and shrunken in the ill-fitting prison uniform, and strangely unfamiliar without his spectacles and dentures. Then the general, who in another week would have been sixty-four years old, mounted the steps of the gallows. And, at precisely one-thirty in the morning of the 23rd of December, 1948, General Hideki Tojo died.

Postscript

Daily Telegraph 23rd December, 1948.
General MacArthur had declined a request by widow of General Tojo to receive her husband's remains. The body will be cremated and ashes scattered.

Pacific Stars and Stripes 23rd April, 1955.
TOKYO (UP) Scraps of the ashes of Japan's wartime premier Hideki Tojo—secretly hidden from Allied occupation officers— were returned Friday to his widow.

Tojo and six other Japanese war criminals were hanged Dec. 23, 1948, after their conviction by an Allied military tribunal.

Their bodies were cremated in Yokohama, and the remains secretly disposed of by Allied officials who feared the ashes might be deified by the Japanese.

But Japanese workers at the crematorium scooped up a few ashes left behind and buried them. They remained hidden until the Allied occupation ended.

Later the salvaged remains were given to the Japanese government's Repatriation Assistance Bureau which turned them over to their families Friday.

"I am only sorry," Tojo's widow said when she received the urn, "that the remains of thousands of Japanese soldiers still have not been returned from the South Pacific and China."

Japan Times 17th August, 1960.

A joint tomb for the seven top Japanese war criminals executed after the war's end, including Gen. Hideki Tojo, was unveiled yesterday in Aichi Prefecture.

The kin of the hanged men, including Mrs. Tojo, widow of the wartime Prime Minister, were invited to the unveiling ceremonies.

The granite tomb has been built atop Sanganesan Hill at Hazu by a group of Japanese leaders sympathizing with the wartime leaders despite the strong opposition of many of their countrymen.

Dr. Ichiro Kiyose, President of the House of Councillors, and a member of the Japanese defense counsel for the war felons when they faced the Allied Far East Tribunal in Tokyo, wrote the inscription placed on the tombstone, reading "The Tomb of Seven Martyrs."

Chapter Notes

Chapter 1

1   Cornelius Ryan and Frank Kelley, *Star Spangled Mikado,* p. 48.

Chapter 2

1   Inazo Nitobe, *Bushido: The Soul of Japan,* p. 104.

2   Words of the 17th-century Tokugawa Shogun, Ieyasu. Quoted in *The World of Dew* by D.J. Enright, p. 13.

3   Dr. Charles Peter Thunberg, 18th-century Swedish traveler. Quoted in *Understanding the Japanese Mind* by James Clark Moloney, p. 100.

Chapter 3

1   *The Complete Journal of Townsend Harris,* edited by Dr. Mario Emilio Cosenza, p. 310.

2   Inazo Nitobe, *Intercourse Between the United States and Japan,* p. 62.

3   From the Memorial by chiefs of the Choshu, Satsuma, Tosa and Hizen clans. Quoted in *A History of Modern Japan* by Richard Storry, p. 105.

Chapter 4

1   Count Hayashi, Japanese diplomat and negotiator of the 1902 Anglo-Japanese Alliance. Quoted in *The Far East in World Politics,* p. 130.

Chapter 6

1   Mrs. Katsuko Tojo interview.

2   Katsuko Tojo, "Twenty Stormy Years for the Tojo Family," *Bungei Shunju* (June 1964).

3   Mrs. Katsuko Tojo interview.

Chapter 7

1   Mrs. Katsuko Tojo interview.

2   Mrs. Katsuko Tojo interview.

Chapter 8

1   Brigadier Rajendra Singh, *Far East in Ferment,* p. 133.

2   Old customs die hard in Japan. In 1952, there was widespread and angry criticism in the country over the deaths of several members of the Japanese Self-Defence Force (Japan, officially, has no army under Article Nine of the American-imposed Constitution). These took place, in what was characterized in the Japanese press as a "death march," as part of a winter training exercise in northern Japan. Many of the officers and n.c.o's conducting it were former members of the Japanese Imperial Army.

3   Hanama Tasaki, *Long the Imperial Way,* p. 38-39.

4   Mrs. Katsuko Tojo interview.

5   Mrs. Katsuko Tojo interview.

Chapter 9

1   Lewis Bush, *Land of the Dragonfly,* p. 179.

2   Takehiko Yoshihashi, *Conspiracy at Mukden,* p. 84n.

Chapter 10

1   Quoted in *I Cover Japan* by Kimpei Sheba, p. 48.

Chapter 11

1   Mrs. Katsuko Tojo interview.

Chapter 12

1   Shigeru Yoshida, *The Yoshida Memoirs,* p. 13-14.

2   Major-General F.S.G. Piggott, *Broken Thread,* p. 265.

3   Kimpei Sheba, *I Cover Japan,* p. 103.

4   Hugh Byas, *Government by Assassination.*

Chapter 13

1   Hessell Tiltman, "General Tojo and History," *Asahi Evening News* (24 December 1958).

Chapter 15

1   Major-General F.S.G. Piggott, *Broken Thread,* p. 336.

2   William Henry Chamberlin, *Modern Japan,* p. 79-80.

3   Chamberlin, p. 79-80.

Chapter 19

1   Lewis Bush, *Land of the Dragonfly,* p. 186.

2   Bush, p. 187.

3   Mrs. Katsuko Tojo interview.

4   From a letter: Ambassador Grew to President Roosevelt, 14 December 1940. (Department of State Publications: "Foreign Relations of the United States, 1941").

5   Telegram from Ambassador Grew to U.S. Secretary of State, Cordell Hull, 27 January 1941. (Department of State Publicacations: "Foreign Relations of the United States, 1941").

Chapter 20

1   Mrs. Katsuko Tojo interview.

2   Otto D. Tolischus, *Tokyo Record.*

3   Shigenori Togo, *The Cause of Japan*, p. 194.

4   Togo, pp. 195-196.

Chapter 21

1   Shigenori Togo, *The Cause of Japan*, pp. 60-61.

2   Togo, pp. 220-221.

3   John Deane Potter, *Admiral of the Pacific*, p. 98.

4   Mrs. Katsuko Tojo interview.

Chapter 22

1   Toshikazu Kase, *Eclipse of the Rising Sun*, p. 132. Toshikazu Kase, a member of the Japanese Foreign Office, took an active part in clandestine moves to have Tojo ousted from office of premier.

Chapter 24

1   Reginald Hargreaves, *Red Sun Rising: The Siege of Port Arthur*, p. 29.

2   Lord Russell of Liverpool, *The Knights of Bushido: A Short History of Japanese War Crimes*, p. 95.

3   Mamoru Shigemitsu, *Japan and Her Destiny*, pp. 343-344.

4   John Morris, "Where East Meets West on Equal Terms," *Manchester Guardian* (29 February 1960).

5   Eric Linklater, *Juan in China*, p. 37.

6   D.J. Enright, *The World of Dew*, p. 15.

7   Fosco Maraini, *Meeting with Japan*, p. 428.

8   Reginald Hargreaves, *Red Sun Rising: The Siege of Port Arthur*, p. 181.

9   Yuji Aida, *Prisoner of the British*, p. 52.

10   Lewis Bush, *Land of the Dragonfly*, pp. 161-162.

11   Fosco Maraini, *Meeting with Japan*, p. 429.

Chapter 25

1   Leonard Mosley, *Hirohito: Emperor of Japan*, pp. 229-230.

2   Lewis Bush, *The Road to Inamura*, pp. 173-174.

Chapter 26

1   Katsuko Tojo, "Twenty Stormy Years for the Tojo Family," *Bungei Shunju* (June 1964).

2   Richard Storry, *A History of Modern Japan*, p. 220.

3   Mrs. Katsuko Tojo interview.

Chapter 27

1   Toshikazu Kase, *Eclipse of the Rising Sun*, p. 90.

2   Kase, p. 79.

3   Mrs. Katsuko Tojo interview.

Chapter 28

1   Mrs. Katsuko Tojo interview.

2   Toshikazu Kase, *Eclipse of the Rising Sun*, p. 92.

3   Mamoru Shigemitsu, *Japan and Her Destiny*, p. 322.

Chapter 29

1   Toshikazu Kase, *Eclipse of the Rising Sun*, p. 103.

2   Mamoru Shigemitsu, *Japan and Her Destiny*, p. 325.

Chapter 30

1   Toshikazu Kase, *Eclipse of the Rising Sun*, pp. 206-207.
2   Toshikazu Kase, *Eclipse of the Rising Sun*, pp. 206-207.
3   Mamoru Shigemitsu, *Japan and Her Destiny*, p. 326.
4   Mrs. Katsuko Tojo interview.
5   Kimpei Sheba, *I Cover Japan*, pp. 210-212.
6   Katsuko Tojo, "Twenty Stormy Years for the Tojo Family," *Bungei Shunju* (June 1964).
7   Tojo, (June, 1964).
8   Mamoru Shigemitsu, *Japan and Her Destiny*, p. 358.
9   Toshikazu Kase, *Eclipse of the Rising Sun*, p. 262.

Chapter 31

1   Mrs. Katsuko Tojo interview.
2   Robert J.C. Butow, *Tojo and the Coming of the War*, pp. 461-462.
3   Mrs. Katsuko Tojo interview.
4   Graham Stanford, "I Saved Tojo the Terrible for the Hangman," *News of the World* (1 January 1962).
5   Stanford, (1 January 1962).
6   Stanford, (1 January 1962).
7   Hessell Tiltman, "General Tojo and History," *Asahi Evening News* (24 December 1958).
8   Katsuko Tojo, "Twenty Stormy Years for the Tojo Family," *Bungei Shunju* (June 1964).
9   Tojo, (June 1964).
10   Gwen Terasaki, *Bridge to the Sun*, p. 227.
11   Kimpei Sheba, *I Cover Japan*, p. 108.
12   Mrs. Katsuko Tojo interview.
13   Mrs. Katsuko Tojo interview.
14   Mrs. Katsuko Tojo interview.

Chapter 32

1   Mrs. Katsuko Tojo interview.
2   Harold Stassen in a statement to the press, 31 August 1945. Stassen, a former Governor of Minnesota and then a Commander in the U.S. Navy, went ashore as Relief Commissioner with the first occupation troops.
3   Mrs. Katsuko Tojo interview.
4   Katsuko Tojo, "Twenty Stormy Years for the Tojo Family," *Bungei Shunju* (June 1964).
5   Colonel A. Kenworthy, "Chief of the American Military Police: Ichigaya Chronicle," *Bungei Shunju* (January 1953).
6   David Bergamini, "High Level Hearsay About Hirohito," *Life* (July 1966).
7   Report from *The Times,* London, 31 December 1947.

Chapter 34

1   Mrs. Katsuko Tojo interview.
2   "The Last Diary of General Hideki Tojo," *Bungei Shunju* (November 1963).

3   "The Last Diary of General Hideki Tojo," (November 1963).

4   "The Last Diary of General Hideki Tojo," (November 1963).

5   Mrs. Katsuko Tojo interview.

6   "The Last Diary of General Hideki Tojo," (November 1963).

7   Mrs. Katsuko Tojo interview.

8   Katsuko Tojo, "Twenty Stormy Years for the Tojo Family," *Bungei Shunju* (June 1964).

Selected Bibliography

AIDA, YUJI, *Prisoner of the British*. Cresset, London, 1966.

AOKI, TOKUZO, *The Pacific War*. Gatujutsu Bunken Fukyukai, Tokyo, 1953.

BEARD, CHARLES A., *President Roosevelt and the Coming of the War*. Yale University Press, New Haven, 1941.

BENEDICT, RUTH, *The Chrysanthemum and the Sword*. Charles E. Tuttle & Co., Tokyo and Vermont, 1946; Houghton Mifflin, Boston, Mass., 1946.

BRINES, RUSSELL, *MacArthur's Japan*. Lippincott, New York, 1948.

BROWN, DELMER M., *Nationalism in Japan*. University of California Press, U.S.A., 1955.

BURTON, HUGH, *Japan's Modern Century*. The Ronald Press Company, New York, 1955.

BUSH, LEWIS, *Land of the Dragonfly*. Robert Hale, London, 1959.

———— *The Road to Inamura*. Robert Hale, London, 1961.

BUTOW, ROBERT J. C., *Japan's Decision to Surrender*. Stanford University Press, California, 1954.

———— *Tojo and the Coming of the War*. Princeton University Press, Princeton, N.J., 1961.

BYAS, HUGH, *Government by Assassination*. Alfred Knopf, New York, 1942.

CAUSTON, E. E. N., *Militarism and Foreign Policy in Japan*. Allen & Unwin, London, 1936.

CHAMBERLIN, WILLIAM HENRY, *Modern Japan*. American Council, I.P.R., Webster, 1942; McGraw-Hill Publishing Co., Berkshire, England, 1954.

CRAIGIE, SIR ROBERT, *Behind the Japanese Mask*. Hutchinson, London, 1945.

The Diaries of Koichi Kido. National Archives, Washington, D.C., 1946.

DULL, PAUL S. and UEMURA, MICHAEL, *The Tokyo Trials*. University of Michigan Press, Ann Arbor, 1957.

250

EICHELBERGER, ROBERT L., *Our Jungle Road to Tokyo.* Viking Press, New York, 1950.

ENRIGHT, D. J., *The World of Dew.* Secker and Warburg, London, 1955.

FAIRSERVIS, WALTER A. JR., *The Origins of Oriental Civilization.* Mentor Books: The New American Library, New York, 1959.

FEIS, HERBERT, *The Road to Pearl Harbour.* Princeton University, U.S.A., 1950.

FLEISHER, WILFRED, *Volcanic Isle.* Doubleday, New York, 1941.

GAYN, MARK, *Japan Diary.* Sloane, New York, 1948.

GREW, JOSEPH C., *Ten Years in Japan.* Simon & Schuster, New York, 1944.

———— *Turbulent Era.* Houghton Mifflin, New York, 1952.

HARGREAVES, REGINALD, *Red Sun Rising: The Siege of Port Arthur.* Weidenfeld & Nicholson, London, 1962; J. B. Lippincott, Philadelphia, 1962.

HARRIS, TOWNSEND, *The Complete Journal of Townsend Harris,* Mario E. Cosenga, ed. Doubleday, Doran & Co., Garden City, New York, 1930; Charles E. Tuttle & Co., Tokyo and Vermont, 1959.

HUDSON, G. F., *The Far East in World Politics.* Oxford University Press, London, 1937.

INOGUCHI, RIKIHEI, NAKAJIMA, TADASHI, and PINEAU, ROGER, *The Divine Wind.* Hutchinson, London, 1959.

JAMES, DAVID H., *The Rise and Fall of the Japanese Empire.* Allen & Unwin, London. 1951.

Japan's Struggle to End the War. U.S. Strategic Bombing Survey, 1946.

JONES, F. C., *Japan's New Order in East Asia.* Oxford University Press, London, 1954.

KASE, TOSHIKAZU, *Eclipse of the Rising Sun.* Jonathan Cape, London, 1951; in U.S. published by Yale University Press under the title *Journey to the Missouri,* 1952.

KELLY, FRANK and RYAN, CORNELIUS, *Star Spangled Mikado.* McBride, New York, 1947.

LANGER, WILLIAM L. and GLEASON, S. EVERETT, *The Challenge to Isolation: 1937-40.* Harper & Row, New York, 1952.

———— *The Undeclared War: 1940-41.* Harper & Row, New York, 1953.

LEE, CLARK, *One Last Look Around.* Duell, Sloan & Pearce, New York, 1947.

LINKLATER, ERIC, *Juan in China.* Jonathan Cape, London, 1937.

LORD, WALTER, *Day of Infamy.* Holt, Rinehart and Winston, New York, 1957.

LORY, HILLIS, *Japan's Military Masters.* Viking Press, New York, 1943.

MARAINI, FOSCO, *Meeting with Japan.* Hutchinson, London, 1959; Viking Press, New York, 1960.

The Memoirs of Cordell Hull. Macmillan, New York, 1948.

Mission Accomplished. U.S. Army Air Force, Washington, D.C., 1946.

MOLONEY, JAMES CLARK, *Understanding the Japanese Mind.* Philosophical Library, New York, 1954.

MOORE, FREDERICK, *With Japan's Leaders*. Chapman & Hall, London, 1943; Scribners, New York, 1942.

MOSLEY, LEONARD, *Hirohito: Emperor of Japan*. Prentice-Hall, New York, 1966; Weidenfeld & Nicholson, London, 1966.

NITOBE, INAZO, *Bushido: The Soul of Japan*. Putnam's and Coward-McCann, New York, 1905.

—— *Intercourse Between the United States and Japan*. John Hopkins Press, Baltimore, Md., 1891.

PIGGOTT, MAJOR-GENERAL F. S. G., *Broken Thread*. Gale & Polden, Aldershot, England, 1950.

POTTER, JOHN DEANE, *Admiral of the Pacific*. Heinemann, London, 1965.

REDMAN, H. VERE, *Japan in Crisis*. Allen & Unwin, London, 1935.

REISCHAUER, EDWIN O., *Japan: Past and Present*. Alfred Knopf, New York, 1964.

—— *United States and Japan*. Harvard University Press, Cambridge, 1957.

RUSSELL, LORD OF LIVERPOOL, *The Knights of Bushido: A Short History of Japanese War Crimes*. Cassell, London, 1958; E. P. Dutton, New York, 1958.

SANSOM, SIR GEORGE, *A History of Japan*. Stanford University Press, California, 1962.

The Secret Diary of Harold L. Ickes. Simon & Schuster, New York, 1954.

SHEBA, KIMPEI, *I Cover Japan*. Tokyo News Service, Tokyo, 1952.

SHIGEMITSU, MAMORU, *Japan and Her Destiny*. Hutchinson, London, 1958; E. P. Dutton, New York, 1958.

SINGH, BRIGADIER RAJENDRA, *Far East in Ferment*. India Army Educational Stores, New Delhi, 1961.

STEIN, GUNTHER, *Far East in Ferment*. Methuen, London, 1936.

—— *Made in Japan*. Methuen, London, 1935.

STIMSON, HENRY L., *On Active Service in Peace and War*. Harper & Row, New York, 1948.

STORRY, RICHARD, *The Double Patriots*. Houghton Mifflin, Boston, Mass., 1957; Chatto & Windus, London, 1957.

—— *A History of Modern Japan*. Penguin Books, Middlesex, England, 1960.

SUZUKI, D. T., *An Introduction to Zen Buddhism*. Arrow Books, London, 1959; Rider, London, 1949.

TASAKI, HANAMA, *Long the Imperial Way*. Victor Gollancz, London, 1951; Houghton Mifflin, Boston, Mass., 1950. Four Square Books, London, 1961.

TERASAKI, GWEN, *Bridge to the Sun*. University of North Carolina Press, Chapel Hill, 1957; Michael Joseph, London, 1958; Penguin Books, Ltd., England, 1962.

TOGO, SHIGENORI, *The Cause of Japan*. Simon and Schuster, New York, 1956.

TOLISCHUS, OTTO D., *Tokyo Record*. Reynal and Hitchcock, New York, 1941.

252

YOSHIDA, SHIGERU, *The Yoshida Memoirs*. Heinemann, London, 1961; Houghton Mifflin, Boston, Mass., 1962.

YOSHIHASHI, TAKEHIKO, *Conspiracy at Mukden*. Yale University Press, New Haven and London, 1963.

YOUNG, MORGAN, *Imperial Japan*. Allen & Unwin, London, 1938.

Index

Other titles of interest